Côte d'Ivoire
a country study

Federal Research Division
Library of Congress
Edited by
Robert E. Handloff
Research Completed
November 1988

On the cover: Detail of hand-painted Sénoufo tapestry from
northern Côte d'Ivoire

Third Edition, First Printing, 1991.

Library of Congress Cataloging-in-Publication Data

Côte d'Ivoire : a country study / Federal Research Division, Library
of Congress ; edited by Robert E. Handloff.
    p. cm. — (Area Handbook Series) (DA pam ; 550-69)
  "Replaces the second edition of the original Area handbook for
the Ivory Coast, which was reprinted in 1973 with an added
summary of events covering the period January 1963 to December
1972"—Pref.
  "Research completed November 1988."
  Includes bibliographical references (pp.223-241) and index.
  Supt. of Docs. no. : D 101.22:550-69/990
  1. Ivory Coast. I. Handloff, Robert Earl, 1942- .
II. Roberts, Thomas Duval, Area handbook for Ivory Coast.
III. Library of Congress. Federal Research Division. IV. Series.
V. Series: DA pam ; 550-69.
DT545.22.C66   1990   90-5878
966.6805—dc20   CIP

Headquarters, Department of the Army
DA Pam 550-69

For sale by the Superintendent of Documents, U.S. Government Printing Office
Washington, D.C. 20402

Foreword

This volume is one in a continuing series of books now being prepared by the Federal Research Division of the Library of Congress under the Country Studies—Area Handbook Program. The last page of this book lists the other published studies.

Most books in the series deal with a particular foreign country, describing and analyzing its political, economic, social, and national security systems and institutions, and examining the interrelationships of those systems and the ways they are shaped by cultural factors. Each study is written by a multidisciplinary team of social scientists. The authors seek to provide a basic understanding of the observed society, striving for a dynamic rather than a static portrayal. Particular attention is devoted to the people who make up the society, their origins, dominant beliefs and values, their common interests and the issues on which they are divided, the nature and extent of their involvement with national institutions, and their attitudes toward each other and toward their social system and political order.

The books represent the analysis of the authors and should not be construed as an expression of an official United States government position, policy, or decision. The authors have sought to adhere to accepted standards of scholarly objectivity. Corrections, additions, and suggestions for changes from readers will be welcomed for use in future editions.

Louis R. Mortimer
Acting Chief
Federal Research Division
Library of Congress
Washington, D.C. 20540

iii

Acknowledgments

The authors wish to acknowledge the contributions of T.D. Roberts, Donald M. Bouton, Irving Kaplan, Barbara Lent, Charles Townsend, and Neda A. Walpole, who coauthored the first edition of *Ivory Coast: A Country Study,* the predecessor of the current volume. The authors also wish to thank Roxanne Donahey, William Kallon, Vincent Kern, Gilda Nimer, and Benjamin Nimer, who updated the original volume with a new section entitled "Summary of Events: January 1963–December 1972." Their collective work provided the organizational outline for the present volume as well as substantial portions of the text. The authors are grateful to those individuals in various public and private agencies who contributed photographs, research materials, and invaluable time and expertise to the production of this book.

The authors also wish to thank those who contributed directly to the preparation of the text. Thomas Collelo, Richard F. Nyrop, and Sandra W. Meditz reviewed all drafts and provided guidance; Martha E. Hopkins and Marilyn Majeska managed editing and production; Mimi Cantwell, Sharon Costello, Vincent Ercolano, Ruth Nieland, and Sharon Schultz edited the chapters; Beverly Wolpert performed the final prepublication review; and Shirley Kessel prepared the index. Also involved in preparing the text were editorial assistants Barbara Edgerton and Izella Watson. Malinda B. Neale of the Library of Congress Composing Unit prepared the camera-ready copy, under the supervision of Peggy Pixley.

David P. Cabitto reviewed draft maps from which he, Kimberly A. Lord, and Harriett R. Blood prepared the final maps. Additional thanks are due also to Kimberly A. Lord for designing the artwork for the cover and the illustrations on the title page of each chapter and, with David P. Cabitto and Sandra K. Ferrell, preparing charts and graphs. Arvies J. Staton provided information on military ranks, uniforms, and insignia.

Contents

Preface

Côte d'Ivoire: A Country Study replaces the second edition of the original *Area Handbook for Ivory Coast* which was reprinted in 1973 with an added summary of events covering the January 1963 to December 1972 period. Like the earlier study, this edition seeks to provide a concise and objective account of the history and dominant social, political, economic, and military aspects of contemporary Côte d'Ivoire. Sources of information included scholarly monographs and journals, official reports of governments and international organizations, periodicals, and foreign and domestic newspapers. Chapter bibliographies appear at the end of the book; brief comments on some of the more valuable sources appear at the end of each chapter. Measurements are given in the metric system; a conversion table to aid readers is included (see table 1, Appendix). A glossary is also included.

Authors have spelled place-names in accordance with usage established by the United States Board on Geographic Names. In transliterating personal names, they have followed standard usage in official Ivoirian sources.

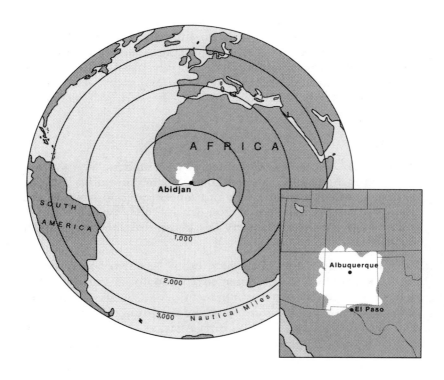

Country

Formal Name: République de Côte d'Ivoire.

Short Form: Côte d'Ivoire.

Term for Citizens: Ivoirians.

Capital: Abidjan.

Date of Independence: August 7, 1960, from France.

Geography

Size: Total area 322,460 square kilometers.

Topography: Southern boundary 515-kilometer coastline on Gulf of Guinea. Southeast marked by coastal lagoons; southern region, especially southwest, densely forested; northern region savanna zone of lateritic or sandy soils, with vegetation decreasing from south to north within region. Terrain mostly flat to undulating plains, with mountains in the west.

Climate: Warm, humid climate transitional from equatorial to tropical. In north, heavy rains between June and October (110 centimeters annually); along equatorial coast, some rain in most months, but heaviest between May and July and August and September (200 centimeters annually), with major dry season from December to April. Temperatures average between 25°C and 30°C and range from 10°C to 40°C.

Society

Population: As of 1987, estimated at 10.6 million, with average annual growth rate of 4.1 percent, one of highest in world. Roughly 50 percent of population urban and concentrated in Abidjan and Bouaké areas. Average population density thirty-two persons per square kilometer in 1987. Forty-five percent of population under age fifteen.

Ethnic Groups: More than sixty ethnic groups. Major ethnic groups included: Baoulé (15 percent), Sénoufo (10 percent), Bété (6 percent), Lagoon peoples (5 percent), Agni (Anyi—3 percent), and Mandé cluster of groups, including Juula, Bambara, and Malinké (17 percent). Non-Ivoirian Africans, Lebanese, Asians, and Europeans composed nearly 27 percent of population.

Languages: Number of African languages (grouped into four branches of Niger-Congo language family) corresponds roughly to number of ethnic groups. Sections of several groups speak different languages. Some languages used as mother tongue by more than one ethnic group. Official language, French; variants of Mandé-kan spoken throughout country as commercial language.

Religion: In 1980s one-fourth of population Muslim, one-eighth Christian (mostly Roman Catholic), and remainder local religions or, in smaller numbers, syncretic religions.

Education: Six-year primary-school system compulsory where available. In 1987 enrolled 75 percent of boys and 50 percent of girls under fifteen. Only 19 percent of primary-school students enrolled in public secondary schools. After four years, students sit for exams for certificate of lower cycle of secondary study (*brevet d'étude du premier cycle*—BEPC). A second three-year cycle led to *baccalauréat*, necessary for university entrance. Public schooling through university controlled and funded by central government. Fourteen percent of primary schools and 29 percent of secondary schools private, mostly Catholic. Some Quranic schools in north tolerated but not supported by government. In 1988 overall literacy rate 43 percent; 53 percent for men and 31 percent for women.

Health: In 1988 health services unable to meet needs of majority of population. Urban-rural and regional imbalances, low ratios of doctors to patients, and severe shortages of nurses and auxiliary health care personnel existed. Public health programs underfunded and personnel lacked adequate training. Nutritional deficiencies and impure water major sources of disease. Malaria, measles, and tropical ailments common; 250 cases of acquired immunodeficiency syndrome (AIDS) reported by end of 1987.

Economy

Salient Features: Economy oriented toward private enterprise with extensive government participation through parastatals, investment, and tax policies. Foreign investment welcomed; multinational corporations heavily involved in two-thirds of largest thirty businesses dealing in commodity exports, food processing, oil refining, textiles, beverages, construction, and commercial wholesaling and retailing. Country's principal resource agricultural land. Major food crops yams, cassava, rice, maize, and plantains.

Agriculture: Thirty-four percent of population engaged in subsistence farming. Cash cropping on small plots (coffee, cocoa, and cotton) and large plantations (bananas, palm oil, pineapples, rubber, and sugar). Agriculture second largest contributor to gross domestic product (GDP—see Glossary) and main source of exports. In late 1990s, not self-sufficient in food production.

Manufacturing: Import substitution consumer goods, some intermediate inputs for domestic markets, and food processing—coffee, cocoa, and sugar—for export. Most industry required imported intermediate materials.

Mining: Some diamonds, manganese, iron ore, cobalt, bauxite, copper, nickel, colombo-tantalite, ilmenite, and gold, but none in significant amounts; offshore oil met about two-thirds of local needs.

Energy: Rural population heavily dependent on wood; urban population, on electric power, natural gas, and kerosene.

Foreign Trade: Principal exports cocoa, coffee, and timber; other exports cotton, sugar, rubber, palm oil, and pineapples. Principal imports petroleum products, machinery, and transport equipment.

Currency: African Financial Community (Communauté Financière Africaine) franc (CFA F) equal in 1988 to 315 per dollar and freely convertible to French francs (FF).

Fiscal Year: January 1 through December 31.

Transportation

Railroads: Government-owned railroad runs 660 kilometers between Abidjan and border with Burkina Faso, where, under different ownership, it continues on to Ouagadougou; one-meter gauge, single track except at stations.

Roads: Extensive system totaling 53,736 kilometers; more than 3,600 kilometers bituminous and bituminous-treated surface; 32,000 kilometers gravel, crushed stone, laterite, and improved earth; 18,136 unimproved. Hard surface roads generally run north-south, linking cities to Abidjan.

Ports and Shipping: Major ports at Abidjan and San-Pédro; minor port at Sassandra. At Abidjan, facilities included total of thirty-five deepwater berths for general, bulk, and container cargo; roll-on/roll-off facility; and specialized quays for bananas, fish, timber, cement, hydrocarbons, and tankers. In 1986 handled 9.5 million tons of cargo.

Civil Aviation: Government-owned Ivoirian Air Transport and Liaison (Groupement Aérien de Transport et de Liaison—GATL), also known as Air Ivoire, provided domestic and regional service; international service provided by Air Afrique, owned by consortium of African countries and based in Abidjan. International airports at Abidjan, Bouaké, and Yamoussoukro, plus 13 major domestic airfields, 17 smaller regional airfields, and 50 private airfields.

Government and Politics

Government: Constitution of 1960 creates republic with strong, centralized presidential government, independent judiciary, and national legislature. President and 175-member National Assembly (Assemblée Nationale) elected by universal suffrage for five-year terms. In the late 1980s, all candidates had to belong to Democratic Party of Côte d'Ivoire (Parti Démocratique de Côte d'Ivoire—PDCI), then the country's only legal party.

Administrative Divisions: Forty-nine prefectures divided into subprefectures; thirty-seven municipalities enjoyed autonomous status.

Judicial System: Laws based on French and, to lesser extent, customary law. Upper-level courts included Supreme Court, High Court of Justice, and State Security Court; lower courts included courts of appeal, courts of first instance, courts of assize, and justice of peace courts.

Politics: As of late 1988, Félix Houphouët-Boigny had served as president since independence. He had not named a successor, encouraging rivalry between National Assembly president Henri Konan Bedié and Economic and Social Council president Philippe Yacé. Economic austerity, calls for multiparty system, and increasing crime were potential threats to stability.

Foreign Affairs: Leading member of Council of the Entente and West African Economic Community; pragmatic foreign policy; staunch ally of France and other Western nations on which Côte d'Ivoire relied for development aid. Supported United States agenda on South Africa and Chad.

National Security

Armed Forces: In 1987 armed forces numbered 9,730 personnel: army numbered 5,500; navy, approximately 700; air force, approximately 930; and Presidential Guard and Militia (Garde Présidentielle et Milice—GPM), approximately 2,600. Military service compulsory; however, volunteers easily filled needs.

Major Tactical Units: Army included four infantry battalions of three companies each, one armored battalion of two squadrons, one antiaircraft artillery battalion, and one engineering battalion, all with support units. Navy included warships, auxiliaries, and service craft. Air force had one fighter-bomber squadron plus twenty transport aircraft and eleven helicopters for training and transport.

Foreign Military Assistance: Relied almost exclusively on French weaponry, communications equipment, and training. Japan provided a training ship plus technical assistance and training; Britain, Netherlands, Sweden, and United States sold support aircraft, small naval craft, trucks, jeeps, and mortars; Switzerland provided assault rifles.

Defense Expenditures: In 1986 defense spending came to CFA F32.4 billion, or less than 7.5 percent of government budget.

Police and Paramilitary Forces: In 1987, National Security Police (Sûreté Nationale), a national police force, numbered 5,300; paramilitary National Gendarmerie (Gendarmerie Nationale), responsible for maintaining law and order in rural areas, numbered approximately 4,500. Municipal police, under local control, maintained law and order in all urban administrations.

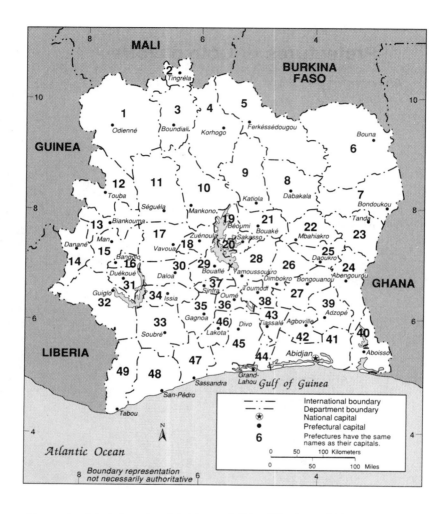

Figure 1. Administrative Divisions of Côte d'Ivoire, 1988

Prefectures of Côte d'Ivoire

Abengourou (24)
Abidjan (41)
Aboisso (40)
Adzopé (39)
Agboville (42)
Bangolo (16)
Béoumi (19)
Biankouma (13)
Bondoukou (7)
Bongouanou (27)
Bouaflé (29)
Bouaké (21)
Bouna (6)
Boundiali (3)
Dabakala (8)
Daloa (30)
Danané (14)
Daoukro (25)
Dimbokro (26)
Divo (45)
Duékoué (31)
Ferkéssédougou (5)
Gagnoa (35)
Grand-Lahou (44)
Guiglo (32)

Issia (34)
Katiola (9)
Korhogo (4)
Lakota (46)
Man (15)
Mankono (10)
Mbahiakro (22)
Odienné (1)
Oumé (36)
Sakasso (20)
San-Pédro (48)
Sassandra (47)
Séguéla (11)
Sinfra (37)
Soubré (33)
Tabou (49)
Tanda (23)
Tiassalé (43)
Tingréla (2)
Touba (12)
Toumoudi (38)
Vavoua (17)
Yamoussoukro (28)
Zuénoula (18)

*Prefectures have the same names
as their respectve capitals.*

Introduction

OBSERVERS OF AFRICA have often characterized Côte d'Ivoire as different from the rest of Africa. Borrowing the metaphor of Félix Houphouët-Boigny, president of Côte d'Ivoire, they have described it as an oasis of political stability and economic prosperity—in short, the "Ivoirian miracle." Indeed, if judged on the basis of political stability and economic performance during its first twenty years of independence, Côte d'Ivoire does appear unique: it has had only one president and no coups since gaining independence, and between 1960 and 1979 the gross national product (GNP—see Glossary) grew by almost 8 percent per year, compared with minimal or negative growth rates elsewhere in Africa. However, that growth produced large—some would have said dysfunctional—disparities in wealth and income and skewed development. Consequently, the country was ill prepared when, in the late 1970s, world prices for coffee and cocoa, Côte d'Ivoire's principal export commodities, dropped, while prices for its principal imports rose. Meanwhile, foreign borrowing to finance massive investments in infrastructure and public enterprises (that lost money) raised Côte d'Ivoire's foreign debt beyond its ability to meet its obligations. Budget reductions and a structural adjustment program forced the vast majority of the population to lower its expectations, which in turn contributed to, among other social ills, heightened frustrations and a sharp increase in violent crime. By the end of the 1980s, Côte d'Ivoire was confronting the same problems of political and economic development as other African countries and having to respond with many of the same difficult and often inadequate solutions.

In the early precolonial period, the dense forests covering the southern half of the area that became Côte d'Ivoire created barriers to large-scale sociopolitical organizations. In the savanna region to the north, dissimilar populations had neither the incentive nor the strength to overcome ethnic differences and forge a larger state. Prior to the eighteenth century, polities consisted of villages or clusters of villages whose contacts with the larger world were filtered through long-distance traders.

European—in this case French—interest in the area remained desultory until late in the nineteenth century. Following the Franco-Prussian War in 1871, for example, the French ministry responsible for colonies offered to exchange Côte d'Ivoire with the British for the Gambia, which bisected the French colony of Senegal. The British refused, and France officially abandoned the territory. By the late 1880s, however, the scramble for colonies gripped both France and Britain. In the western Sudan (see Glossary), French military officers and freebooters extended French domains, often without the knowledge or consent of the home government. Unsubstantiated rumors of gold and a lucrative trade in the hinterland of Côte d'Ivoire once again stimulated French interest in the colony. In 1886 France again exercised direct control over the trading posts on the Ivoirian coast, and in 1887 and 1888 Captain Louis Binger and Maurice Treich-Laplène negotiated a series of agreements with local chiefs in the north-central and northeastern regions of Côte d'Ivoire to bolster French claims of effective occupation. Thus, by the end of the decade, France exercised sovereignty over most of the coastal region of Côte d'Ivoire and claimed influence over certain regions of the interior. In 1893 Côte d'Ivoire became a colony, and Binger served as its first governor.

Over the next twenty years, French administrators used the military to subdue African populations that, with few exceptions, openly resisted French intrusions. In the 1890s, Samori Touré, seeking to construct a kingdom across much of the Sahel, including northern Côte d'Ivoire, withstood French (and British) forces until he was captured in 1898. At about the same time in eastern Côte d'Ivoire, the Agni (Anyi) and Abron peoples first resisted the French and, after military setbacks, either sabotaged or circumvented the colonial administration. In the early twentieth century, the Baoulé of central Côte d'Ivoire openly defied colonial authorities until forcibly subdued in a bloody, so-called pacification campaign undertaken in 1906 by Governor Gabriel Angoulvant.

The French administered Côte d'Ivoire in a more direct, systematic style than did their British counterparts, who preferred indirect rule. French authorities routinely dismissed locally selected chiefs, replacing them with others having no legitimate claim to authority, and regrouped or consolidated villages in an attempt to impose a uniform administration throughout the country. As late as 1958, Paris still appointed governors, who administered the colony using a system of direct, centralized rule that left little room for Ivoirian participation. Most of the inhabitants were considered subjects of France with no political rights and a separate system of law. Thus, all adult males were forced to work ten days for no pay each year, often on plantations owned by the French, as part of a tax obligation to the state, and rural males were routinely drafted to work, again for no pay, on public works projects like roads and the railroad.

World War II profoundly affected all of French West Africa (Afrique Occidentale Française—AOF; see Glossary). The rapid surrender of France and the institution of highly discriminatory policies under the Vichy regime alienated the African political elite, many of whom had served France in World War I and expected greater respect. During the immediate postwar years, an emergent, educated African elite demanded reforms in colonial policy. In response, France joined with its colonies in 1946 to form a community known as the French Union and granted to African members rights of free speech, free association, and free assembly. France also eliminated separate legal codes and the practice of unlimited forced labor.

Despite these concessions, wealthy Ivoirian planters were still incensed at having to work on the plantations of French settlers, who by law received more for their crops than they themselves did. As a result, the Ivoirian planters formed the African Agricultural Union (Syndicat Agricole Africain—SAA) to fight for equal rights. In 1946 the SAA gave rise to Côte d'Ivoire's sole political party, the Democratic Party of Côte d'Ivoire (Parti Démocratique de Côte d'Ivoire—PDCI) under the leadership of Félix Houphouët-Boigny. During the postwar years, the party, in cooperation with a regional coalition of anticolonialist groups, militantly challenged French policies in Côte d'Ivoire. Confrontation led to such violence and repression that by 1951 the party was in near ruin. To stave off a collapse, Houphouët-Boigny abandoned his alliance with the French Communist Party and the radical politics of earlier years in favor of practical cooperation with French authorities. France then granted significant political and economic concessions to the colony, which soon became the wealthiest in French West Africa.

In 1956 the French government authorized for all of its African colonies a series of momentous and fundamental reforms, which in effect substituted autonomy for integration with France as the cornerstone of French colonial policy. Two years later, under the leadership of President Charles de Gaulle, the Constitution of the French Fifth Republic provided for the free association of autonomous republics within the French Community, in which France was the senior partner. Côte d'Ivoire voted in favor of the Constitution, which was thought to be a more pragmatic course than complete independence. Nevertheless, following the lead of Senegal and Mali, Côte d'Ivoire withdrew from the French Community and in August 1960 declared its independence. Houphouët-Boigny became Côte d'Ivoire's first president, an office he still held in late 1989.

The original drafters of the Ivoirian Constitution of October 1960 intended to establish a democratic government with a presidential system incorporating the principles of the separation of powers and an independent judiciary. Within a short time, however, governance became highly authoritarian. Party leadership equated a unified state with unanimous support for the PDCI under the untested belief that competition among parties would waste resources, lead to corruption, and destroy unity. By circumscribing the prerogatives of the National Assembly and tailoring election laws, Houphouët-Boigny effectively denied the assembly an independent voice; and by doling out patronage, co-opting opponents, and pitting rivals against one another, he tightened his grip on government.

Even those who objected to Houphouët-Boigny's style admired the results of his policies: twenty years of economic growth and political stability. Nevertheless, invidious habits and attitudes that had developed over the twenty years of economic growth posed a potential threat to the political order. In few other countries was materialism as open and avowed an ideology. By the 1980s, the elite, using its official positions and connections to obtain wealth, had replaced the struggle for independence with the pursuit of privilege, leading to manifest extremes of wealth and poverty. This elite was infected with consumerism, and it could not afford to lose or even share power. At the same time, the sharp economic downturn of the 1980s and Houphouët-Boigny's advancing age caused fears that the ethnic rivalries he sought to dampen might ignite under a less charismatic successor.

For Côte d'Ivoire, ethnicity was a particularly thorny problem. The population included some sixty indigenous ethnic groups. The largest group (that of Houphouët-Boigny) was the Baoulé, which comprised 15 percent of the population and was centered in the forest region southeast of Bouaké. The Baoulé were part of the larger Akan ethnic cluster, which also included the Abron and the Agni groups. The chief rivals of the Baoulé were the Bété, who in the 1980s made up approximately 6 percent of the population. During the twentieth century, the Bété achieved recognition for their success in cash cropping and for their widespread acceptance of Christianity. Because the Bété nurtured strong beliefs in the superiority of their culture and had a long history of resistance to foreign domination, they have often been accused of fomenting anti-government dissent. Other major ethnic groups included the Dan, the Malinké, the Juula, the Sénoufo, and the Agni. The largest single foreign minority group was the Burkinabé (natives of Burkina Faso, formerly known as Upper Volta), who were generally Mossi. They were concentrated in rural areas, where they worked as farm laborers. The Lebanese, officially estimated at 60,000 but possibly numbering 180,000, dominated sectors of the wholesale and retail trade. In 1988 there were approximately 30,000 French citizens in Côte d'Ivoire, or about the same number as at independence.

Because no single ethnic group held a preponderance of power, none could automatically impose its will. Ethnic politics, therefore, were important in Côte d'Ivoire, notwithstanding presidential statements to the contrary. And because of that cultural diversity, Houphouët-Boigny, making a virtue of necessity, perfected the politics of inclusion. All major ethnic groups were represented in his cabinet and the major policy-making bodies of the PDCI, making it easier to deflect responsibility at a time when the rising expectations of Ivoirians were being thwarted.

The Ivoirian economy in the late 1980s continued its downward spiral, primarily because world prices for coffee and cocoa, the country's two principal exports, remained low. At the same time, exports of timber, the third largest source of foreign exchange, declined because of continued overexploitation. Two offshore petroleum fields, which in the early 1970s were projected to make Côte d'Ivoire self-sufficient in fuel, failed to achieve projected outputs, let alone self-sufficiency. Because of the relatively low world prices for petroleum and Côte d'Ivoire's high production costs, all the wells in one field were capped.

Beginning in the mid-1970s, the government undertook a major effort to diversify the export economy by expanding production of palm oil, natural rubber, coconut oil, cotton, sugar, and tropical fruits. Ten years later, the government implemented a program to modernize its import substitution industries, sell off unprofitable parastatals, and further expand exports to include processed foods, textiles, wood, and such nonagricultural products as building materials, chemicals, and electronics.

The results of all three plans were mixed. The market for palm and coconut oils was eroded by substitutes with less saturated fat; sugar, produced by a grossly inefficient parastatal, simply added to a world surplus; and in other areas Côte d'Ivoire was competing with other states of Africa and Asia producing many of the same tropical agricultural goods. Exports produced under the industrial expansion program were more expensive—at least initially—than similar goods produced elsewhere and so required export subsidies. Subsidies, however, required scarce funds. Meanwhile, Houphouët-Boigny adamantly refused to cut producer prices for coffee and cocoa; consequently, production levels increased—some estimates for the 1988–89 cocoa harvest were as high as 700,000 tons—which further depressed commodity prices. Finally, divestment from parastatals yielded lower returns than anticipated.

Moreover, the larger, more profitable companies were purchased by foreign interests, further adding to capital flight.

The lack of investment capital was the undoing of the Ivoirian miracle. To finance development, Côte d'Ivoire borrowed substantial amounts abroad, especially during the mid-1970s when unusually high coffee and cocoa prices led planners to overestimate the potential of the economy. Thus, by 1976 high debt payments together with repatriated profits and foreign worker remittances had produced a negative net reserve position for the first time in the country's history. Debt servicing costs continued to mount to the extent that in May 1987 the government announced that it would suspend payments on its foreign debt.

To stave off a financial collapse, Côte d'Ivoire negotiated an economic recovery and structural adjustment program with the Paris Club (see Glossary), the International Monetary Fund (IMF—see Glossary), and the London Club (see Glossary) that provided a respite from debt repayment. The subsequent retrenchments mandated by the programs affected all income groups in the country, but they had the greatest impact on the poor. These measures gave rise to such symptoms of violent social dislocation as drug abuse and crime—which required additional expenditures and new political options from the government.

The party-government of Côte d'Ivoire in the mid-1980s most closely resembled an old-fashioned political machine. Although it called itself a one-party democracy, Côte d'Ivoire was not a democracy in the Western sense: the government controlled the press, limited civil liberties, and allowed no institutionalized opposition to frame debate. As economic austerity exacerbated political tensions, individuals and informal groups called for greater political choice, which the government seemed unprepared to grant.

Meanwhile, students protested against the role of foreigners in the economy and the government, which they saw as controlled by a small number of party leaders for the benefit of a privileged class of bureaucrats and landowners. Corruption in the business community, long considered an affliction of other African states, was becoming embarrassingly obvious in Côte d'Ivoire. Reduced services, coupled with wage freezes and higher costs, were alienating mid-level civil servants and professionals. And increasingly brazen attacks against expatriates by well-armed bandits were affecting tourism and foreign investment. A growing number of Ivoirians was questioning whether these problems could be solved by a government dominated by an octogenarian president with no apparent successor.

In the late 1980s, the choice of a successor to Houphouët-Boigny remained a dominant issue in Ivoirian politics. Because the style, form, tone, and policies of the government were the personal creation of the president, the succession question had substantial implications. Two plausible contenders in 1989 were Philippe Yacé and Henri Konan Bedié, representing, respectively, the first and second generations of Ivoirian politics. Houphouët-Boigny refused to designate an heir and left the decision to the political process, believing that the Ivoirian polity was mature enough to make a decision without recklessly endangering national security or precipitating military intervention into civilian politics.

With the exception of a small uprising (the true size of which has never been documented) in 1970 near Gagnoa in the Bété region, the military has played no role in domestic peacekeeping. Moreover, Houphouët-Boigny co-opted the military with sufficiently attractive perquisites (including high salaries and positions in the party) so that the senior officer corps had little interest in political meddling. To further promote satisfaction, the military was equipped with advanced equipment purchased from France.

In its foreign affairs, Côte d'Ivoire either befriended or attempted to isolate its immediate neighbors. Recognizing that the "oasis never encroaches upon the desert," Houphouët-Boigny sought mutually beneficial ties with Côte d'Ivoire's neighbors despite ideological differences. And for good measure, he insisted that France maintain a battalion of marines near Abidjan to buttress his own military.

As Côte d'Ivoire faced the 1990s, the problems of finding a successor to Houphouët-Boigny, discontent on the campus of its only university, an ossified party, and a beggar-thy-neighbor materialism concerned Ivoirians. At the same time, a history of political stability coupled with a tradition of civilian rule and an apparent willingness on the part of the second and third generation of Ivoirian politicians to liberalize the political process and accommodate divergent views promised a less troubled future for the country.

October 6, 1989

*   *   *

In mid-1989, as the economy continued its decline, even leading members of the establishment began voicing discontent, albeit in guarded terms. In September 1989, Houphouët-Boigny invited political leaders—critics and supporters—to Abidjan for what was called "five days of dialogue." Uncharacteristically sharp and candid criticisms of the party and government over the five days conveyed a lack of confidence in the ruling elite, which was labeled narrow and selfish, and called for a more responsive party in a multi-party system. Less than a month later on October 16, 1989, Houphouët-Boigny reshuffled his cabinet and, in response to World Bank (see Glossary) recommendations, reduced it from 29 to 21 members.

Four months later, students protested recently announced wage cuts, tax increases, and the longstanding issue of single party rule with large-scale demonstrations that at times turned into violent confrontations with police in the streets of Abidjan and, in one instance, in Abidjan's Roman Catholic cathedral. In April and May 1990, army and air force recruits protesting the cost-cutting decision to limit their military service to a single tour of duty demonstrated in bases across Côte d'Ivoire; a group of armed air force recruits even took over the international airport outside Abidjan for twelve hours. Police and firefighters also staged highly visible protests for higher wages. By mid-May, Houphouët-Boigny had capitulated on the issues of military duty and higher wages for police and firefighters, and he scrapped plans to increase income taxes. Most significantly, he pledged for the first time to legalize opposition parties and promised to name a successor, although as of June 1990, he had not yet done either.

July 1, 1990   Robert Handloff

Chapter 1. Historical Setting

Nineteenth-century mud-brick mosque in the Sudanic style

SINCE THE 1950s, CÔTE D'IVOIRE has been one of the few sub-Saharan African countries to enjoy political stability and a relatively sound economy. Much of the credit for Côte d'Ivoire's success goes to Félix Houphouët-Boigny, the country's most prominent politician since 1944, who methodically shaped personal and institutional controls and carefully cultivated and maintained close ties with Western industrialized countries.

Côte d'Ivoire remained relatively isolated for much of its early history. Islam, which penetrated most other regions of West Africa before the sixteenth century, made only minor inroads into Côte d'Ivoire's forest belt. The country's rugged coastline and lack of suitable harbors discouraged European exploration until the mid-nineteenth century. Before that time, the only French contact with Côte d'Ivoire occurred in 1637, when missionaries landed at Assini, on the southern Ivoirian coast. This remote region was neither politically nor economically significant and therefore held little attraction for settlement or exploitation by European powers.

In the 1880s, France pursued a more vigorous colonial policy. Driven by the growing forces of European imperial competition for foreign influence, as well as the promise of wealth to be found in a West African empire, French explorers, missionaries, trading companies, and soldiers gradually extended the area under French domination. They achieved control over the population, sometimes through deceit and coercion, by signing treaties with local rulers, who agreed to come under French protection in return for economic favors and protection from neighboring enemies. After Côte d'Ivoire officially became a French colony in 1893, France engaged in a so-called pacification campaign clearly intended to subjugate the indigenous population and to establish French sovereignty. Before World War I, the many instances of violent and protracted resistance to the French, especially among the Baoulé, were the longest wars fought between Europeans and Africans in West Africa. In many instances, these were contained only when Ivoirians in positions of power recognized the tremendous economic advantages accorded them by France.

By the 1940s, sources of strong opposition to the French colonial administration had emerged. At that time, France was neither able nor willing to crush opposition as in the past. Moreover, the opposition, which focused on the administration's institutionalization of forced labor and its discrimination in favor of French

3

planters, intended—at least initially—simply to change colonial policy rather than to achieve independence. Because all Ivoirians were affected by at least one of these discriminatory practices, many were hostile to the administration. Ivoirian planters, in particular, suffered from French discriminatory policies. In 1943, for example, they were forbidden to recruit their own labor and were sometimes removed from their own plantations to work for European enterprises. This group thus stood to benefit greatly from the abolition of colonial labor recruitment policies and had strong reasons to struggle against certain aspects of French colonialism. They were behind the formation of an anticolonialist movement that in 1944 resulted in the birth of the African Agricultural Union and later of the Democratic Party of Côte d'Ivoire.

In other ways, French colonial rule had significant consequences for the modern history of Côte d'Ivoire. The French colonial system introduced modern technology and economic development. It also reinforced the position of relatively privileged groups like the Ivoirian planters, when discriminatory practices were abolished after World War II. As a result of economic and social changes in France after World War II, French investments in the West African colonies grew at the same time as Paris thrust greater responsibilities and powers on its African colonies. There emerged in Côte d'Ivoire a group whose economic interests were closely linked to those of France and whose continuing close relations with France ensured the stability of French economic interests in Côte d'Ivoire. Thus, when Côte d'Ivoire became independent in 1960, France was able to maintain a secure economic grip on the country and continued to influence Ivoirian political decisions, much as it did before independence.

The most significant features of modern Ivoirian history have been the development of the one-party state, which Houphouët-Boigny established to assure his own autocratic rule, and economic growth. When Côte d'Ivoire gained independence in 1960 under the leadership of Houphouët-Boigny, the new president immediately assumed strong powers as head of state, head of government, and leader of the ruling Democratic Party of Côte d'Ivoire. Houphouët-Boigny's political strength derived from the country's economic prosperity. Until the late 1970s, Côte d'Ivoire experienced enormous economic growth, based largely on agricultural exports. The benefits of economic prosperity were not equally distributed, however. Benefiting most was a bourgeoisie made up of wealthy politicians, who were often also business people and owners of prosperous coffee and cocoa plantations. But the president successfully prevented significant pockets of resistance to his rule from

4

forming through a combination of co-optation and mild repression. So successful was he that most of those whose rights were abused nonetheless recognized that they were materially better off than their neighbors. The greatest source of Houphouët-Boigny's popular appeal was, and continued to be in mid-1988, the strength of his charismatic personality.

Pre-European Period

Little is known about the original inhabitants of Côte d'Ivoire. Historians believe that they were all either displaced or absorbed by the ancestors of the present inhabitants. The first recorded history is found in the chronicles of North African traders, who, from early Roman times, conducted a caravan trade across the Sahara in salt, slaves, gold, and other items. The southern terminals of the trans-Saharan trade routes were located on the edge of the desert, and from there supplemental trade extended as far south as the edge of the rain forest. The more important terminals— Djenné, Gao, and Timbuctu—grew into major commercial centers around which the great Sudanic empires developed. By controlling the trade routes with their powerful military forces, these empires were able to dominate neighboring states.

The Sudanic empires also became centers of Islamic learning. Islam had been introduced into the western Sudan (see Glossary) by Arab traders from North Africa and spread rapidly after the conversion of many important rulers. From the eleventh century, by which time the rulers of the Sudanic empires had embraced Islam, it spread south into the northern areas of contemporary Côte d'Ivoire.

Ghana, the earliest of the Sudanic empires, flourished in present-day eastern Mauritania from the fourth to the thirteenth century. At the peak of its power in the eleventh century, its realms extended from the Atlantic Ocean to Timbuctu. After the decline of Ghana, the Mali Empire grew into a powerful Muslim state, which reached its apogee in the early part of the fourteenth century. The territory of the Mali Empire in Côte d'Ivoire was limited to the northwest corner around Odienné. Its slow decline starting at the end of the fourteenth century followed internal discord and revolts by vassal states, one of which, Songhai, flourished as an empire between the fourteenth and sixteenth centuries. Songhai was also weakened by internal discord, which led to factional warfare. This discord spurred most of the migrations of peoples southward toward the forest belt.

The dense rain forest covering the southern half of the country created barriers to large-scale political organizations as seen farther

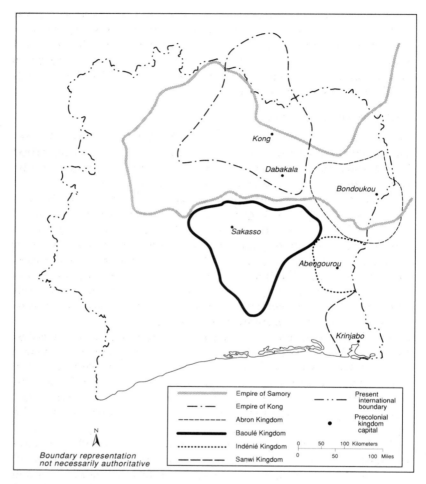

Source: Based on information from J.-N. Loucou, "Histoire," in Pierre Vennetier (ed.), *Atlas de la Côte d'Ivoire* (2d ed.), Paris, 1983, 25.

Figure 2. Precolonial Kingdoms

north. Inhabitants lived in villages or clusters of villages whose contacts with the outside world were filtered through long-distance traders. Villagers subsisted on agriculture and hunting.

Five important states flourished in Côte d'Ivoire in the pre-European era (see fig. 2). The Muslim empire of Kong was established by the Juula in the early eighteenth century in the north-central region inhabited by the Sénoufo, who had fled Islamization under the Mali Empire (see Ethnic Groups and Languages, ch. 2).

Although Kong became a prosperous center of agriculture, trade, and crafts, ethnic diversity and religious discord gradually weakened the kingdom. The city of Kong was destroyed in 1895 by Samori Touré (see Local Resistance and Establishment of Protectorates, this ch.).

The Abron kingdom of Jaman was established in the seventeenth century by an Akan group, the Abron, who had fled the developing Asante confederation in what is present-day Ghana. From their settlement south of Bondoukou, the Abron gradually extended their hegemony over the Juula in Bondoukou, who were recent émigrés from the market city of Begho. Bondoukou developed into a major center of commerce and Islam. The kingdom's Quranic scholars attracted students from all parts of West Africa.

In the mid-eighteenth century in east-central Côte d'Ivoire, other Akan groups fleeing the Asante established a Baoulé kingdom at Sakasso and two Agni kingdoms, Indénié and Sanwi. The Baoulé, like the Asante, elaborated a highly centralized political and administrative structure under three successive rulers, but it finally split into smaller chiefdoms. Despite the breakup of their kingdom, the Baoulé strongly resisted French subjugation. The descendants of the rulers of the Agni kingdoms tried to retain their separate identity long after Côte d'Ivoire's independence; as late as 1969, the Sanwi of Krinjabo attempted to break away from Côte d'Ivoire and form an independent kingdom.

Arrival of the Europeans

The African continent, situated between Europe and the imagined treasures of the Far East, quickly became the destination of the European explorers of the fifteenth century. The first Europeans to explore the West African coast were the Portuguese. Other European sea powers soon followed, and trade was established with many of the coastal peoples of West Africa. At first, the trade included gold, ivory, and pepper, but the establishment of American colonies in the sixteenth century spurred a demand for slaves, who soon became the major export from the West African coastal regions. Local rulers, under treaties with the Europeans, procured goods and slaves from inhabitants of the interior. By the end of the fifteenth century, commercial contacts with Europe had spawned strong European influences, which permeated areas northward from the West African coast.

Côte d'Ivoire, like the rest of West Africa, was subject to these influences, but the absence of sheltered harbors along its coastline prevented Europeans from establishing permanent trading posts. Seaborne trade, therefore, was irregular and played only a minor

Côte d'Ivoire: A Country Study

role in the penetration and eventual conquest by Europeans of Côte d'Ivoire. The slave trade, in particular, had little effect on the peoples of Côte d'Ivoire. A profitable trade in ivory, which gave the area its name, was carried out during the seventeenth century, but it brought about such a decline in elephants that the trade itself virtually had died out by the beginning of the eighteenth century.

The earliest recorded French voyage to West Africa took place in 1483. The first West African French settlement, Saint Louis, was founded in the mid-seventeenth century in Senegal, while at about the same time the Dutch ceded to the French a settlement at Ile de Gorée off Dakar. A French mission was established in 1687 at Assini, and it became the first European outpost in that area. Assini's survival was precarious, however, and only in the mid-nineteenth century did the French establish themselves firmly in Côte d'Ivoire. By that time, they had already established settlements around the mouth of the Senegal River and at other points along the coasts of what are now Senegal, Gambia, and Guinea-Bissau. Meanwhile, the British had permanent outposts in the same areas and on the Gulf of Guinea east of Côte d'Ivoire.

Activity along the coast stimulated European interest in the interior, especially along the two great rivers, the Senegal and the Niger. Concerted French exploration of West Africa began in the mid-nineteenth century but moved slowly and was based more on individual initiative than on government policy. In the 1840s, the French concluded a series of treaties with local West African rulers that enabled the French to build fortified posts along the Gulf of Guinea to serve as permanent trading centers. The first posts in Côte d'Ivoire included one at Assini and another at Grand-Bassam, which became the colony's first capital. The treaties provided for French sovereignty within the posts and for trading privileges in exchange for fees or *coutumes* (see Glossary) paid annually to the local rulers for the use of the land. The arrangement was not entirely satisfactory to the French because trade was limited and misunderstandings over treaty obligations often arose. Nevertheless, the French government maintained the treaties, hoping to expand trade. France also wanted to maintain a presence in the region to stem the increasing influence of the British along the Gulf of Guinea coast.

The defeat of France in the Franco-Prussian War (1871) and the subsequent annexation by Germany of the French region of Alsace-Lorraine caused the French government to abandon its colonial ambitions and withdraw its military garrisons from its French West African trading posts, leaving them in the care of resident merchants. The trading post at Grand-Bassam in Côte d'Ivoire

8

The mosque at Kong, ca. 1897. Engraving from Louis Gustave Binger,
Du Niger au Golfe de Guinée, *Paris, 1892.*

was left in the care of a shipper from Marseille, Arthur Verdier, who in 1878 was named resident of the Establishment of Côte d'Ivoire.

French Expansion in Côte d'Ivoire

In 1885 France and Germany brought all the European powers with interests in Africa together at the Berlin Conference. Its principal objective was to rationalize what became known as the European scramble for colonies in Africa. Prince Otto von Bismarck also wanted a greater role in Africa for Germany, which he thought he could achieve in part by fostering competition between France and Britain. The agreement signed by all participants in 1885 stipulated that on the African coastline only European annexations or spheres of influence that involved effective occupation by Europeans would be recognized. Another agreement in 1890 extended this rule to the interior of Africa and set off a scramble for territory, primarily by France, Britain, Portugal, and Belgium.

Local Resistance and Establishment of Protectorates

In 1886, to support its claims of effective occupation, France again assumed direct control of its West African coastal trading posts and embarked on an accelerated program of exploration in the interior.

In 1887 Lieutenant Louis Binger began a two-year journey that traversed parts of Côte d'Ivoire's interior. By the end of the journey, he had concluded four treaties establishing French protectorates in Côte d'Ivoire. Also in 1887, Verdier's agent, Maurice Treich-Laplène, negotiated five additional agreements that extended French influence from the headwaters of the Niger River Basin through Côte d'Ivoire.

By the end of the 1880s, France had established what passed for effective control over the coastal regions of Côte d'Ivoire, and in 1889 Britain recognized French sovereignty in the area. That same year, France named Treich-Laplène titular governor of the territory. In 1893 Côte d'Ivoire was made a French colony, and then Captain Binger was appointed governor. Agreements with Liberia in 1892 and with Britain in 1893 determined the eastern and western boundaries of the colony, but the northern boundary was not fixed until 1947 because of efforts by the French government to attach parts of Upper Volta (present-day Burkina Faso) and French Sudan (present-day Mali) to Côte d'Ivoire for economic and administrative reasons.

Throughout the process of partition, the Africans were little concerned with the occasional white person who came wandering by. Many local rulers in small, isolated communities did not understand or, more often, were misled by the Europeans about the significance of treaties that compromised their authority. Other local leaders, however, thought that the Europeans could solve economic problems or become allies in the event of a dispute with belligerent neighbors. In the end, the loss of land and freedom by all the local rulers resulted more from their inability to counter European deception and brute strength than from a loss of will to respond to European encroachment.

Throughout the early years of French rule, French military contingents were sent inland to establish new posts. The African population resisted French penetration and settlement, even in areas where treaties of protection had been in force. Among those offering greatest resistance was Samori Touré, who in the 1880s and 1890s was establishing an empire that extended over large parts of present-day Guinea, Mali, Burkina Faso, and Côte d'Ivoire. Samori's large, well-equipped army, which could manufacture and repair its own firearms, attracted strong support throughout the region. The French responded to Samori's expansion of regional control with military pressure. French campaigns against Samori, which were met with fierce resistance, intensified in the mid-1890s until he was captured in 1898.

Akan chief in traditional attire
Courtesy Robert Handloff

France's imposition of a head tax in 1900, aimed at enabling the colony to undertake a public works program, provoked a number of revolts. Ivoirians viewed the tax as a violation of the terms of the protectorate treaties because it seemed that France was now demanding the equivalent of a *coutume* from the local kings rather than the reverse. Much of the population, especially in the interior, also considered the tax a humiliating symbol of submission.

Repression and Conquest

In 1906 Gabriel Angoulvant was appointed governor of Côte d'Ivoire. Angoulvant, who had little prior experience in Africa, believed that the development of Côte d'Ivoire could proceed only after the forceful conquest, or so-called pacification, of the colony. He thus embarked on a vigorous campaign, sending military expeditions into the hinterland to quell resistance. As a result of these expeditions, local rulers were compelled to obey existing antislavery laws, supply porters and food to the French forces, and ensure the protection of French trade and personnel. In return, the French agreed to leave local customs intact and specifically promised not to intervene in the selection of rulers. But the French often disregarded their side of the agreement, deporting or interning rulers regarded as instigators of revolt. They also regrouped villages and established a uniform administration throughout most of the colony.

Finally, they replaced the *coutume* with an allowance based on performance.

French Rule Until World War II

Evolution of Colonial Policy

French colonial policy incorporated concepts of assimilation and association. Assimilation presupposed the inherent superiority of French culture over all others, so that in practice the assimilation policy in the colonies meant extension of the French language, institutions, laws, and customs.

The policy of association also affirmed the superiority of the French in the colonies, but it entailed different institutions and systems of laws for the colonizer and the colonized. Under this policy, the Africans in Côte d'Ivoire were allowed to preserve their own customs insofar as they were compatible with French interests. An indigenous elite trained in French administrative practice formed an intermediary group between the French and the Africans.

Assimilation was practiced in Côte d'Ivoire to the extent that after 1930 a small number of Westernized Ivoirians were granted the right to apply for French citizenship. Most Ivoirians, however, were classified as French subjects and were governed under the principle of association.

Until 1958, governors appointed in Paris administered the colony of Côte d'Ivoire, using a system of direct, centralized administration that left little room for Ivoirian participation in policy making. The French colonial administration also adopted divide-and-rule policies, applying ideas of assimilation only to the educated elite. The French were also interested in ensuring that the small but influential elite was sufficiently satisfied with the status quo to refrain from any anti-French sentiment. In fact, although they were strongly opposed to the practices of association, educated Ivoirians believed that they would achieve equality with their French peers through assimilation rather than through complete independence from France, a change that would eliminate the enormous economic advantages of remaining a French possession. But after the assimilation doctrine was implemented entirely, at least in principle, through the postwar reforms, Ivoirian leaders realized that even assimilation implied the superiority of the French over the Ivoirians and that discrimination and inequality would end only with independence.

Colonial Administration

French expansion in Africa during the last quarter of the nineteenth century was so rapid that it was difficult to find enough

Captain Louis Binger and Maurice Teich-Laplène. Engravings from Louis Gustave Binger, Du Niger au Golfe de Guinée, *Paris, 1892.*

administrators to govern the growing number of possessions effectively. For a brief period, therefore, the French adopted a system of indirect rule using indigenous leaders as their surrogates. The local rulers, however, exercised authority only by sanction of the French administrators. Those rulers who refused to submit to French directives were deposed and replaced with more cooperative ones.

With the consolidation of French power in West Africa at the end of the nineteenth century, French officials increasingly assumed direct administrative powers, and they reduced local rulers to the level of low-ranking civil servants. In 1895 France grouped the French West African colonies of Côte d'Ivoire, Dahomey (present-day Benin), Guinea, Niger, French Sudan (present-day Mali), Senegal, Upper Volta, and Mauritania together and subordinated their governors to the governor of Senegal, who became governor general. A series of additional decrees in 1904 defined the structure of this political unit and organized it into French West Africa (Afrique Occidentale Française—AOF; see Glossary).

France divided the individual colonies into districts known as *cercles,* each of which was governed by a district commander

13

(commandant du cercle) who, because of poor communications between the *cercles* and the colonial governors, exercised his responsibilities with relative autonomy. Within a *cercle,* the commander ruled through a hierarchy of local rulers, whom he appointed and could dismiss at will. He was advised by a council of notables *(conseil des notables)* consisting of these local rulers and of other individuals appointed by him.

Most of the inhabitants of the colonies were subjects of France with no political rights. Moreover, they were drafted for work in mines, on plantations, as porters, and on public projects as part of their tax responsibility. They were also expected to serve in the military and were subject to the *indigénat* (see Glossary), a separate system of law.

Economic Development and Social Change

As France consolidated its holdings in Côte d'Ivoire, it began to take steps to make the colony self-supporting. In 1900 the French initiated a policy that made each colony responsible for securing the resources—both money and personnel—needed for its administration and defense; France would offer assistance only when needed.

The public works programs undertaken by the Ivoirian colonial government and the exploitation of natural resources required massive commitments of labor. The French therefore imposed a system of forced labor under which each male adult Ivoirian was required to work for ten days each year without compensation as part of his obligation to the state. The system was subject to extreme misuse and was the most hated aspect of French colonial rule. Because the population of Côte d'Ivoire was insufficient to meet the labor demand on French plantations and forests, which were among the greatest users of labor in the AOF, the French recruited large numbers of workers from Upper Volta to work in Côte d'Ivoire. This source of labor was so important to the economic life of Côte d'Ivoire that in 1932 the AOF annexed a large part of Upper Volta to Côte d'Ivoire and administered it as a single colony.

In addition to the political and economic changes produced by colonial rule, the French also introduced social institutions that brought about fundamental changes to Ivoirian culture. Catholic missionaries established a network of churches and primary schools, which in time provided the literate Ivoirians needed by government and commerce. Some of the wealthier and more ambitious Ivoirians continued their educations at the few secondary schools and at French universities, adopting European culture and values

Koulango village. Engraving from Louis Gustave Binger, Du Niger au Golfe de Guinée, *Paris, 1892.*

15

and becoming members of a new African elite. The members of this elite were accepted as cultural and social equals by their white counterparts and were exempt from military and labor service.

Except in remote rural areas, the colonial government gradually destroyed the traditional elite by reducing the local rulers to junior civil servants and by indiscriminately appointing as rulers people with no legitimate claims to such titles. In areas where traditional leaders retained their position and power, they often developed strong rivalries with educated Ivoirians who tried to usurp that leadership on the grounds that their education and modern outlook better suited them for the position.

Impact of World War II

World War II had a profound effect on the future of all French West Africa. The fall of France and the establishment of the German-allied Vichy government in France forced the French colonies to declare loyalty either to the Vichy regime or to the Free French under General Charles de Gaulle. Although all the AOF governors remained loyal to the Vichy government, Ivoirians largely favored the Free French.

The Vichy government, espousing Nazi racial theories, subjected French West Africa to economic exploitation and overt racism. French planters intensified their labor recruitment practices and military conscription. Farmers were forced to meet production quotas to supply the armed forces at the expense of the local residents, whose standard of living had already been greatly lowered by the cutoff of imports from Europe.

The onset of World War II and the rapid surrender of France, the self-described purveyor of a so-called higher civilization, sharply revised political thinking in Côte d'Ivoire. Ivoirians resented Vichy policies and began to express feelings of Ivoirian nationalism. Ivoirian intellectuals were attracted by some of the Marxist ideas introduced by anti-Nazi movements and by some French teachers and labor organizers. In 1943 branches of an organization known as Communist Study Groups were established in the principal cities of West Africa, including Abidjan in Côte d'Ivoire. Many African intellectuals in these groups later became prominent as postwar national leaders.

Brazzaville Conference

After the defeat of France and the alignment of many West Africans with the Free French, the political maturity of the indigenous populations developed. De Gaulle recognized the need to revise the relationship between France and its colonies in Africa. In

January 1944, Free French politicians and high-ranking colonial officials from the French African colonies met in Brazzaville (in present-day Congo). The Brazzaville Conference, as it came to be known, recommended political, social, and economic reforms. It accepted the representation of the colonies in the French Constituent Assembly, which was to draw up a new French constitution after the war, and the subsequent representation of the colonies in whatever parliamentary body the constitution established. The conference also recommended that the colonies be administered with greater autonomy and that both French citizens and Africans be permitted to elect a legislative assembly. In addition, the conference committed the French government to respect local customs, abolish the *indigénat,* adopt a new penal code, end labor conscription, improve health and educational facilities, and open positions in the colonial administration to Africans.

The only immediate effect of the conference was the passage of a law in August 1944 granting workers in the AOF the right to organize. In October 1945, after the defeat of Germany and the end of the war, the first countrywide elections were held in Côte d'Ivoire to choose two delegates for the French Constituent Assembly, which was to meet in Paris before the end of the year. French citizens residing in Côte d'Ivoire elected one delegate, and a restricted African electorate chose Félix Houphouët-Boigny as the other delegate. Houphouët-Boigny, a wealthy African planter and French-educated physician, was the cofounder of the African Agricultural Union (Syndicat Agricole Africain—SAA), which was formed in 1944 to fight for the abolition of forced labor and the rights of African planters. Much of Houphouët-Boigny's support came from the SAA, whose members included some 20,000 African planters as well as laborers, civil servants, traders, and other Africans engaged in the money economy. In spite of his popularity, however, Houphouët-Boigny won by only a narrow margin.

Two factors explain the closeness of the vote. First, the French colonial administration disapproved of the SAA and consequently supported the candidacy of a Mossi, costing Houphouët-Boigny the votes of the majority of Mossi, who constituted one of the largest ethnic groups in Upper Volta. And second, Houphouët-Boigny, a Baoulé, faced rival candidates from the Bété and Agni ethnic groups. Houphouët-Boigny's support came from most of the rural voters in the south and the forest area, but he would not have won the election without the support of most of the voters in the Bobo Dioulasso region in Upper Volta (a part of Côte d'Ivoire's annexed territory).

When the French Constituent Assembly met in Paris, 63 of the 600 delegates represented the African colonies. The African delegates, all members of the educated elite, demanded liberal reforms in the colonial system, for which they received support from French socialist and communist delegates. In the end, the assembly reevaluated colonial policy and drafted a plan for the union of France and the colonies.

In addition to abolishing the *indigénat* and forced labor system, in 1945 and 1946 the French government decreed a number of other important reforms concerning Africans. It granted freedom of speech, association, and assembly to the residents of the colonies; it provided funds for economic and social development; it permitted the AOF to adopt a new penal code; and it granted all inhabitants of French colonies French citizenship. France's failure to define closely the rights of citizenship, however, prevented the indigenous populations of the colonies from the full exercise of civil rights on the grounds that they were not yet ready for it.

French Union

The first draft of the French Fourth Republic's constitution, which included whole passages of the Brazzaville recommendations, proved too liberal for the French electorate, which rejected it in a May 1946 referendum. When a second Constituent Assembly convened in June, pressure from conservative elements in France and in the colonies was strong, and sharp differences of opinion developed among the delegates. The advocates of colonial autonomy included all the colonial deputies and the French political left wing. Most African deputies, including Houphouët-Boigny, supported the idea of local self-government and political equality for the French and the Africans. The French political right and center, however, favored a nominally federalist system, within which France would preserve its dominant position. A compromise was finally reached, and the plan for the French Union was written into a new draft constitution, which was adopted by the assembly on September 28, 1946. It was approved as the constitution of the Fourth Republic in a referendum held in France and the overseas possessions on October 13, 1946.

Under the French Union, the French West African colonies were designated as overseas territories. The French government exercised all legislative and executive powers, and the administration of Côte d'Ivoire continued under the French Ministry of Overseas Departments and Territories.

Despite the acceptance of the French Union in Côte d'Ivoire, longstanding economic grievances gave rise to the development of

Colonial architecture,
Grand-Bassam
Courtesy Eszti Votaw

anticolonial sentiment. With the large-scale introduction of cash crops between World War I and World War II, a wealthy African planter class emerged. These Africans competed with Europeans who had come to Côte d'Ivoire to make their fortunes. Colonial policies strongly favored the Europeans: they received free labor under the forced labor system, higher prices for their crops, and access to protected markets. African resentment against this discrimination grew during World War II, when economic hardships weighed especially heavily on African plantation owners.

The rights to free speech and assembly, guaranteed by the constitutional reforms of 1946, permitted the formation of African political parties. A number of parties based on ethnic and regional interests were organized in Côte d'Ivoire and elected members to the Territorial Assembly, created as a result of the 1946 reforms, and the Abidjan municipal council. The Democratic Party of Côte d'Ivoire (Parti Démocratique de Côte d'Ivoire—PDCI), created in 1946 out of the SAA to appeal to a wider following than its predecessor, became the dominant party. It soon attracted the radical intellectuals from the wartime Communist Study Groups and became a significant political force in French West Africa. Its leader, Houphouët-Boigny, was rapidly becoming a prominent national figure. Having successfully sponsored the law abolishing forced labor, he had regained support from the Mossi of Upper Volta. He served in 1946 as a delegate to the French Constituent Assembly and, later that year, to the newly constituted French National Assembly.

Regional Political Cooperation

Increasing political activity and a growing national consciousness were both responsible for and stimulated by the postwar constitutional reforms. Pressure from the SAA and similar organizations in other territories brought about most of the 1946 reforms. The reforms grouped the territories into the AOF under one elected council, the Grand Council in Dakar, thereby encouraging cooperation across territorial boundaries. As a result, in 1947 Houphouët-Boigny and several other French West African leaders formed the African Democratic Rally (Rassemblement Démocratique Africain—RDA).

The RDA was established during a critical period in French history. In 1946 and 1947, France was confronted by open rebellion in Indochina and Madagascar and by unrest in North Africa. Internally, the alliance between conservatives and communists, uneasy from the start, was collapsing. The French viewed the RDA, which called for full equality and consequently enjoyed the support of African and French communists, as another serious threat to French colonial interests. As a result, the French colonial administration harassed the RDA, which was also opposed by Africans allied with the more moderate French Socialist Party. Nevertheless, the RDA soon emerged as the dominant political force in French West Africa, and Côte d'Ivoire, where African and European planters were in direct competition, provided the most fertile ground for recruiting a militant African party. Consequently, Côte d'Ivoire became the stronghold of the RDA, and Houphouët-Boigny became the RDA leader. Thus, France also considered Côte d'Ivoire and Houphouët-Boigny's party, the PDCI, as threats to French colonial rule.

After a strongly conservative and discriminatory colonial administration was installed in 1947, relations between the PDCI and the administration became openly hostile. The administration actively sponsored rival parties and manipulated elections. It dismissed PDCI supporters from government jobs and jailed most PDCI leaders. Only his parliamentary immunity enabled Houphouët-Boigny to escape imprisonment. The PDCI retaliated by organizing strikes, boycotts of European goods and services, and mass demonstrations. In 1949 the hostility erupted into violence as government troops fired on African demonstrators on several occasions.

By 1951 the PDCI was close to collapse. Its alliance, through the RDA, with the French Communist Party had alienated the more moderate elements of the party. Government-sponsored rival parties had eroded much of its popular support and drastically weakened its position in elective bodies of the French Union. Houphouët-Boigny, in a radical effort to preserve the PDCI, severed connections with the French Communist Party and expelled the RDA's secretary general, who supported the communist association. He then abandoned the PDCI policy of militant opposition to the administration and embarked on a policy of practical cooperation. This policy change restored the strength and prestige of the PDCI at home and of the RDA in the rest of the AOF and France. Also, it led to political concessions as well as significant economic cooperation with France and members of the local French community. Within a short time, Côte d'Ivoire became the wealthiest territory in the AOF.

Transformation of the Democratic Party of Côte d'Ivoire

By the end of 1946, the PDCI achieved its political monopoly by bargaining with potential contenders, rather than through open competition. In any event, the party received widespread support throughout the country. For example, an African could be elected in Côte d'Ivoire only with the endorsement of the PDCI.

The organization of the PDCI, based on that of the French Communist Party, was determined during the party's First Territorial Congress in October 1947. The Executive Committee presided over party cells located throughout the country. Although the PDCI became a direct party, operating on the principle of democratic centralism, it deviated from French Communist Party organization in that it was not a vanguard party with restricted membership. Instead, it became a mass organization whose members were required only to purchase a party card and pay annual dues.

Ideologically, the PDCI discouraged the transition to independence or even greater democracy on the pretext that intraparty disagreements prevented the party from implementing its democratic governing mechanisms. Instead, the PCDI's leadership gave Houphouët-Boigny almost autocratic control. In addition, *sous-section* (subsection at the *cercle* level) officials and others in positions of responsibility frequently nominated village committees in rural areas instead of allowing them to be elected. As a result, most rural party committees reflected the preexisting ethnic imbalance. At the national level, PDCI leaders had stipulated from the party's birth that party congresses would be held annually as part of the democratic process. In fact, by 1956 only two had been held: in

1947 and 1949. Consequently, those in party offices enjoyed long, uncontested tenures.

Reform and the French Community

The reforms of 1956, or *loi cadre,* passed by the French Fourth Republic, acknowledged the growing nationalism and a developing political consciousness in the AOF. From its inception, the *loi cadre* drew on the suggestions of African leaders who were permitted to participate in the decision-making process.

Conceptually, the *loi cadre* ended the integrationalist phase of French colonial policy and granted considerable internal autonomy to the overseas territories. Universal suffrage and the elimination of the dual college electoral system led to the creation of district and local representative councils and a great enlargement of the powers of the territorial assemblies. Each territory could formulate its own domestic policies, although the territories continued to rely on France for decisions concerning foreign affairs, defense, higher education, and economic aid. As its most important provision, the *loi cadre* established the Council of Government, which assumed the major executive functions of each territory, until that time carried out by a colonial official appointed in Paris.

After the dissolution of the French Fourth Republic in 1958, General Charles de Gaulle, the first president of the Fifth Republic, had even more extensive reforms written into a new constitution, reflecting not only de Gaulle's own pragmatic and anti-imperialist ideas but also the economic and political changes that had occurred since 1946. The French Constitution of 1958, creating the Fifth Republic, provided for the free association of autonomous republics within the newly created French Community, in which France was the senior partner. The community had jurisdiction over foreign policy, defense, currency, common ethnic and financial policy, policy on strategic raw materials, and, unless specifically excluded by agreement, higher education, internal and external communications, and the courts. An elected president, who was also the president of the Fifth Republic, presided over the community's executive, which consisted of an executive council and a senate elected indirectly by each member state in proportion to the population. Each member state was to have its own government and a separate constitution.

In September 1958, France presented a referendum to the community. Each member could accept the Constitution and consequent membership in the community or reject it and immediately sever all ties with France. Côte d'Ivoire voted almost unanimously in favor of the Constitution, further confirming the almost mystical feeling of brotherhood with France that more than fifty years of cultural assimilation had instilled, particularly among the economic and political elite. The elite prudently recognized that although Côte d'Ivoire was the wealthiest French African territory, it lacked the financial resources and the trained work force to develop as rapidly as it could as a member of the community. Also, because Africanization of high-level posts within the government had barely begun in 1957, too few trained Ivoirians were available to staff the administration. A continued association with France was seen as the pragmatic course.

In March 1959, Côte d'Ivoire adopted its first constitution as a self-governing republic. It provided for a unicameral legislature elected by universal, direct suffrage and an executive headed by a prime minister elected by a majority vote of the legislature and responsible to it. The PDCI won all seats of the newly formed legislature, and Houphouët-Boigny resigned his post in the French government to form the first government of Côte d'Ivoire.

Independence and the Institutionalization of the One-Party System

In 1959 several West African members of the French Community formed the Mali Federation. Although the federation initially included Senegal, French Sudan, Upper Volta, and Dahomey, all but Senegal and French Sudan withdrew quickly under pressure from Houphouët-Boigny, who regarded the federation's desire for independence from France as a threat to the economic development of the former French colonies. Nonetheless, the federation gained independence in June 1960 and split into the two independent nations of Senegal and Mali.

Meanwhile, to counterbalance the Mali Federation, Houphouët-Boigny in 1959 successfully convinced several other West African leaders to form the Council of the Entente (Conseil de l'Entente—Entente)—a loose grouping that included Niger, Dahomey (present-day Benin), Upper Volta (present-day Burkina Faso), and Côte d'Ivoire—to pool their resources for economic development.

Houphouët-Boigny's argument against independence quickly lost its appeal among other members of the French Community following the independence of Senegal and Mali. In addition, in early 1960 the French government sponsored an amendment to the 1958 Constitution that permitted community members to gain complete independence but remain within the community. Houphouët-Boigny was opposed to this reconstituted community, which he considered a new federation, and in August 1960 Côte d'Ivoire withdrew from the community and became independent. Houphouët-Boigny was the first head of state.

On October 31, 1960, the National Assembly of Côte d'Ivoire adopted a constitution establishing an independent republic. Those involved in the drafting of the Constitution, including Houphouët-Boigny and other PDCI members, wanted to establish a strong and stable government based on democratic principles. They also wanted a presidential system based on the separation of powers between the executive and legislative branches of government and an independent judiciary. In practice, however, a gap developed between the democratic principles written into the Constitution and political practice. The PDCI leadership equated national unity with unanimous support for the PDCI and believed that competition among political parties would waste resources and destroy unity. Therefore, election provisions made it almost impossible for another party to win seats in the National Assembly. As the sole political party, the PDCI came to exercise political control over all branches of government.

By the late 1960s, power was concentrated in the hands of Houphouët-Boigny, who, in addition to his position as president, was also titular president of the PDCI. Loyal colleagues received positions of authority within the police and armed forces, as well as in the government and PDCI. Philippe Yacé, who held the positions of secretary general of the PDCI and president of the National Assembly, was the second most powerful figure in Côte d'Ivoire. The president appointed the administrative heads of the 6 departments *(départements)*, 24 prefectures *(préfectures)*, and 107 subprefectures *(sous-préfectures)*, which constituted the administration of Côte d'Ivoire (see Local Government, ch. 4). Houphouët-Boigny also selected the thirty-five members of the Economic and Social Council (Conseil Economique et Social), a government body, and, with the Political Bureau, chose the members of the National Assembly.

Houphouët-Boigny further consolidated his power by circumscribing the prerogatives of the National Assembly (see The National Assembly, ch. 4). Presidential and PDCI control of assembly membership precluded an independent or opposition role by the assembly in the decision-making process. At the same time, the existence of an assembly with responsibility for approving proposed laws legitimized the government's democratic pretensions. Moreover, the PDCI used the assembly as a means of co-opting potential government opponents and securing their loyalty by providing deputies with a variety of privileges and amenities. Finally, the government channeled its major decisions through the assembly to the ethnic and interest groups that its members supposedly represented, thereby again giving the appearance of legitimate government.

Houphouët-Boigny also took steps to ensure the new regime's security. Although Côte d'Ivoire had no military until more than a year after independence, one was finally organized and strengthened with French assistance. Ivoirian members of the French colonial marine infantry who had been born in Côte d'Ivoire were transferred to Abidjan in October 1961 and formed the core of the first battalion. By late 1962, the military comprised about 5,300 soldiers organized into four battalions (see Constitutional, Legal, and Administrative Structure, ch. 5).

Internal Dissent and Further Consolidation of Power

Despite Houphouët-Boigny's efforts to consolidate power and build a strong military, several events in the early 1960s demonstrated the vulnerability of the new regime. In 1962 a group of young radical PDCI members, displeased with the regime's moderate policies, allegedly planned to capture Houphouët-Boigny and other party leaders. More than 125 people were arrested and secretly tried in the president's hometown of Yamoussoukro. Forty-four of the alleged plotters were convicted. In 1963 the government announced the discovery of another plot, which allegedly involved a coalition of hostile groups, including left-wing youth, discontented politicians, and northerners who resented southern domination in the government. In April 1971, Houphouët-Boigny released the last of those who had been jailed following the 1963 trials and virtually admitted that the charges had been baseless.

Changes in Government and Party Structures

In 1965 Houphouët-Boigny reorganized his administration to accommodate the growing number of Ivoirians qualified to fill government positions. The four existing *départements* were redivided into six *départements* with twenty-four *préfectures*. A corresponding increase in the number of prefects *(préfets)* took place. By the end of 1972, there were 115 subprefectures. This rise in the number of administrative subdivisions facilitated public access to government offices that the new civil code, implemented in 1964, necessitated.

Houphouët-Boigny also purged the party of more than 200 party leaders in mid-1964. The group included five members of the Political Bureau and six members of the Executive Committee of the party's Youth Auxiliary, who had been implicated in alleged treasonous activities. In the ensuing overhaul of the party structure, party leaders modified the PDCI's organization to parallel the reorganized state bureaucracy; forty-five new party sections, corresponding to the number of new subprefectures in 1965, were added to the existing sections. Each was led by an elected secretary general. The number of party sections was increased again in 1970 to correspond to the increase in the number of subprefectures. The new sections were subdivided into village committees in rural areas and into ward and ethnic subcommittees in towns.

Sources of Popular Discontent

After independence, the production of export cash crops such as coffee and cocoa supported the development of nonagricultural economic growth, particularly in the Abidjan area (see Growth and Structure of the Economy, ch. 3). The commercial development of Abidjan and its growing status as the administrative center of the country consequently attracted even more French private investment and personnel. This concentration of economic and political activity in Abidjan led to population shifts toward the south and the creation of a modern capital, the life of which contrasted sharply with Côte d'Ivoire's up-country village life.

The country's increasing economic wealth, however, did not benefit all segments of the population. Rapid urbanization brought massive urban unemployment and rising conflict. Labeled by the government as the *sans-travail,* unemployed Ivoirians in Abidjan began to organize protest demonstrations in 1969 to pressure the government to achieve greater Ivoirianization of low-level jobs. On September 30, 1969, about 1,600 demonstrators were arrested in the capital, leading to resentment of both government and foreign workers among the *sans-travail.*

Another problem area existed between Ivoirian intellectuals and some elites on the one hand and white Europeans, mainly the French, who held numerous skilled jobs in the economy and civil service, on the other hand. The Ivoirian government was reluctant to undertake a large-scale Ivoirianization of the economy. It wanted to preserve Côte d'Ivoire's economic ties to France and to avoid staffing the administration with untrained bureaucrats. Consequently, many Ivoirians perceived Houphouët-Boigny as favoring Europeans over Ivoirians in employment.

Another rift resulted from the influx from other African countries of hundreds of thousands of unskilled workers, most of whom were Mossi from Upper Volta. The Ivoirian government encouraged the import of cheap foreign African laborers, who worked on the large coffee and cocoa plantations and in industry. Competition between Ivoirian and foreign workers exploded into violence in September and October 1969, when widespread attacks on Mossi workers occurred in Abidjan.

A fourth area of conflict resulted from the antagonism between students and the PDCI government. This antagonism manifested itself in recurrent protests by university students. Large numbers of Ivoirian students who had studied in France or were influenced by students from many other sub-Saharan African countries rejected the PDCI's ideological movement away from socialism that had begun in 1950. They rejected what they perceived as the regime's neocolonial policies vis-à-vis France. Many students also objected to the government's placement of the major student organization under the control of the PDCI.

A confrontation between the students and the government occurred in May 1969, when the student organization, the Movement of Ivoirian Primary and Secondary School Students (Mouvement des Etudiants et Elèves de Côte d'Ivoire—MEECI), presented a list of demands to the government for specific reforms at Abidjan University (present-day National University of Côte d'Ivoire) and held a strike in which 150 students participated. The government arrested all Ivoirian student protesters in Abidjan, expelled all foreign students, and closed the university for two weeks, leading to further expressions of student discontent at the university. The government's crackdown aroused the sympathy of other discontented groups, including the *sans-travail* and secondary students in other towns. For its part, the government considered student activity as a threat to its authority and political stability, and it blamed the strike on outside communist influences.

Consolidation of Power in the 1960s and 1970s

After the 1963 alleged coup plot, Houphouët-Boigny took steps to ensure party and military loyalty. His success over the ensuing years lay in his carefully crafted system of checks and balances, using ethnic differences, political animosities, and co-optation to guarantee his own supremacy. To satisfy the political elite, he resorted to state and party patronage, mostly in the form of high-paying jobs. To diffuse the potential for ethnic conflict resulting from perceived inequalities in the development process, he divided cabinet appointments among representatives of Côte d'Ivoire's major ethnic groups.

To fortify his hold over the armed forces, Houphouët-Boigny assumed direct control of the police and military, the size of which he reduced from 5,300 to 3,500 members. He divided responsibility for internal security among seven groups—a 3,000-man militia linked to the party and composed almost exclusively of Baoulé

(Houphouët-Boigny's ethnic group); a 3,000-man gendarmerie; the police; a special presidential guard; a small navy; a small air force; and the army. He also broadened his executive powers so that he alone could appoint and promote senior military officers. With the removal of political rivals following the 1962 and 1963 conspiracy trials, Houphouët-Boigny's position was unchallengeable.

In the 1970s, as the Ivoirian polity became somewhat more sophisticated, Houphouët-Boigny of necessity refined his style. He began replacing aging and loyal party militants with younger intellectuals and highly trained technocrats for whom he often created positions in his government—and who therefore owed him fealty. After the 1970 party congress, Houphouët-Boigny also began naming younger members to the political bureau and as candidates to the National Assembly. He ingratiated himself with the middle and lower classes by speaking out frequently about the failures of government officials. His preferred method of addressing popular issues was through dialogues in which the public could air their grievances to their seemingly attentive leader. During the first dialogue in January 1974 with 2,000 party workers, Houphouët-Boigny invited criticisms and appointed various committees to study and recommend reforms. In March a second dialogue with foreign and local business leaders elicited resolutions and warnings to inefficient and corrupt cadres and to the Lebanese and French business communities. No reforms of substance occurred following either of these sessions, but by allowing public criticism, albeit in a tightly controlled environment, the president remained informed about popular dissatisfaction. Subsequently he could take steps either to remedy or to suppress problems while maintaining his firm grip over Ivoirian politics.

Houphouët-Boigny also continued to invite traditional, or ethnic, leaders to participate in both party and government at the local level so that he could maintain constructive ties with the traditional elite. Nevertheless, he was not always able to extinguish all micronationalist sentiments. For example, the Agni of Sanwi claimed that their kingdom had become part of Côte d'Ivoire without their consent (see Ethnic Groups and Languages, ch. 2). In December 1969, the Sanwi king called for the kingdom to secede and led a separatist revolt. Government troops swiftly suppressed the rebellion. In November 1970, a Bété leader, Gnagbé Niabé (also known as Gnabé Opadjelé) proclaimed himself grand chancellor of Côte d'Ivoire. When Houphouët-Boigny refused to accept Gnabé's candidacy for president or grant his request for a cabinet post, Gnabé gathered a large group of supporters and marched on Gagnoa.

Again, government troops captured the rebel leader, ending the small rebellion.

Houphouët-Boigny's ability to maintain stability lay in his belief in strong management and organization, which led him from independence to building an administration based on the solid, bureaucratic institutions left by the French. In fact, the large number of French bureaucrats and entrepreneurs remaining in Côte d'Ivoire supported Houphouët-Boigny's monopoly on political power and thereby contributed to the perceived effectiveness of the public and private sectors of the Ivoirian economy. In November 1975, he was reelected president, claiming nearly 100 percent of the vote.

In the early 1970s, notwithstanding political calm and rapid economic growth, underemployment and unemployment continued to pose problems in Côte d'Ivoire. Immigrants continued to flood the lowest end of the job market, while whites continued to dominate the top executive jobs. In addition, the uneven distribution of social services and jobs throughout the country exacerbated the regional economic disparities arising from the growing concentration of wealth in the south. And finally, the adverse effects of the 1973 Sahelian drought on northern farmers caused even greater dissatisfaction among the rural population.

Houphouët-Boigny relied on his charisma and the government's coffers to dispel discontent. In the late 1960s and early 1970s, he gained popular favor by alternating Ivoirian independence festivities between Abidjan and the different prefecture capitals. Prefecture capitals hosting the festivities underwent massive rehabilitation, which included jobs in construction for new governmental buildings, streets, and housing. And when neither charisma nor largess mollified his critics, Houphouët-Boigny skillfully blamed others. In July 1977, he reorganized his cabinet, dismissing four of the country's most influential political figures, who, although instrumental in the growth of the Ivoirian economy, were also accused of involvement in fraudulent schemes to enrich themselves. These figures became useful scapegoats for continuing fraud and maldistribution of the nation's wealth.

On two occasions in the early 1970s, Houphouët-Boigny traveled to the north to convince local populations that he was not to blame for the state of affairs and to dispense politically timely aid in the form of development programs. The enthusiasm generated by the president's northern visits spread to other regions seeking largess from a presidential visit. Eager to exploit this nationwide burst of personal support, the government scheduled presidential trips throughout the country over the next several years.

The military also showed signs of restlessness. An alleged coup conspiracy by a group of discontented young officers, in June 1973 followed by the 1974 military overthrow of Niger's Hamani Diori, Houphouët-Boigny's lifelong friend, undermined Houphouët-Boigny's confidence in the government's security and precipitated changes in the military. Although many Ivoirian political observers thought that the conspirators of the alleged coup had done nothing more than discuss among themselves the need for greater economic equality in Côte d'Ivoire, the government dealt with them harshly. Shortly thereafter, Houphouët-Boigny replaced two senior French military officers, who had allegedly fomented discontent among Ivoirian officers, with Ivoirians. Further changes, designed to instill military loyalty by giving the armed forces more scope in national affairs, took place in July 1974, when Houphouët-Boigny appointed military officers to both high- and low-level positions in the civil administration. And finally, in February 1979, Houphouët-Boigny appointed eight army officers as prefects and subprefects to give the military a greater stake in maintaining the status quo.

Economic and Political Issues of the Late 1970s and 1980s

Growing Economic Problems

The worldwide economic recession at the beginning of the 1980s caused the prices of cocoa and coffee, Côte d'Ivoire's principal exports, to drop sharply, resulting in a significant economic slowdown. Combined with soaring commercial interest rates, the recession abruptly truncated the growth of the Ivoirian economy and exacerbated tensions in the labor force, where underemployment and unemployment had become acute. In mid-1978 complaints about inflation, the public debt, decreasing exports, the role of foreigners in the economy, and the succession question appeared in antigovernment tracts distributed in Abidjan. Popular manifestations of discontent with the regime's rigid policies, as well as with declining revenue, high urban unemployment, and the atrophied one-party political system, continued into the early 1980s. As was by now typical, Houphouët-Boigny dealt quickly with the complaints by proposing more rapid Ivoirianization and steps to decentralize and democratize local administrations. The government also trimmed the budget of several development programs.

Perhaps foreseeing political problems, Houphouët-Boigny took steps to consolidate further his own control. In 1980, again running unopposed, he was elected to a fifth term in office. In the same year, the Seventh Party Congress of the PDCI, following instructions from the president, abolished the post of PDCI secretary general and established Houphouët-Boigny as the party's executive chairman, assisted by the new nine-member Executive Committee of the Political Bureau.

Succession Question

The question of who would succeed Houphouët-Boigny became the significant political issue by the beginning of the 1980s. Many political observers believed that if Houphouët-Boigny did choose a successor, internecine feuds would erupt within the PDCI. They also believed that, at least initially, no one could combine Houphouët-Boigny's prestige, charisma, and experience with the political acumen that he had exercised over Ivoirian politics for almost thirty years.

In 1980 a constitutional amendment created the office of vice-president, who was to succeed to the presidency in the event of a midterm vacancy and who would be chosen by and elected at the same time as the president. The next elections, however, were not scheduled until 1985, and Houphouët-Boigny had given no indication of his plans for a vice-presidential running mate. (In 1985 Houphouët-Boigny resolved the problem by amending the constitution, eliminating the position of vice-president.)

In the 1970s, Philippe Yacé, the president of the National Assembly and PDCI secretary general, seemed to be the most likely successor. In 1975 the National Assembly adopted a law stipulating that power would pass to the president of the assembly, confirming Yacé as the second most powerful man in the country. Nevertheless, Yacé, who was popular with party officials, had many enemies, mostly because of his role as chief accuser in the fabricated 1963 plot.

In 1980 the prospects for designating a presidential successor were even more obscured when Houphouët-Boigny abolished the post of PDCI secretary general held by Yacé, who had fallen into disfavor with the president because he was thought guilty of pride. Shortly thereafter, Yacé was also stripped of his position as president of the National Assembly.

By the early 1980s, the list of possible successors included members of the old guard in the top echelons of the party as well as technocrats—middle-aged, university-educated Ivoirians—who filled executive positions in the administrative bureaucracy and the economy. Among the old guard who enjoyed great support inside the PDCI were Minister of State Mathieu Ekra; Senior Minister of State Auguste Denise; and president of the Economic and Social Council Mamadou Coulibaly. The most likely candidate,

31

however, was Henri Konan Bedié, a Baoulé, a technocrat, and the new National Assembly president. According to Article 11, amended, of the Constitution, the president of the National Assembly takes over the office of the president of the republic should the latter die or become incapacitated. The provisional president can then run for a full term in elections, which are to take place within sixty days. As provisional president, Bedié would have an edge over possible rivals. Moreover, demographic trends favored Bedié, who as a second-generation politician enjoyed growing support from younger and middle-aged Ivorians who believed perhaps that Yacé, a first-generation figure, was now too old. A third group of political rivals was a younger generation of politicians, most in their thirties, who were known for their effectiveness in the economic sphere and favored closer ties with the United States and the Federal Republic of Germany (West Germany).

In the mid-1980s, political infighting threatened to spill over boundaries of the narrow circle of the party leadership, however. That Houphouët-Boigny continued to resist naming a successor proved disconcerting to all those in positions of power, as well as to the West and especially to France, which had extensive investments in Côte d'Ivoire.

Party Decentralization

As the Ivoirian bureaucracy assumed a more prominent position in the postindependence years, the PDCI withered steadily. Increasingly it became a sinecure for the old guard, who lacked the ability to hold government office but remained personally loyal to the president. Also, by the early 1970s the one-party political structure was based on a purely ethnic system of representation at the local level that lacked any democratic procedures and that had produced an economically privileged political class. Moreover, the party and government hierarchies were characterized by nepotism and corruption. And finally, the poorly defined and overlapping responsibilities of party officials caused infighting and political rivalry.

In the late 1970s, Houphouët-Boigny, faced with growing party disarray, began to decentralize the PDCI at the local level, where a substantial change in party leadership took place. For the first time, the local party secretary generals, previously elected as part of a slate, were now to be chosen in open elections.

Discontent on Campus

The academic community was the most vocal protest group. The first sign of difficulty occurred in 1982, when the union of students went on strike to protest government efforts to halt political speeches on the National University of Côte d'Ivoire campus. Houphouët-Boigny responded in his typical paternalistic fashion: he chastised the students, dissolved their movement, and forced them to return to their villages until they all had apologized in writing to the government. Laurent Gbagbo, a young professor who during the strike spoke out on the need for a multiparty system, went into voluntary exile in France and became a symbol for young Ivoirians who wanted to liberalize the ruling party.

Further disturbances occurred in 1983, when approximately 4,000 secondary-school teachers, members of the National Union of Secondary School Teachers of Côte d'Ivoire (Syndicat National des Enseignants du Secondaire de Côte d'Ivoire—SYNESCI), went on strike to protest the elimination of their housing allowances. Their strike was also an expression of solidarity with those students and professors who had protested over issues of free speech the year before and, more significant, had voiced their basic opposition to Houphouët-Boigny. Because the teachers' union was the only union independent of the PDCI (SYNESCI refused to affiliate with the official government union), the government dissolved the union during the strike. In addition, the teachers complained that Houphouët-Boigny had unfairly penalized them and ignored cabinet members who, they alleged, had mismanaged the economy. Reacting once again in an arbitrary manner that further alienated teachers and students alike, Houphouët-Boigny closed all the secondary schools and sent the 200,000 students home.

Other Sources of Discontent

The teachers' strike quickly expanded into a major political issue at a time when underlying popular discontent had already come close to the surface. Shortly before the strike, the president had announced an expensive move of the capital from Abidjan to his village birthplace, Yamoussoukro. The move promised to increase vastly the value of land in the region, much of which was owned by the president and his family. And then, after the strike, Houphouët-Boigny delivered an extraordinary speech to the PDCI's Political Bureau in which he divulged the sources and use of his own extensive wealth. The consequent publication of the speech surprised much of the population, many of whom had been adversely affected by the country's increasing economic difficulties, and aroused tremendous popular disapproval.

In 1984, despite record harvests and prices for cash crops and a rescheduling of the external debt, the political atmosphere remained glum. Public investigations revealed high levels of corruption in the public housing sector and led to a protracted trial and the subsequent imprisonment of a number of high-ranking officials. More important, the trial implicated higher authorities, including past and present ministers and members of the president's family, none of whom was brought to justice.

Popular discontent also increased in response to the president's implementation of austerity measures. In the public sector, the government froze salaries. Throughout 1984 the employees retaliated by threatening strikes, work stoppages, and absenteeism. In the private sector, where politicians who were also business people had always enjoyed privileged treatment, financial irregularities were usually ignored. But the austerity measures took aim at the business people, eliminating their privileges and exposing financial scandals. For example, Emmanuel Dioulo, Abidjan's mayor, reportedly defrauded the National Agricultural Development Bank of US$32 million. At the end of March 1985, when the PDCI's Executive Committee lifted Dioulo's parliamentary immunity so that he could be tried on criminal charges, Dioulo fled the country. Following the Dioulo affair, Houphouët-Boigny launched a series of tax investigations of Yacé and other prominent political figures who had acquired personal fortunes.

During Houphouët-Boigny's 1984 annual summer vacation in Europe, a number of political tracts, published by unidentified opposition groups, appeared in the capital. The tracts questioned the president's political views and denounced the failure of the PDCI to manage the economy. The PDCI leadership responded to the attacks by organizing a series of trips to the interior to speak personally to the population. This measure, however, only created more tension because the leaders competed among themselves for coverage in the national media and exposed their sometimes bitter rivalry. One reason for the increasing intensity of the rivalry was the scheduled September 1985 Eighth Party Congress of the PDCI, to be followed by legislative and presidential elections.

In addition to the succession issue and the economic crisis, urban populations were faced with a worsening crime wave for which Ivoirians blamed foreigners primarily from Ghana and Burkina Faso (see Crime and Punishment, ch. 5). Some gangs, however, were directed by the Ivoirian underworld, an organized crime group that sometimes recruited unemployed youths from Burkina Faso. Many of the attacks were aimed at affluent French and Lebanese business people.

Thus, by the end of 1984, uncertainty and instability permeated the Ivoirian political and economic sectors, replacing the growth and optimism of a decade earlier. The most pressing issue, however, as viewed by the Ivoirian political elite and Western governments (France in particular), was whether Houphouët-Boigny would designate an official successor for the 1985 elections. The Ivoirian elite seemed committed to a stable transition of power, mostly to protect their economic interests. Clearly, many Ivoirian politicians believed that this designation would eliminate much of the then-pervasive popular discontent.

* * *

Detailed written accounts of Côte d'Ivoire's early history simply are not available because the archaeological record has yet to be fully explored. There do exist numerous transcriptions of oral accounts, with their limitations in reassembling the historical record, by ancestors of the indigenous population. Two secondary sources that include sections on the early history of the region are Virginia Thompson and Richard Adloff's *French West Africa* and Robert W. July's *A History of the African People.*

More recent literature on Côte d'Ivoire is copious and varied. Aristide R. Zolberg's *One-Party Government in the Ivory Coast* is the best known and most detailed source for an analysis of recent Ivoirian politics, and Michael A. Cohen's *Urban Policy and Political Conflict in Africa* is an excellent source for a discussion of the country's contrasting urban and rural life. Other analytical studies of Ivoirian politics, both precolonial and postcolonial, include Christian Potholm's chapter in *Four African Political Systems* titled "The Ivoirian Political System"; two articles by Bonnie Campbell, one in John Dunn's *West African States* titled "The Ivory Coast"; and the other in Paul M. Lubeck's *The African Bourgeoisie* titled "The State and Capitalist Development in the Ivory Coast;" and an article by Martin Staniland titled "Single-Party Regimes and Political Change: The P.D.C.I. and Ivory Coast Politics."

Literature that deals extensively with the nature and extent of Houphouët-Boigny's personal power is found in Claude Welch's *No Farewell to Arms?* and Robert H. Jackson and Carl G. Rosberg's *Personal Rule in Black Africa.* One other article of note, which deals in great depth with the Ivoirian succession issue, is Tessilimi Bakary's "Elite Transformation and Political Succession" in I. William Zartman and Christopher Delgado's *The Political Economy of Ivory Coast.*

One of the best sources for a critical assessment of Houphouët-Boigny is Laurent Gbagbo, a government opponent, whose book, *Côte d'Ivoire: Economie et société à la veille de l'Indépendance (1940–1960),* examines the events and conditions that brought Houphouët-Boigny to power. (For further information and complete citations, see Bibliography.)

Chapter 2. The Society and Its Environment

Sculpted door from northern Côte d'Ivoire showing Sénoufo symbolic figures

CULTURAL DIVERSITY is impressive in Côte d'Ivoire. Urban and agricultural workers, herders, traders, and fishermen; matrilineal and patrilineal organizations; villages and chiefdoms; and progressive and conservative political tendencies contribute to this national mosaic. Added to this indigenous variety are French, Lebanese, and African immigrants and visitors who live and work throughout the country. This complex nation is changing, however, and attitudes toward change vary among and within these groups. During the 1980s, the pace of change was affected by the numerous oppositions that characterized Ivoirian society—rich-poor, urban-rural, modern-traditional, and south-north. Côte d'Ivoire was developing its own balance of these tensions, with a result far more complex than a simple combination of indigenous cultures and colonial legacies.

Religious systems have changed in ways that reflect other social trends. In this nation of "miraculous" economic development, as it is so often dubbed, with its clearly privileged elite, people have on the whole retained traditional African religious beliefs. Usually combined with Christian or Muslim precepts, or both, local religions nonetheless permeate views regarding the nature of cause and effect. The syncretisms emerging from these strains of continuity and change are, like the nation itself, unique, despite similarities with other African states.

Political systems, like religions, reflect elements of modern and indigenous values in their development, and in Côte d'Ivoire these influences were especially evident in the practice of justifying authority in personal terms. The patrimonial style of President Félix Houphouët-Boigny indelibly marked political development through the early decades of independence. He crafted, although not single-handedly, a nation that exemplified moderation in some respects, resisting political trends and social extremes. Social development was generally steady and gradual rather than abrupt or catastrophic. The resulting society was marked by a general optimism regarding the possibility of benefiting from the system. The lure of affluence fostered an individualism that was absent in traditional cultures, as materialism "caught on" but did not obliterate traditional beliefs about the nature of the universe. Alienation was moderated by the hope of participation in the nation's material growth.

Efforts to improve educational opportunities were important in this changing social environment, both for individual advancement and for social control. The government placed a high priority on schools, adapting the system inherited from France to advance local interests—but still relying heavily on French assistance. In health care service delivery as well, Côte d'Ivoire made substantial improvements in the system it inherited from colonial times, raising material standards of living, at least for some. Like many benefits of development both before and after independence, however, these advantages were most readily available to those who were already able to exploit the changing social system to their own advantage.

Physical Setting

Location and Size

Côte d'Ivoire lies on the West African coast on the Gulf of Guinea (see fig. 3). Its outline is roughly that of a square, 560 kilometers on a side, with an area of 322,460 square kilometers—nearly the same as New Mexico. It is bounded on the east by Ghana, on the north by Burkina Faso and Mali, and on the west by Guinea and Liberia. The entire southern border is Gulf of Guinea coastline.

Physical Features

The nation consists of a large plateau rising gradually from sea level to almost 500 meters altitude in the north. Vegetation changes from lagoon and semitropical growth in the south to savanna grassland and scrub in the north (see fig. 4). Mountain ranges extend along the western border, and a few peaks dot the northeast corner. Four major river systems flow southward forming parallel drainage basins. Cutting across these basins are three geographic regions roughly parallel to the coast—the lagoon region, the forest region, and the savanna region.

The Lagoon Region

The lagoon region (*zone lagunaire*) is a narrow coastal belt extending along the Gulf of Guinea from the Ghana border to the mouth of the Sassandra River. It consists of a strip of low, sandy islands and sandbars built by the combined action of heavy surf and ocean currents. These barrier islands, known as the *cordon littoral,* have almost closed the rivers flowing into the gulf. The resulting series of lagoons range in width from about a hundred meters to seven or eight kilometers, and adjacent lands seldom rise more than thirty meters above sea level, leaving the area subject to frequent flooding during rainy seasons.

Most of the lagoons are narrow, salty, and shallow and run parallel to the coastline, linked to one another and the gulf by small watercourses or canals. Where large rivers empty into the gulf, broad estuaries extend as much as ten to twenty kilometers inland. The sandy soil supports the growth of coconut palms and salt-resistant coastal shrubs. The dense rain forest that once came down to the water's edge along the continental side of the lagoons has been largely supplanted by clearings for farms and towns and by second-growth woodlands. In the few remaining undisturbed areas, dense mangrove thickets appear along the edges of marshy inlets.

The Forest Region

A broad belt of dense forest covers nearly one-third of the country, extending north of the lagoon region in the east and reaching down to the coastline in the west between the Sassandra River and the mouth of the Cavally River. Its northern boundary stretches from the city of Man in the west to Bondoukou in the east, dipping down in the center of the country to the confluence of the Bandama Blanc and Bandama Rouge rivers. This boundary marks the transition from forest to grassy woodlands where plantation agriculture and burning have encroached on the forest. From the border with Ghana west to the Sassandra River, the gently rolling relief of the forest region is broken by small hills. West of the Sassandra, the Dan Mountains and the Toura Mountains reach 1,300 meters elevation. Mt. Nimba, near the border with Liberia and Guinea, reaches 1,752 meters.

The Savanna

The northern half of the nation is generally characterized as savanna—a large plateau consisting primarily of rolling hills, low-lying vegetation, and scattered trees. Vegetation varies from woodlands to grasslands and occasional patches of dry scrub in the far north. Some narrow strips of forest extend toward the north along watercourses and drainage lines. The southern portion of the savanna is sometimes referred to as the transition zone *(zone de transition)* and the northern portion as the sudanic zone *(zone soudanienne)*, although the entire region is transitional between the narrow belt of forest paralleling the coastline and the Sahara Desert. The gently rolling plains are broken occasionally by granite domes or small hill masses, the most extensive being the Komonos Hills. In the northwest, a number of peaks exceed 800 meters elevation.

A major divide extends across the northeastern corner of Côte d'Ivoire near Burkina Faso, separating the main southward drainage system from the Volta River Basin, which drains to the

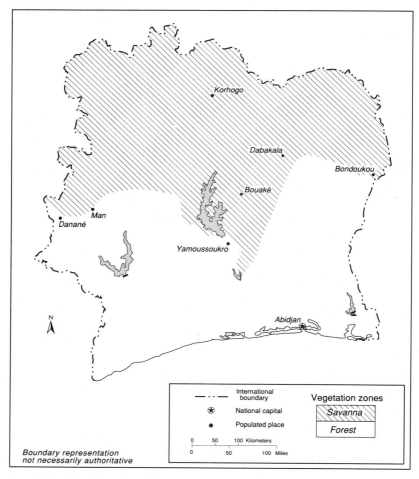

Source: Based on information from Y. Monnier, "Végétation," in Pierre Vennetier (ed.), *Atlas de la Côte d'Ivoire* (2d ed.), Paris, 1983, 17.

Figure 4. Vegetation Zones, 1983

north. Near Bondoukou, where the divide crosses the Ghana border, Mt. Bowé de Kiendi reaches 725 meters elevation. In the north, Mt. Yélévé reaches an altitude of 685 meters.

Rivers

Four major river systems follow meandering courses from north to south, draining into the Gulf of Guinea. From west to east these are the Cavally, Sassandra, Bandama, and Comoé—all relatively untamed rivers navigable only short distances inland from the coast. In the north, many smaller tributaries change to dry streambeds between rains.

The Cavally River has its headwaters in the Nimba Mountains of Guinea and forms the border between Côte d'Ivoire and Liberia for over half its length. It crosses rolling land and rapids and is navigable for about fifty kilometers inland from its exit to the sea near Cape Palmas.

The Sassandra River Basin has its source in the high ground of the north, where the Tienba River joins the Férédougouba River, which flows from the Guinea highlands. It is joined by the Bagbé, Bafing, Nzo, Lobo, and Davo rivers and winds through shifting sandbars to form a narrow estuary, which is navigable for about eighty kilometers inland from the port of Sassandra.

The Bandama River, often referred to as the Bandama Blanc, is the longest in the country, joining the Bandama Rouge (also known as the Marahoué), Solomougou, Kan, and Nzi rivers over its 800-kilometer course. This large river system drains most of central Côte d'Ivoire before it flows into the Tagba Lagoon opposite Grand-Lahou. During rainy seasons, small craft navigate the Bandama for fifty or sixty kilometers inland.

Easternmost of the main rivers, the Comoé, formed by the Léraba and Gomonaba, has its sources in the Sikasso Plateau of Burkina Faso. It flows within a narrow 700-kilometer basin and receives the Kongo and Iringou tributaries before winding among the coastal sandbars and emptying into the Ebrié Lagoon near Grand-Bassam. The Comoé is navigable for vessels of light draft for about fifty kilometers to Alépé.

Large dams were built in the 1960s and 1970s to control the flow of major rivers to the south. These projects created reservoirs, now referred to as lakes bearing the names of the dams—Buyo on the Sassandra, Kossou and Taabo on the Bandama, and Ayamé on the small Bia River in the southeast corner of the country. Lake Kossou is the largest of these, occupying more than 1,600 square kilometers in the center of the country.

Climate

The climate is generally warm and humid and is, overall, transitional from equatorial to tropical. Seasons are more clearly distinguishable by rainfall and wind direction than by temperature. Continental and maritime air masses, following the apparent movement of the sun from north to south, determine the cycle of the seasons that is associated with heat and cold farther from the equator.

During half of the year, a warm maritime air mass pushes north-ward across Côte d'Ivoire in response to the movement of the sun. Ahead of it, a low pressure belt, or intertropical front, brings warm air, rain, and prevailing winds from the southwest. As the solar cycle reverses, a dry continental air mass moves southward over the nation, permitting the dusty harmattan to dominate. Surface winds are gentle, seldom exceeding fifteen to twenty kilometers per hour.

Two climatic zones are created by the alternating wind patterns. In the north, rainfall amounts delineate two major seasons. Heavy rains fall between June and October, averaging 110 centimeters annually. Along the coast, four seasons prevail. Some rain falls in most months, with an average of 200 centimeters annually, but four seasons are generally distinguishable. Heavy rains fall between May and July in most years, followed by a short dry season during August and September. A second rainy season comes during October and November, followed by the major dry season from December to April.

Temperatures and humidity generally follow the same pattern, with average temperatures between 25°C and 30°C and ranges from 10°C to 40°C. Temperatures are higher in the north but may exceed 30°C even in the south. Annual and daily ranges of both temperature and humidity are small along the coast but increase progressively toward the north. The average relative humidity is 85 percent in the south and 71 percent in the north.

Population

Côte d'Ivoire's first national census in 1975 counted 6.7 million inhabitants, allowing 1987 estimates of 10.6 million. The 1987 annual growth rate was 4.1 percent. Regional variations were marked, with annual growth of only 1 percent in the far north, but throughout the country, population growth rates, which included high net immigration rates, were increasing. In the late 1980s, population projections for the year 2000 exceeded 20 million people.

Country-wide, life expectancy rose from thirty-nine to fifty-one years between 1960 and 1988, and during the same period, the average annual birth rate also increased steadily to 45.9 per 1,000 population. Fertility rates were about average for West Africa at 6.6 births per adult female. Fertility rates were lowest in Abidjan and highest in rural areas, where infant mortality also remained relatively high.

Mortality rates overall declined sharply after 1960, when one-third of all infants died before the age of five. Infant mortality in

Granite outcropping near Mankono
Courtesy Robert Handloff

the first year of life declined to 110 deaths per 1,000 births in the late 1980s. The crude death rate was just over 14 per 1,000 population.

Distribution

Population density increased steadily from twenty-one inhabitants per square kilometer in 1975 to thirty-two in 1987. This national average masked uneven distribution, however, with much of the population concentrated in the south and fewer than ten inhabitants per square kilometer in parts of the north. The southwestern corner of the country presented a low-density exception to this pattern. Population distribution reflected Ivoirian history more than physical environment. Most areas of high density corresponded to the first centers of settlement by major ethnic groups, especially the Akan and Mandé, altered in the north by nineteenth-century conquests by Samori Touré (see Pre-European Period, ch. 1). Colonial policy moved villages nearer transportation routes in order to control the population and to provide a ready labor supply. In the late 1980s, the population was still distributed along main roads as the result of resettlements, which had continued into the 1930s in the southwest.

Ivoirian settlement patterns in the late 1980s also revealed continued southward migration from the savanna to the forest, a process first set in motion by precolonial invasions from the north and continued by colonial policies emphasizing cash crop and plantation agriculture. This migration pattern was aided by postindependence urban and industrial development, which took place primarily in the southeast.

Composition

Urbanization was rapid after 1950, as the urban population grew by an average of 11.5 percent per year until 1965 and about 8 percent per year from 1966 to 1988. As a result, Côte d'Ivoire had a high urban-rural population ratio compared with the rest of sub-Saharan Africa. Roughly one-half of the 1987 population lived in urban areas, defined as localities of more than 10,000 inhabitants and those of more than 4,000 inhabitants where more than half of all households depended on nonagricultural incomes. In 1988 about 20 percent of the total population lived in the capital city of Abidjan.

Foreigners—mostly West Africans—made up from 27 percent to 50 percent of the population and were more highly urbanized than indigenous groups. Foreign migrants have sought jobs in Ivoirian industry, commerce, and plantation agriculture since the beginning of the twentieth century, especially after World War II. Most have found work in urban areas, but in 1980 the number of Ivoirians who migrated from rural to urban areas was almost equaled by the 75,000 migrant farm workers from neighboring states.

Because of moderately high fertility, falling mortality rates, and labor immigration, the Ivoirian population was fairly young by world standards (see fig. 5). About 45 percent of the 1987 population was under the age of fifteen, and the dependency ratio—the number of elderly and young dependents in relation to 100 working-age adults—was 92 nationwide. There were 110 males per 100 females, reflecting the largely male immigrant work force.

Ethnic Groups and Languages
Ethnic Diversity

The population of Côte d'Ivoire is ethnically diverse. More than sixty indigenous ethnic groups are often cited, although this number may be reduced to seven clusters of ethnic groups by classifying small units together on the basis of common cultural and historical characteristics. These may be reduced to four major cultural regions—the East Atlantic (primarily Akan), West Atlantic (primarily Krou), Voltaic, and Mandé—differentiated in terms of environment, economic activity, language, and over~ll cultural characteristics. In the southern half of the country, East Atlantic and West Atlantic cultures, separated by the Bandama River, each make up almost one-third of the indigenous population. Roughly one-third of the indigenous population lives in the north, including Voltaic peoples in the northeast and Mandé in the northwest (see fig. 6).

In Côte d'Ivoire, as across Africa, national boundaries reflect the impact of colonial rule as much as present-day political reality, bringing nationalism into conflict with centuries of evolving ethnic identification. Each of Côte d'Ivoire's large cultural groupings has more members outside the nation than within. As a result, many Ivoirians have strong cultural and social ties with people in neighboring countries. These centrifugal pressures provided a challenge to political leaders in the 1980s, as they did to the governors of the former French colony.

Most representatives of East Atlantic cultures are Akan peoples, speakers of languages within the Kwa branch of the Niger-Congo language family. Many are descendants of eighteenth-century migrants from the kingdom of Asante. The largest Akan populations in Côte d'Ivoire are the Baoulé, who make up nearly 15 percent of the total population, and the Agni (Anyi), who make up only about 3 percent of the total (see fig. 7). Much larger Akan populations live in Ghana and Togo. Akan societies are generally organized into farming communities but have a history of highly centralized chiefdoms and kingdoms tracing descent through maternal links. In the region that is now Côte d'Ivoire, they did not form large empires like the Asante of Ghana.

Smaller groups live in the southeastern lagoon region, where contact and intermarriage between the Akan and earlier inhabitants have resulted in ways of life that reflect elements of several cultural traditions. These Lagoon cultures comprise about 5 percent of the population. They depend on fishing and crop cultivation for subsistence and are not organized into centralized polities above the village level.

Across the Bandama River, West Atlantic cultures are represented by Krou peoples, probably the oldest of Côte d'Ivoire's present-day ethnic groups. Traditional Krou societies were organized into villages relying on hunting and gathering for subsistence and descent groups tracing relationships through male forebears. They rarely formed centralized chiefdoms. The largest Krou population in Côte d'Ivoire is the Bété, who made up about 6 percent of the population in the 1980s.

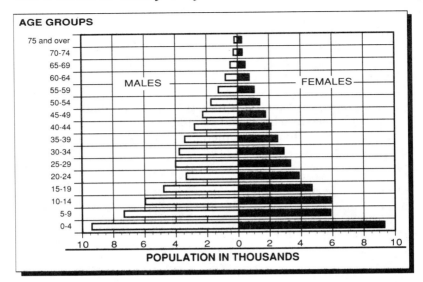

AGE GROUPS

Source: Based on information from World Bank, March 17, 1988.

Figure 5. Population by Age and Sex, 1988

In the north, cultural differences are greater than in the south. Descendants of early Mandé conquerors occupy territory in the northwest, stretching into northern Guinea and Mali. The nation of Mali took its name from one of the largest of these societies, the Malinké. In the 1980s, Mandé peoples—including the Malinké, Bambara, Juula, and smaller, related groups—made up about 17 percent of the population of Côte d'Ivoire.

To the east of the Mandé are Voltaic peoples. The most numerous of these, the Sénoufo, made up about 10 percent of the total population in the 1980s. The Sénoufo migrated to their present location from the northwest in the sixteenth and nineteenth centuries. Both historical periods are still in evidence in two forms of social organization found in the area—one based on small descent groups and the other on more complex confederations similar to those of the Mandé.

Language Diversity

French is the official language and is used throughout the country, but linguistic diversity still reflects the ethnographic mosaic of its peoples. Four of the eight major branches of the Niger-Congo language family are represented, including the Kwa, Atlantic, Mandé, and Voltaic (Gur). Language areas correspond closely, but not exactly, to the four cultural regions of the nation.

Agni and Baoulé, both Kwa languages and to some extent mutually intelligible, are the most widely spoken languages in the south. Variants of Mandé and Sénoufo are the most widely spoken in the north but are also heard in virtually all southern trading areas. Most Ivoirians speak two or more languages fluently, but no single African language is spoken by a majority of the population.

French is used in schools and commerce and is spoken more frequently by men than by women. Most publications, including government documents, are also printed in French. Vernacular newspapers are not widely available, although biblical texts and educational materials have been translated into major African languages.

Arabic is taught in Quranic schools, which are most common in the north, and is spoken by immigrants from Lebanon and Syria. Non-Ivoirian African languages are also heard, including Mossi, Gourounsi, Fanti, Ewe, Fon, and Wolof. Many Ivoirians understand English, which is taught in high school and at the National University of Côte d'Ivoire (formerly the University of Abidjan), but English is not popular even among educated people.

Lineage Patterns

In Côte d'Ivoire, as in most of Africa, family relationships reflect beliefs about kinship that differ markedly from those of most Europeans and Americans. Kinship groups are relatively resistant to change through modernization, and, as a result, one traditional descent group—the lineage—is so common that it can be discussed in general terms, without reference to specific Ivoirian cultures. The organization of the lineage is based on the belief that relationships traced through males and those traced through females are substantially different. Kinship terms and behavioral expectations differ accordingly.

The patrilineage, or group formed by tracing descent through male forebears to a male ancestor, is an important social unit throughout most of Africa. In eastern Côte d'Ivoire, however, many societies are organized into matrilineages, tracing descent through female forebears to one female ancestor. Each type of lineage includes both men and women, sometimes five or six generations removed from the founding ancestor, but the linking relatives are of one gender. In this way, second and third cousins within the same lineage may be considered closer relatives than first cousins in two different lineages, i.e., children of a brother and sister.

Lineages generally share corporate responsibility for socializing the young and maintaining conformity to social norms. Lineage elders often meet to settle disputes, to prescribe or enforce rules

51

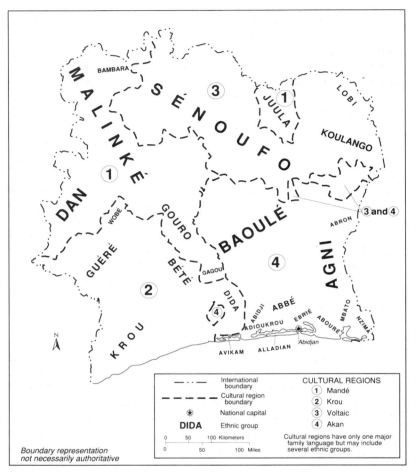

Source: Based on information from J.-C. Arnaud, "Ethnies," in Pierre Vennetier (ed.),
Atlas de la Côte d'Ivoire (2d ed.), Paris, 1983, 27.

Figure 6. Major Ethnic Groups, 1983

of etiquette and marriage, to discuss lineage concerns, and in general to preserve the group itself. They also serve as pressure groups on individuals, bringing nonconformists in line with socially accepted standards. Lineage rules usually require individuals to marry outside their lineage, and the resulting alliances are important sources of social cohesion. Although these practices were widely condemned by some of the teachings of early European missionaries and by colonial officials, they have been preserved nonetheless because they provide a coherent set of expectations by which people can live in harmony with the universe as it is perceived in that society.

Lineage ties serve to emphasize the unity of living and deceased relatives by descent through ritual observances and ceremonies. At times, however, lineages break apart in response to the pressure of interpersonal rivalries or when they become too large to maintain close ties. When such fission occurs, related lineages usually maintain some ties and celebrate occasions together. If they consider their alliance important enough to be preserved for several generations, the resulting confederation of lineages, usually termed a *clan,* may include thousands of individuals and become a powerful interest group in the regional or national context. Aside from their political potential, many aspects of lineage behavior and expectation are still important in Côte d'Ivoire, giving people their sense of history and social responsibility and serving to define the role of the individual in society.

East Atlantic Cultures

Akan

Akan societies are best known for the large kingdom of Asante, which evolved in what is now Ghana. The westernmost Akan peoples—the Agni, Baoulé, and several smaller groups—are descendants of people who fled from Asante and now make up about one-fifth of the Ivoirian population.

Historians believe that Akan civilization evolved in stages, beginning about A.D. 1000, forming urban settlements by about A.D. 1400, and giving rise to the Asante and other large kingdoms by about A.D. 1600. They became known for their elaborate use of gold, their military organization, and their success in international trade. Military expertise probably provided the basis for their regional dominance, but their dramatic success from A.D. 1600 on also resulted from their use of slaves in gold mining and agriculture and from the spread of Islam.

Most Akan societies are organized into matrilineages *(abusua).* Each lineage is identified with a home village or section of a town, although lineage members may be dispersed. Lineages demonstrate their autonomy with respect to other similar groups through the ownership of a symbolic chair or stool, named for the female founder of the lineage. Possession of the ritually important stool is seen as vital to the existence of the group. Large lineages may segment into branches, each led by an elder or headman, but a branch does not possess a stool as a symbol of its social autonomy.

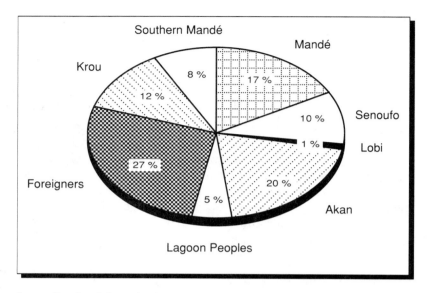

Source: Based on information from United States, Department of State, "The Tribes of the Ivory Coast," April 1970; and Côte d'Ivoire, National Census Information, 1976.

Figure 7. Percentage of Population by Ethnic Cluster, 1988

Despite their matrifocal center, Akan societies are dominated by men. Men occupy most leadership positions, but they succeed former leaders based on their relationship through their mothers and sisters. Thus, a leader is succeeded, and his valuable property is inherited, by his brother or his sister's son.

Matrilineal descent and inheritance produce particular strains in the social fabric under the pressures of modernization. Tensions often arise between a man's sons, who help him acquire wealth and property, and his sister's sons, who may inherit it. Similarly, a man is expected to support children of deceased maternal relatives, a demand that may conflict with the interests of his own children. Akan people used to cope with this contradiction by allowing a senior woman in the lineage to rule that a matrilineal relative had to relinquish his rights in favor of a man's son. More recently, the Ivoirian government has refused to enforce legal claims to matrilineal rights and has condemned, but not eliminated, practices related to matrilineal descent.

Agni political organization was derived from its lineage foundations, in that lineages grouped in villages were united as a chiefdom. The chief served as the guardian and protector of this domain and as priest, judge, administrator, and custodian of the sacred stool, which in the 1980s was still recognized as a symbol of unity of the entire chiefdom. An Agni chief was succeeded by a man nominated by the senior women of the lineage. This nominee, usually one of the deceased chief's matrilineal heirs, was confirmed, or on rare occasions rejected, by a council of lineage elders. Most of the chiefs' traditional political authority has been eroded or transformed by modern national law, but their ritual authority remained important in the 1980s, confirmed by their custody of the sacred stool.

The Agni were particularly successful at assimilating other groups into their political organization, with the result that many people in the southeast trace their ancestry both to Agni chiefdoms and to smaller, distinct societies that fell under Agni control. One mechanism of assimilation was grouping semiautonomous chiefdoms under an Agni paramount chief, who held ultimate authority over his subjects. In at least four regions, these polities evolved into kingdoms—Indénié, Moronou, Comoénou, and Sanwi—which still evoke strong loyalties and ethnic pride. The continuing importance of the kingdoms was demonstrated in 1959 and 1969, when Sanwi attempted to secede from Côte d'Ivoire in the hope of demonstrating Agni autonomy from Baoulé domination.

In 1988 the Baoulé constituted about 15 percent of the population, making this the nation's largest indigenous ethnic group, although the Agni population in neighboring states was larger. Baoulé society was less highly centralized than the Agni, with villages grouped into small chiefdoms. Baoulé agricultural successes were remarkable, however, partly because of careful control of land, which was held in common by an entire village and redistributed each year to those most efficient at cultivating it. Hunting supplemented agriculture.

The Baoulé were also successful in absorbing neighboring peoples into their society by political means and intermarriage. Baoulé women married freely into other societies, in part because their children inherited their lineage membership from their mother. As a result, many Baoulé still have extended kin ties reaching into other ethnic communities, and this network provides political support for Baoulé politicians. Assimilation by the Baoulé also involved the transfer of their myth of origin—which emphasized the value of agriculture, respect for authority, and individual sacrifice for society—to smaller neighboring groups.

Ivoirian president Houphouët-Boigny has used his Baoulé identity pragmatically to pursue political goals. For example, he refused to name a successor to his presidency, saying that to do so was not in keeping with tradition. At the same time, he condemned the Baoulé traditional practice of matrilineal inheritance and descent for failing to strengthen the unity of the nuclear family, which he considers the pillar of modern Ivoirian society and the mainstay of economic development.

Most influential among smaller Akan cultures of eastern Côte d'Ivoire are the Abron (Brong in Ghana), Abouré, Ehotilé, and Nzima. Together they make up only about 2 percent of the total population. All are matrilineal peoples with a heterogeneous population and mixed economy. None achieved the elaborate political centralization of the Agni nor the postindependence importance of the Baoulé.

Lagoon Cultures

Along the coastline from the nation's eastern border to the Bandama River is a series of lagoons, where fishing and trading dominate local economies. Lagoon societies include the Mekyibo, Attié, Mbato, Ebrié, Abidji, Adioukrou, Alladian, Avikam, Abbé, and others, each of which, in turn, is known by a variety of names within the region and is subdivided into smaller groups.

Residents of inland villages are subsistence farmers, and many lagoon peoples produce cash crops. Although not Akan language speakers, they speak related Kwa languages and are organized into matrilineages and chiefdoms similar to the Agni and Baoulé to the north. This cultural assimilation reflects the local history of occasional domination by Akan armies from the north. Ebrié, Attié, and Adioukrou societies are further segmented into age classes organized for warfare, mutual aid, and communal work projects. Age-groups continued to operate in the 1980s, providing an important source of social cohesion.

Although the nation's capital, Abidjan, is in traditional Ebrié territory, the Ebrié made up less than 10 percent of the population of the city in the late 1980s. Many local groups have been displaced by Akan peoples and others moving into the densely populated southeast corner of the nation. Some of these survive in scattered villages; others were absorbed into the coastal economy by early French arrivals and flourished under this arrangement. As a result, this complex and heterogeneous lagoon region exhibits an eclectic variety of cultural and linguistic traits that defy simple classification.

West Atlantic Cultures

Krou

The dominant peoples in the southwest region, where the forest zone reaches the coastal lagoons, are the Krou. Krou languages are

Lobi homestead, northeastern
Côte d'Ivoire
Courtesy Robert Handloff

a subgroup within the Kwa branch of the Niger-Congo language family, related to those of the Akan and lagoon peoples to their east. Krou societies are found along the coast from Monrovia, Liberia, to the Bandama River in Côte d'Ivoire. They include the Bété, Dida, Guéré, Wobé, and several smaller groups.

Krou cultures generally lack the centralization characteristic of the Akan to the east. The basic social unit is the patrilineage, tracing descent through males to a common male ancestor for both men and women. The lineage, which usually coincides with a village, is further subdivided into segments or branches. Village leadership may be exercised by a council of elders, sometimes headed by a chief whose power is limited by the council. The result is an uncentralized, but not anarchic, society. Few status distinctions are recognized other than age and lineage membership, although many Krou people kept slaves from neighboring societies before the arrival of European slave traders. Villages maintain ties based on presumed common descent, reinforced by ceremonial exchanges and gifts. Unrelated villages maintained neutral relations but were rarely united into a larger polity until the colonial era.

For their livelihood, the Krou rely on farming supplemented by hunting in forest areas. Land is held collectively by members of a village but is worked by individual lineage branches or families. Age-groups were traditionally assigned military and religious responsibilities, and they still organized communal work projects

57

in the late 1980s. Women were important in the village, with responsibilities for most activity concerning crops. They also formed age-groups or village councils, which were traditionally consulted before implementing political decisions, although women's councils lost influence under colonial rule.

The Bété, the largest Krou society, are probably the descendants of groups pushed southward from savanna woodland to forested areas by warfare to the north. They are divided into patrilineage-based villages, often allied with other villages by tracing descent to a common ancestor. Lineage exogamy prohibits marriage within the patrilineage and contributes to links among patrilineages through intermarriage.

Marriage is a family responsibility, as it is in many societies. The family of the groom compensates the family of the bride for their loss, a practice crudely translated as "bride-price." This exchange legitimizes children of the marriage, who are considered members of their father's patrilineage, while their mother retains her membership in her father's lineage.

Polygyny, or plural marriage by Bété men, remained relatively common in the 1980s, although as in all societies, it was an expensive means of gaining prestige, sexual access, and children, and it was not recognized by Ivoirian law. Divorce, although not common, was socially acceptable and allowed children to retain their membership in their father's patrilineage even if they continued to live with their mother.

In the twentieth century, the Bété have been recognized for their success in cash cropping and for their widespread acceptance of Christianity. They have a strong ethnic consciousness despite these foreign influences and have been active both within the government and in antigovernment dissent groups since independence. They also have a long history of resistance to foreign domination and strong beliefs in their own cultural superiority.

Around the Bété are a number of smaller groups, including the Dida, Guéré, Wobé, Neyo, Niaboua, and several others. Most are organized into farming villages, with a greater dependence on fishing along the coast. Many villages share common basic features with neighboring groups, and most have an ethnically mixed labor force and large immigrant population. Some have adopted myths of origin of other groups to legitimize their pride in their past, and many maintain strong loyalties to the region, despite their apparent mixed origins.

The Southern Mandé

Dan and Gouro cultures of western Côte d'Ivoire share numerous culture traits in common with the Krou peoples to their south, but they speak languages related to that of the Mandé to their north. Their traditional political organization was not complex, resembling the villages of the southwest more than the highly centralized polities of the Mandé. /Because of their cultural eclecticism, the Dan, Gouro, and smaller, related groups of west-central Côte d'Ivoire are sometimes classified as Southern Mandé or "Peripheral Mandé," a label they would reject. They made up slightly less than 8 percent of the total population in the late 1980s.

Mandé Cultures

The largest cultural complex in northwestern Côte d'Ivoire is that of the Mandé peoples, descendants of renowned inventors of West African agriculture—independent of, but approximately coincident with, early crop domestication in the Middle East. As traders, artisans, and cultivators, they developed highly complex political structures. Two large empires are still remembered today—the Soninké Empire of Ghana, which dates from about the fourth to the thirteenth century, and the Malinké Empire of Mali. The Malinké, like the Soninké, extended their dominion into what is now northern Côte d'Ivoire between the thirteenth and fifteenth centuries (see Pre-European Period, ch. 1). In about 1670, their Bambara subjects threw off Malinké rule and established several independent states, which were attacked by Fulani armies in the nineteenth century and subsequently fell under the domination of a Malinké conqueror, Samori Touré.

Most Mandé societies are organized into patrilineages and agricultural homesteads. Animal husbandry plays an important role in the economy, although commerce is also well developed, with large markets in both rural and urban settings.

Among the three Mandé groups that continue to dominate the northwest are the Malinké, also found in neighboring Guinea and Mali, and the Bambara, most of whom live in Mali. More recent Mandé immigrants to the region include the Juula, who are dispersed throughout the nation but are identified with the area near the city of Kong. None of these three groups retains its ancient hierarchical political structure, but each has a hereditary nobility and fairly extensive social stratification. The Malinké and Bambara group men and women according to fairly narrow age ranges, and the resultant sororities and fraternities serve to strengthen social solidarity and organize communal work projects.

Most Mandé people speak variants of a common language, sometimes referred to as Mandé-kan, and they share numerous other cultural traits. At the same time, they have different histories and myths of origin, and, most important from their point of view, they have different religions.

The Bambara have retained the substance of local beliefs and practices and are known locally as pagans. The Malinké have adapted tenets of Islam to their native beliefs, creating a wide variety of Islamic and syncretic sects. The Juula are strongly Muslim— so much so that many Bambara refer to themselves as Juula if they convert to Islam. Similarly, in other areas of Côte d'Ivoire, Muslim Malinké are referred to as Juula outside their home area, in recognition of their Islamic beliefs. Non-Muslims in the northwest are often called Bambara, regardless of ethnic affiliation.

The term *Juula* is also a local term for a trader and is used ambiguously in the region to refer to merchants and sedentary descendants of former Juula. The lines of ethnic identity are also blurred because traders are often recognized authorities on Islamic law and may be Juula in both senses of the term.

The Juula have a history of itinerant preaching, teaching, and trading, and they won converts easily in areas characterized by patrilineal descent, patriarchal family organization, and plural marriage. The Wattara clan *(jaamu)* among the Juula was centered in the region of Kong, where it developed into a mini-kingdom surrounded by Sénoufo people and was destroyed by Samori Touré in the nineteenth century.

Voltaic Cultures

Voltaic cultures are found in northeastern Côte d'Ivoire, northern Ghana, and Burkina Faso. They share cultural similarities with the Mandé peoples to their west but have not influenced the political history of the region to the same extent. Northern Voltaic peoples—such as the Mossi, who are based outside Côte d'Ivoire— built large empires, but the Sénoufo and the Lobi are organized into small chiefdoms based on unilineal descent.

The Sénoufo occupy north-central Côte d'Ivoire, Mali, and Burkina Faso and are also known as the Seniambélé and Siena. Sénoufo is a Juula word meaning "speaker of Séné," but language is among the few culture traits that unify this heterogeneous group. They have several myths of origin, each popular in a different area. Several of these involve an ancestor known as Nangui or Nengué, who left the Juula capital of Kong to establish the Sénoufo city of Korhogo, which means "heritage." Sénoufo history refers to Juula traders as early as the thirteenth century, when Islam arrived in the region. The territory was raided by Samori Touré in the late nineteenth century, and the resulting decline continued into colonial times.

The Sénoufo economy is primarily agricultural. Commerce is well developed in the area, but in most cases it is conducted by Juula rather than Sénoufo traders. The close relationship between the Sénoufo farmer and the land is emphasized in religious observances and mediated through the lineage. Each lineage has a mythical ancestor, often identified with an animal that is said to have helped found the lineage. This animal, or "totem," occupies a special niche in the Sénoufo worldview, as the subject of a ritual taboo and symbol of social unity. The head of the lineage exercises moral and religious authority and is believed to propitiate local gods and ensure good harvests. Aside from the lineage head, status distinctions are relatively few, although many people kept slaves from other societies until well into the twentieth century.

Villages are unified by male age-grades, uniting youths close in age within secret brotherhoods known as *poro* in this region and parts of Sierra Leone and Liberia. *Poro* societies have survived in part because they help maintain order, especially in times of social upheaval. They also serve as repositories of social customs and religious values, providing a conservative balance against the rapid acculturation in Ivoirian society as a whole.

Akan influence is fairly strong among the Sénoufo, some of whom have adopted matrilineal descent systems resembling that of the Akan. Villages were unified under the authority of an appointed chief during colonial times, a practice that drew villagers into the national system but also disrupted established channels of authority and was resisted by many of the culturally conservative Sénoufo people.

Adjacent to Sénoufo territory are the Lobi, Koulango, and several smaller Voltaic societies. They inhabit an isolated, relatively undeveloped corner of the country. They probably arrived in the area from the east and organized themselves in autonomous villages. They resisted the spread of Islam, which was brought by Juula traders and teachers over several centuries. More recently, they have rejected many aspects of European acculturation and lack the overall fascination with economic progress that characterizes much of the nation.

Foreigners

The presence of a large foreign population—estimated by some to be as high as 50 percent of the total in 1985—complicates ethnic relations in Côte d'Ivoire. The area was the scene of population migration and mobility long before the imposition of national boundaries. Many ethnic groups overlap present boundaries, placing citizenship and ethnic loyalties in conflict, and some foreigners

61

Donvagne, a village in eastern Côte d'Ivoire
Courtesy Robert Handloff

have remained in Côte d'Ivoire long enough to feel they are Ivoirians. Official demographic and employment data often include immigrant workers and residents. Despite these complications, the government has attempted tó codify the legal distinction between citizen and noncitizen, and this distinction is becoming increasingly important to many people.

In the mid-1980s, the largest single foreign minority group was the Burkinabé, most of Mossi ethnic identity, who numbered about 1.2 million—nearly one-half of the foreign population. Unlike most other foreigners, Mossi immigrants were concentrated in rural areas, where they worked as agricultural laborers. Some Mossi workers were also found in low-wage urban jobs.

Other ethnic groups represented in the foreign population included Krou peoples from Liberia, Fanti and Ewe from Ghana, and smaller numbers of Bobo, Gourounsi, Dogon, Hausa, Djerma, and Fulani from neighboring states. Lebanese immigrants, officially estimated at 60,000 but possibly numbering close to 200,000 in 1987, worked in commerce and business in many towns. The French population, once as high as 60,000, had declined to about 30,000, or the same number as at independence. Other Europeans and Africans were also found in this complex and cosmopolitan nation.

The Role of Religion

Most Ivoirians practice local religions, which are sometimes infused with elements of Christianity or Islam, or both. Government estimates in the 1980s suggested that about one-fourth of the population was Muslim and one-eighth, Christian—mostly Roman Catholic.

Islam and Christianity are practiced in a variety of forms throughout the country, as different social and spiritual problems bring forth a variety of responses. Islam has been practiced in the far north for roughly seven centuries, shifting its appeal over this time from its strength as a world religion and its basis in written testaments to its symbolic importance as an alternative to European religions. Christian missionaries arrived at the coast in the seventeenth century but did not win converts in large numbers until the nineteenth century. Christianity's appeal was strongest among educated Africans and those who sought advancement through European contact. Christian holidays are officially recognized, but Muslim celebrations are also held, and, as in many areas of national life, tolerance is the general attitude toward the practice of religion.

Religious communities generally coexist peacefully, in part because no world religion has been enthusiastically embraced by a majority of people. Conversions have been an individual matter in most cases, and many families include Muslims and Christians living together. Religious tolerance is also part of government policy. The president personally contributes to the cost of building mosques and churches, and he encourages both Muslims and Christians to assist in projects undertaken by other religious communities. Religious practitioners have also earned substantial goodwill through the services they offer their communities, especially in health and education, and by their overall contribution to social harmony.

The Constitution calls for a secular state, although this is not interpreted as strict separation of church and state. Officials often attend religious ceremonies as representatives of the state, and some mission schools receive government aid. Missionaries are generally welcomed throughout the nation, although their teachings seldom replace centuries-old systems of spiritual belief and practice that form the basis of cultural unity.

African religions have maintained their credibility because they provide effective explanations for many of life's dilemmas in ways that can only be understood in their cultural context. Local religions reassure people that they are living in harmony with the universe and that this harmony can be preserved by maintaining proper relationships with all beings. For this reason, separating religion from other aspects of life serves to distort, rather than clarify, its meaning.

According to most local belief systems, spiritual beings—a creator, ancestral spirits, and spirits associated with places and objects—can influence a person's life and luck. This is the major premise on which belief and practice are based. The distinction between the spiritual and physical "worlds," in Western secular terms, is unimportant in the face of what is interpreted as overwhelming evidence that physical events may have spiritual causes.

Lineages are also important in understanding the organization of many Ivoirian religions. The spiritual unity of the descent group transcends distinctions among the unborn, the living, and the deceased. In this context, religious differences are not based on disagreements over dogma or doctrine. Rather, groups living in different social and physical environments encounter different spiritual and physical dangers, and their religious needs differ accordingly. This diversity accounts, in part, for early missionaries in West Africa who often described the spiritual "chaos" they encountered, when they were actually observing different social groupings, each with different spiritual obligations to ancestral and other

65

spirits, acting in accordance with common beliefs about the nature of the universe.

Local Religions

Religions of the South

Most Akan recognize a supreme being, *Nyame*, who created all things and from whom lesser gods derive their power. *Nyame* is not worshiped directly but is approached through intermediaries. These lesser gods *(abosom)* may inhabit lakes, streams, rivers, or trees. Below them are minor deities whose power is invoked through amulets or charms *(suman)* worn for protection.

Ancestral spirits *(samanfo)* surpass these deities in importance among most Akan peoples, as it is the ancestors who safeguard the prosperity of the lineage and provide assistance in meeting daily challenges. Ancestral spirits are often consulted, offered food and drink, and reminded that people are depending on them, in the hope that an individual will be able to act with confidence, especially in dealing with others in the lineage. Failure to perform sacrifices to ancestral spirits not only damages a person spiritually but also brings forth the wrath of the ancestor and can result in tragedy or unhappiness.

An individual's spirit, or soul *(elaka* among the Agni; *okra* among the Baoulé), is immortal and indestructible. A living individual also possesses other spiritual substances, including *sunsum,* which is adaptable and determines a person's character, and *mogya,* which determines a person's membership in a matrilineage. Through transgressions—failure to perform rituals or obey moral precepts—an individual can damage the soul or lose it entirely. Upon death, the soul (or in some areas, part of the soul) may enter the kingdom of the dead, where its existence is happy and peaceful, or it may reenter a human being to continue on its path toward fulfillment.

Akan religious practitioners include lineage heads, village chiefs (when the head and the chief are not the same individual), and priests who officiate at ritual observances for cults honoring specific deities. These priests *(akomfo)* undergo extensive training as apprentices to established practitioners. Priests can also act as diviners, and the most esteemed among them are believed to be clairvoyant, able to locate the source of spiritual difficulty for their clients, who consult them for a fee. They also give instructions for coping with adversity. Priests sometimes act as doctors, since many diseases are believed to have spiritual causes.

Sorcerers *(obayifo)* are spiritual practitioners who, in the Akan worldview, bring about evil. Their actions are believed to be

Man with a radio, Bondoukou
Courtesy Robert Handloff
Drummer, Broukro
Courtesy Robert Handloff
Mauritanian shopkeeper,
Bondoukou
Courtesy Karen Peterson

motivated by envy or hatred, and, it is feared, they may be employed by one's enemies. Sorcery often consists of poisoning, which may be counteracted by a priest or detected by a diviner, but one of the hazards of dealing with the spiritual realm is that sorcerers are sometimes disguised as priests or diviners. A person may use amulets or other objects to ward off the evil effects of sorcery, but these are sometimes powerless against the anger of an ancestor.

Collective religious ceremonies are important to the life of many Akan peoples. The most important of these is the yam festival, which serves several functions. It is a memorial service for the dead and begs for their protection in the future; it is a time of thanksgiving for good harvests; and it is a ritual of purification that helps rid the group of evil influences. It also provides an opportunity to recall the discovery of the yam—now an important part of the diet of many Akan people—and to salute the Akan chief who, it is said, risked his life by tasting this unknown food before others in his chiefdom. The yam festival is considered vital to the group's survival, and it serves important social functions—it defines the group, symbolizes its unity, and reminds people of their obligations to others.

Religion among the Krou peoples of the southwest resembles that of the Akan, with an important difference in the presence of a second powerful deity alongside the creator. This second god is an evil deity or devil, who works against the creator god, producing a duality that is an important theme in Krou culture. All individuals exhibit a balance of good and evil, in this view, and maintaining this balance is important both to the individual and to the entire universe.

Religions of the North

Northern religions contain the notion of dual deities found in the southwest, although the two often complement rather than oppose each other. Ancestral spirits are especially important because it is believed that they can directly influence an individual's fortunes in this life.

The cosmology of the Mandé peoples of the northwest is described in their myth of origin, variants of which are retold throughout the region. The myth recounts God's creation of the universe and of four sets of twins from seeds. They were commanded to populate the earth and teach their offspring how to grow crops. They used the first music to plead for rain, and the Niger River was formed from the resulting series of floods. Each area along the river is associated with a wild animal that either prevented the sowing of seeds or protected the fields. Features of the river and surrounding terrain are also associated with activities of the first ancestors, reinforcing the bond between the group's spiritual existence and the land—a bond that has confused foreign missionaries, government officials, and development workers in recent decades.

In Lobi society in the northeast, divination is important as a means of determining the cause of death, disease, or other misfortune. Diviners do not predict the future; rather, they prescribe a course of action that emphasizes accepted social values in an effort to help people cope with present-day dilemmas. The diviner's role is similar to that of a counselor or confessor, who reminds people of the need to maintain proper relationships with all beings and provides them with a new perspective on relationships that have gone wrong.

Secret societies are found in several areas of northern Côte d'Ivoire (see Voltaic Cultures, this ch.). They serve important functions in the initiation and education of the young, and they provide vehicles for preserving beliefs about the past. Senior members are responsible for ritual instruction of new members and for the observance of funerals and ceremonies to ensure agricultural prosperity. Blacksmiths have secret societies of their own, and in some areas this occupational group is believed to have special spiritual powers. Medical and ritual specialists also undergo apprenticeships with established practitioners, thereby reinforcing their status.

World Religions

Islam

Islam is a monotheistic religion based on revelations received in seventh-century Arabia by the Prophet Muhammad. His life is recounted as the early history of the religion, beginning with his travels from the Arabian town of Mecca about 610. Muhammad preached a series of divine revelations, denouncing the polytheistic religions of his homeland. He became an outcast from Mecca and in 622 was forced to flee to the town of Yathrib, which became known as Medina (the city) through its association with him. The flight (hijra) marked the beginning of the Islamic Era and of Islam as a powerful force in history, and it marked the year 622 as the beginning of the Islamic calendar. Muhammad ultimately defeated his detractors in battle and consolidated his influence as both temporal and spiritual leader of most Arabs before his death in 632.

After Muhammad's death, his followers compiled those of his words that were regarded as coming directly from God in the Quran, the holy scripture of Islam. Muhammad's teachings and the precedents of his behavior as recalled by those who knew him became the hadith (sayings). From these sources, the faithful constructed the Prophet's customary practice, or sunna, which they endeavor to emulate. The Quran, hadith, and sunna form a comprehensive guide to the spiritual, ethical, and social life of the faithful in most Muslim countries.

Islam came to West Africa in three waves. In the ninth century, Berber traders brought the faith from North Africa to the ancient empire of Ghana. Beginning in the thirteenth century, the Malinké rulers of the Mali Empire contributed to its spread throughout much of the savanna, a process that continued into the eighteenth century, when the Juula established a Muslim kingdom in what is now northern Côte d'Ivoire. Finally in the nineteenth century, the Malinké warrior Samori Touré contributed to the southward spread of Islam (see Pre-European Period, ch. 1).

The central requirement of Islam is submission to the will of God (Allah), and, accordingly, a Muslim is a person who has submitted his will to God. The most important demonstration of faith is the *shahadah* (profession of faith), which states "There is no God but God (Allah), and Muhammad is his prophet." *Salat* (daily prayer), *zakat* (almsgiving), *sawm* (fasting), and *hajj* (pilgrimage to Mecca) are also required.

In Côte d'Ivoire, only the most devout Muslims pray, fast, and give alms as required by strict tenets of Islam, and only the most wealthy perform the hajj. Most Ivoirian Muslims are Sunni, following the Maliki version of Islamic law. Sufism, involving the organization of mystical brotherhoods *(tariqa)* for the purification and spread of Islam, is also widespread, laced with indigenous beliefs and practices. The four major Sufi brotherhoods are all represented in Côte d'Ivoire, although the Qadiriya, founded in the eleventh century, and the Tidjaniya, founded in the eighteenth century, are most popular. The Qadiriya is prevalent in the west, and the Tidjaniya, in the east. The other two major Islamic brotherhoods have few adherents in Côte d'Ivoire. The Senoussiya is identified with Libya, where its influence is substantial. The Ahmadiya, a Shiite sect originating in nineteenth-century India, is the only non-Sunni order in Côte d'Ivoire.

The significant religious authority is the *marabout*. He is believed to be a miracle worker, a physician, and a mystic, who exercises both magical and moral authority. He is also respected as a dispenser of amulets, which protect the wearer—Muslim or non-Muslim—against evil. The influence of *marabouts* has produced a number of reactions in Ivoirian society, among them a series of reformist movements inspired by Wahabist puritanism, which

originated in nineteenth-century Saudi Arabia. These reform movements often condemn Sufism and *marabouts* as un-Islamic, but the poor see that *marabouts* often speak out on behalf of the downtrodden and that reform movements appear to support the interests of wealthier Muslims.

Hamallism began as an Islamic reform movement in the French Sudan early in the twentieth century and has provided a channel for expressing political and religious discontent. Its founder, Hamallah, was exiled from the French Sudan to Côte d'Ivoire during the 1930s. He preached Islamic reform tempered by tolerance of many local practices, but he condemned many aspects of Sufism. Orthodox brotherhoods were able to convince the French authorities in Côte d'Ivoire that Hamallah had been responsible for earlier political uprisings in the French Sudan. Authorities then expelled Hamallah from Côte d'Ivoire and banned his teachings.

The relative success of Islam may be related to its compatibility with many aspects of African culture—for example, plural marriage for men, which was opposed by Christian missionaries. Nonetheless, Islam was also embraced because it provided symbolic identification with successful traders and travelers throughout the world, and it was seen as an alternative to European religion. Its agents were black, and it preached on behalf of those who lacked the trappings of Western civilization. In the 1980s, about one-fourth of all Ivoirians, including most Juula and Malinké people, called themselves Muslims.

Christianity

Only about one-eighth of the population was Christian in the 1980s. In general, Christianity was practiced by the middle class and in urban centers of the south. It was most prevalent among the Agni and lagoon cultures of the southeast, least so among the Mandé of the northwest. Roman Catholicism was the largest Christian religion, but Methodist, Baptist, and a number of smaller mission churches also existed.

Roman Catholicism made a brief appearance in Côte d'Ivoire in the mid-seventeenth century and reappeared two centuries later when French missionaries began to work among the Agni. The first African Roman Catholic mission in Côte d'Ivoire was established in 1895, and the first African priest was ordained in 1934. In the 1980s, the Roman Catholic Church operated seminaries and schools throughout the country. Although Côte d'Ivoire is officially a secular state, the president expressed pride in Abidjan's large Roman Catholic cathedral and alone funded construction of a basilica at Yamoussoukro, his birthplace, by 1990. Some villages have also adopted patron saints, whom they honor on both secular and religious holidays.

The largest Protestant religion as of the mid-1980s was Harrism, begun in 1914 by William Wade Harris, a Liberian preacher who proselytized along the coast of Côte d'Ivoire and Ghana. Harris set an example for his followers by leading a simple life and eschewing conspicuous wealth. He condemned the use of amulets and fetishes as idolatry, and he preached against adultery, theft, and lying. His was a simple, fairly austere form of Christianity, which was open to Roman Catholics and Protestants and did not preach open defiance of colonial authority.

In 1915 Harris was expelled from the region by an uneasy colonial governor, an action that revitalized his church, leaving dozens of small "Harrist" churches along the coast. A decade later, Methodist missionaries made contact with Harris and attempted to continue his work among the lagoon peoples. Harris succeeded in part because of his ethnic background—he was African but not Ivoirian—but also because he converted women as well as men—a practice that had been scorned by earlier Christian missionaries who failed to recognize the impact of matrilineal descent on an individual's spiritual life. Harrism was subsequently recognized as a branch of Methodism.

Syncretic Religions

Both Islam and Christianity have been adapted to indigenous religions in a variety of ways. Beyond these localized versions of world religions, however, are complex systems of belief and practice that incorporate many elements of more than one religion. Most widely recognized among these syncretic religions are numerous offshoots of Harrism along the coast, where new prophets, preachers, and disciples blend traditional beliefs, Harrism, and modern-day political advice to help deal with the problems of everyday life.

Syncretic religions are generally more common among minorities in a particular area or among groups that perceive themselves to be resisting political domination by their neighbors. The Agni have remained heavily Catholic, for example, whereas the neighboring Baoulé have evolved a variety of syncretisms, following prophets that promise good fortune as a reward for allegiance to them. Small groups in the far northeast have also evolved a variety of belief systems to maintain their traditions, incorporate selected aspects of Islam, and resist domination by outsiders.

Social Organization and Social Change

For centuries Côte d'Ivoire has been the scene of social and economic change brought about by cross-cultural contact, trans-Saharan and coastal trade, and innovation by local inhabitants. Established patterns of change were dramatically altered by the imposition of colonial rule and the transition to independence, and by the 1980s patterns of social and cultural change reflected responses to these disruptions and to the processes and policies of government.

The colonial imposition of plantation agriculture allowed the emergence of the first nontraditional African elite, when those who could claim rights to land began to employ farm laborers to produce cash crops for the colonial regime (see Economic Development and Social Change, ch. 1). This group of planters, as they came to be known, formed the core of the earliest Ivoirian political machine, which continued to influence the course of change in the 1980s. Alongside the rural elite, a fledgling civil servant middle class also appeared in response to the needs of the bureaucracy, as new levels of political awareness and activism surfaced throughout the region.

The African Agricultural Union (Syndicat Agricole Africain—SAA), formed in 1944 as a union of planters, led the opposition to colonial agricultural policies (see Brazzaville Conference, ch. 1). Félix Houphouët-Boigny, a Baoulé elder and French-trained

medical doctor, became head of the SAA and of the preindepen
dence movement, the Democratic Party of Côte d'Ivoire (Part
Démocratique de Côte d'Ivoire—PDCI), which emerged to leac
the struggle. The PDCI emphasized participation through traditional ethnic group leaders and ethnic committees *(comités ethniques)*.
Ethnic committees helped channel grass-roots participation in the
political process, but in 1985 they were replaced by local committees *(comités de base)*.

From the French perspective, those who had gained wealth and
prestige by exploiting new opportunities in the changing environment were considered most qualified for political decision making
on behalf of the colony (see Evolution of Colonial Policy, ch. 1).
Houphouët-Boigny gained a multiethnic constituency as leader of
the PDCI by acting as a broker between colonial officials and emerging African elites, and especially by opposing colonial forced-labor
policies. During the 1950s, the PDCI gradually adopted a strategy
of collaboration with colonial officials, a strategy Houphouët-Boigny
pursued successfully enough to become the nation's first president
at independence in 1960.

Even as an early leader in the preindependence PDCI, Houphouët-
Boigny had defined interest groups and grievances for the nation.
In 1974, after a decade of moderate discontent and dissidence, he
convened a series of dialogues that served the dual purpose of air-
ing cross-ethnic grievances and maintaining the president's image
as a traditional-style leader, using the analogy of the African "palaver"
(palabre). Teachers, students, former students, parents of students,
tenants, union members, union leaders, transporters, the military,
and the party youth wing, the Movement of Ivoirian Primary and
Secondary School Students (Mouvement des Etudiants et Elèves de
Côte d'Ivoire—MEECI), were invited. Excluded were representatives of the growing number of unemployed and of ethnic groups,
with the notable exception of the Lebanese community.

Economic modernization paralleled political and social change
in the shift from colonial to African power arrangements. Spurred
by the opening of the Vridi Canal to the Gulf of Guinea in 1950
and the concentration of government functions in the southeastern
port of Abidjan, population migration toward the south increased,
and secondary towns developed along routes to Abidjan. Modernization essentially became the process of urbanization, and the
distinction between urban and rural came to symbolize the widening
rift between rich and poor.

Urban Society

Urban ethnic associations performed important social functions,
from the initial reception of new migrants to the burial of urban

The basilica Notre Dame of Peace at Yamoussoukro
Courtesy Clair Votaw
Muslims kneeling in prayer
Courtesy Robert Handloff

residents. They also served as important mutual aid networks and facilitated communication with home villages. Rapid urbanization brought together people from numerous ethnic groups, however, and these contacts contributed to changing values and produced demands that went beyond the reach of traditional leadership roles. In this changing environment, ethnic organizations lost influence as cultural and economic brokers. Most grievances arose in response to government policy choices, and because these policies were not phrased in terms of ethnic groups, neither were grievances against them. Neighborhood and citywide problems demanded broader solutions, and multiethnic associations emerged as important interest groups.

Ethnicity was further diminished as a factor in urban politics as foreigners were drawn to Côte d'Ivoire's lucrative job market and as Houphouët-Boigny maintained fairly balanced ethnic representation among political appointments, without bringing traditional leaders into top levels of administration. He encouraged the most ambitious and educated young men from different regions to participate in nation building, and to do so through his patronage.

Houphouët-Boigny's patrimonial style of governing began to shape the social landscape, as the political skills he acquired during the waning years of colonial rule—his expertise as a strategist, his nonconfrontational manner of dealing with political rivals, and his paternalistic approach to allies—helped consolidate his support. In the late 1980s, he continued to emulate the style of his Baoulé elders, softening strong leadership enough to maintain broad popular support, satisfying crucial popular demands, and co-opting potential opponents (see Political Issues, ch. 4).

As a result of these factors—the urban emphasis, the relative unimportance of ethnic differences, and Houphouët-Boigny's patrimonial style of governing—a self-perpetuating elite emerged. Social relations were ordered more by access to status, prestige, and wealth than by ethnic differences, and for most people the locus of this access was the government. Wealth and government service became so closely linked that one was taken as a symbol of the other.

Elites

Access to land, housing, secondary education, jobs, and social services determined paths of opportunity and social mobility in Ivoirian society, where, for the first three decades after independence, there were clear-cut cleavages between a ruling elite and people who lacked privileged access to resources. This self-reinforcing system allowed a wealthy, urban, privileged minority to receive most of the benefits available to the society as a whole. For example, most urban land concessions were granted to people in government and administration and to their relatives and clients. In fact, political appointments were often accompanied by land concessions in Abidjan, and many Ivoirians attributed the scarcity of land and high levels of rent to this form of patronage.

Urban housing was also a fairly good measure of political status. Cabinet ministers received monthly housing allowances and lived in relative luxury. Government housing policy favored construction of expensive quarters for upper-income families. Rents were high as a proportion of income and often required deposits of several months or years rent in advance. Building a private home required ''good standing'' within the community in order to meet credit and permit restrictions.

Secondary education was also an important urban resource and vehicle of social mobility. Although primary schools were found throughout the country, secondary schooling was primarily an urban activity, channeling graduates into urban occupations and contributing to the rural exodus. A large proportion of pupils who entered primary school were eliminated at crucial points in the education ladder, especially through limits on secondary school and university admissions, but many also dropped out throughout the system. In general, students' educational attainments reflected their parents' level of education. Even when the government achieves its goal of universal primary education, access to secondary schooling is expected to remain an extremely limited, highly valued resource.

By the 1980s, employment had become the most significant indicator of social status. High-level government employees earned salaries several times the national average, and public sector salaries generally exceeded those in the private sector, although this situation was changing in the late 1980s as the government succeeded in freezing civil service pay scales. Rural wages lagged far behind those in urban areas, where the number of unemployed far exceeded the number of available jobs. In a circular fashion, those who were employed had an edge in the job market and in most other areas of social life. Social services were more readily available to those who had jobs or had just lost them, and social service organizations tended to be located in wealthier sections of town. In general, the distribution of government subsidies helped to maintain the distance between urban elites and the rural and urban poor.

The Ivoirian middle class was still a small minority, primarily traders, administrators, teachers, nurses, artisans, and successful farmers. The middle class constituted the highest social stratum in rural areas and some small towns, but the majority of small farmers were not included, nor were the many low-wage earners in urban areas. Middle-class status was, in Côte d'Ivoire as elsewhere, marked by continual striving, for one's self and one's children, to acquire the symbols of wealth. In cities, opportunities for social mobility were limited for the middle class and the poor, who continued to depend on the patronage of the elite to achieve most of their goals.

The Role of Women

Houphouët-Boigny's political style and longevity shaped Ivoirian elites into a wealthy, male, educated social stratum. By the late 1980s, women were beginning to emerge within this group, as education and acculturation enabled them to challenge the established order. Official attitudes toward the status of women were pragmatic, like most official attitudes in Côte d'Ivoire. Beliefs about the role of women in society were partly the result of ethnic conditioning, however, and the cultural bias against equality between the sexes was embodied in customary law, where ethnic diversity and cultural conservatism slowed the pace of modernization of regulations regarding women.

Role expectations for women changed, however, altered by colonial legislation, which liberated captives throughout francophone Africa in 1903, and then by the Mandel Decree of 1939, which fixed the minimum age of marriage at fourteen and made mutual consent a formal necessity for marriage. The Jacquinot Decree of 1951 invoked the power of the state to protect women from claims to their services—by their own or their husband's family—after marriage. Moreover, it enabled women to obtain a divorce more easily and invalidated in-laws' claims to any brideprice that had been paid to a woman's family to legitimize the marriage. This decree also recognized monogamy as the only legal form of marriage and allowed couples to marry without parental consent. These changes altered popular perceptions of marriage and established the colonial government as the authority on most aspects of the status of women.

At independence, the government of Houphouët-Boigny acknowledged existing decrees affecting the status of women and went on to establish the primacy of the nuclear family, raise the minimum age for marriage to eighteen, and condemn in general terms the notion of female inferiority. At the same time, however, legislation during the 1960s established a husband's right to control much of his wife's property, and it required a woman to obtain her husband's permission to establish a bank account or obtain a job. The government also placed restrictions on a woman's right to divorce, denied legal recognition of matrilineal rights of inheritance (inheritance by a man's nephews before his sons), and finally, condemned the practice of bride-price.

In 1963 women reacted to the extent and direction of government control by forming the Association of Ivoirian Women (Association des Femmes Ivoiriennes—AFI). They also persuaded the president to establish the Ministry of Women's Affairs (Ministère de la Condition Féminine) in 1976 and to appoint AFI leader Jeanne Gervais as minister. Gervais's goals were to obtain better educational and employment opportunities for women and to establish judicial equality for women. Legislation was enacted in 1983 to allow a woman to control some of her property after marriage and to appeal to the courts for redress of a husband's actions.

The status of women, in practice and in the law, was still well below that of men through most of the 1980s, but educational opportunities for women were improving at all levels. In 1987 about one-sixth of the students at the National University of Côte d'Ivoire were women, and the number of women in the salaried work force had also increased. Women made up almost one-fourth of the civil service and held positions previously closed to them, in medicine, law, business, and university teaching.

Social Attitudes

Despite official descriptions of their society as "classless" and egalitarian in the 1980s, Ivoirian citizens were acutely aware of the distinction between the rich and the poor. People perceived "temporary distortions" in the social fabric—as social inequities were described by the president—as continuing trends. They attributed these distortions to a variety of factors but rarely to the role of the government in maintaining and subsidizing the elite. Regional and international competition in commodity markets was cited as a source of economic recession and hardship in general. Within Côte d'Ivoire, regional inequities were often blamed on mismanagement by presidential advisers but not on the president himself. Cabinet ministers, in particular, were often blamed for poor policy decisions and implementation and were often subjected to invidious comparisons with presidential wisdom and imagination.

Ivoirians were also adept at generalizing about each other and about immigrants to their nation, placing blame for social ills on ethnic groups more often than on socioeconomic forces. The Baoulé, the president's own constituency, were "too dominant" among high officeholders, in their critics' view. The related, and rival,

Agni often expressed anti-Baoulé sentiments, while the Agni them-selves, because of their tradition of hierarchical organization, were criticized for elitist attitudes toward other ethnic groups. Groups that avoided centralization among indigenous polities, such as the Bété, were stereotyped, in turn, as "unsophisticated." The Lobi and related groups from the northeast were similarly stereotyped. Non-Africans, even those born in Côte d'Ivoire, were blamed for "draining the wealth from the nation." Within the foreign work force, Mossi farm laborers were looked down upon, whereas French white-collar workers were both despised and emulated. These and other social reactions served to legitimize popular views of Ivoiri-an society and to confirm ethnic pride.

At the same time, Ivoirian society was permeated with a sense of apathy about social development, except among those in or very close to political office. Even those who acknowledged the nation's strengths often did not feel like active participants in its develop-ment. The large foreign presence within the economy, the en-trenched political machine, and the relatively unchanging living conditions among the poor contributed to this sense of alienation from the overall progress that has marked Côte d'Ivoire since in-dependence.

Education

The Ivoirian education system is an adaptation of the French system, which was introduced at the end of the nineteenth century to train clerks and interpreters to help administer the colony. The education system was gradually expanded to train teachers, farm-ers, and artisans, but by 1940, only 200 Africans had been admit-ted to primary schools. In 1945 the nation had only four university graduates, despite an official policy, described as "assimilationist," aimed at creating a political elite that would identify with France and French culture. The education system was made into a depart-ment of the French national system under the jurisdiction of the minister for education in Paris in the last decade of colonial rule, but by limiting access to a tiny minority of Africans, it generally failed to supplant Ivoirian values with French ones.

Education assumed much greater importance as independence approached, leading some village elders to establish and support village schools. Primary-school enrollments increased eightfold dur-ing the 1950s; secondary-school enrollments increased ninefold. Schools began to prepare students for the university, and scholar-ship programs were implemented to send a select few to Europe or to Dakar, Senegal, for further study.

During the 1980s, education was an important national priority; it received nearly one-third of the national budget in 1985. Responsibility for educational development lay with the Ministry of National Education and Scientific Research, which also prescribed curricula, textbooks, and teaching methods; prepared qualifying examinations; and licensed teachers, administrators, and private educational institutions.

As a result of its emphasis on education, Côte d'Ivoire boasted a 43 percent literacy rate overall, 53 percent for men and 31 percent for women in 1988. About 15 percent of the total population was enrolled in some type of educational institution, but enrollments were still much higher in urban than rural areas.

The Education System

The education system comprised three stages: primary school lasted six years, leading to a certificate of primary studies; secondary school lasted seven years, leading to a certificate or *baccalauréat* (see fig. 8). University education, available only in Abidjan, culminated in a university degree. A large number of technical and teacher-training institutions also provided postprimary and postsecondary education. There was no system of adult education, although many adults attended night courses or, in rural areas, received literacy and other instruction via radio.

Most public schools were tuition free, although students paid an entrance fee and bought uniforms. Most supplies were free, and some students received government scholarships, usually in return for a period of government employment after graduation.

In 1980 approximately 14 percent of primary schools and 29 percent of secondary schools were private. Most of these were Catholic, staffed by religious and lay teachers, with salaries partially subsidized by government funding. Catholic schools operated primarily in the south and east but were also located throughout the country. Religious instruction was not permitted in government schools. Quranic schools were common in the north and were tolerated, but not supported, by the government. Some students attended both public and Quranic schools.

The school year was divided into three terms, beginning in September and separated by short Christmas and Easter holidays and a two-month summer recess. The average week consisted of approximately thirty hours of classes, Monday through Saturday morning. Most instruction encouraged mental discipline more than analytical thinking or creativity by emphasizing rote memorization and oral recitation.

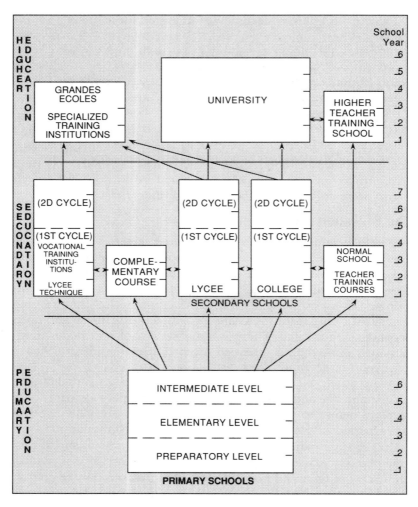

Source: Based on information from *International Yearbook of Education*, 32, New York, 1980, 112–3.

Figure 8. Public Education System, 1988

Primary Education

Approximately 1.5 million pupils attended primary school in 1987, representing about 75 percent of boys and 50 percent of girls below age fifteen. Primary-school enrollments increased at a rate of about 7.2 percent per year from 1960 to 1980, climbing to 9.1 percent between 1976 and 1980. This rate slowed after 1980, averaging 4.2 percent from 1981 to 1984 and 2.2 percent after 1984.

Children entered primary school at the age of seven or eight and passed through six grades, divided into preparatory, elementary, and intermediate levels. In the first six months, students mastered French, the language of instruction. Classes in reading, writing, and arithmetic were taught, gradually supplemented by history, geography, natural sciences, music, art, and physical education. Rural schools also required students to work in school gardens and learn basic agricultural methods. Standard school-leaving exams led to the certificate of elementary education *(certificat d'études primaires élémentaires*—CEPE) and determined entrance to secondary institutions.

Secondary Education

About 250,000 students, or about 19 percent of primary-school graduates, attended government-funded secondary schools in 1987. Most of those preparing for university attended a *collège* or lycée, both of which included seven years of study divided into two cycles. Significant differences between these two institutions almost disappeared in the decades following their introduction by the French, but the lycée was generally administered by the national government and the *collège* by the municipal government with national funding.

After the first cycle or four years of secondary school, students took exams and were awarded the certificate of the lower cycle of secondary study *(brevet d'étude du premier cycle*—BEPC). This qualification generally allowed them to continue at the *collège* or lycée, enter a teacher-training institution, or find an entry-level job in commerce or government. After the second cycle of three years of study, graduates earned the *baccalauréat,* which indicated a level of learning roughly equivalent to one or two years of university study in the United States. In Côte d'Ivoire, as in France, it qualified a student for university entrance.

Secondary-school enrollments grew at a rate of about 11 percent per year from 1960 to 1984, but that rate has declined since 1984. The dropout rate was especially high for girls, who made up only 18 percent of the student body during the last two years of secondary school. An average of one-fourth of all secondary students received the *baccalauréat.*

Complementary courses were the most common type of alternative secondary education, administered as four-year programs to improve the academic education of those who did not qualify for *collège* or lycée. Complementary courses were established during the 1950s, when expanding educational opportunities was a high priority, and they were located throughout the country to

83

compensate for the urban bias in secondary education. Complementary courses often provided a combination of academic and practical training, leading to an elementary certificate *(brevet élémentaire*—BE) or the BEPC, and enabled some students to enter the second cycle at a *collège* or lycée, or a vocational training institution.

Additional secondary-level courses were administered by religious organizations, most often the Catholic Church. These courses consisted of seven years of study divided into two cycles, with a certificate of completion awarded after each cycle. Teacher-training was available, often as an alternative to academic university preparation, at a variety of postprimary levels. Secondary-level teacher training could lead to a BE certificate and admission to a normal school *(école normale)*, which might also be attended by students who left lycées or *collèges* after the first four years of study.

Vocational training, attended by 47,000 students in 1982–83, was available at a variety of postprimary institutions. This training included courses in agriculture, engineering, public works, transportation management, secretarial and commercial subjects, and building trades. Graduates often worked as apprentices or pursued further training at higher technical institutes.

Higher Education

The National University of Côte d'Ivoire, which was founded as the Center for Higher Education at Abidjan in 1959 and became the University of Abidjan in 1964, had an enrollment of 18,732 in 1987. Of this number, about 10,000 were Ivoirians and 3,200 were women. Still heavily dependent on French assistance, it included faculties of law, sciences, and letters and schools of agriculture, public works, administration, and fine arts. Other institutions of higher learning, known as *grandes écoles,* awarded certificates of training in specialized fields in cooperation with, but not as part of, the national university.

Teachers

In the mid-1980s, five classes of teachers were distinguished by their educational preparation and salary level: professors, who taught at the secondary or university level; assistant professors at the secondary level; and *instituteurs, instituteurs-adjoints,* and monitors at the primary level. Teachers' salaries were generally higher than salaries of civil servants with similar qualifications in the mid-1980s, although many people still left teaching for more lucrative professions. The government responded to teacher shortages with a variety of training programs and short courses and by recruiting expatriates to teach at the secondary and postsecondary levels.

Administration building, National University of Côte d'Ivoire
Courtesy Eszti Votaw

Teachers were organized into a number of unions, most of them incorporated into the government-controlled central union federation, the General Federation of Ivoirian Workers (Union Générale des Travailleurs de Côte d'Ivoire—UGTCI). The National Union of Secondary School Teachers of Côte d'Ivoire and two smaller unions remained outside the UGTCI and were outspoken in their criticism of government educational policies and educational finances in particular. Despite this tradition of criticism, many government officials achieved political office through leadership positions in the teachers union (See Interest Groups, ch. 4).

Problems in Education

During the early 1980s, Côte d'Ivoire spent a higher share of its gross national product (GNP—see Glossary) and of its national budget on education than any other country in the world. Although this served as an indication of the nation's high regard for education, expatriate teachers' salaries accounted for a disproportionate share of current expenditures, reducing the benefits to the nation itself. Generous scholarships for secondary-school students also reduced funds available for younger children.

The Ministry of National Education and Scientific Research assigned highest priority to problems of financing educational development and reducing the number of school dropouts. Reducing regional inequities was also important; in 1986 enrollments in the south averaged about four times those in the north. The government employed innovative methods to improve the education system, including the use of televised instruction in primary schools in the 1970s—a project that was abandoned as too expensive. Computers and automated data processing equipment were being used at the National University in 1987 and were to be introduced at lower levels of the educational system by 1990. By the late 1980s, the government was also producing its own textbooks, previously purchased in France, to reflect local rather than foreign cultural values.

The internal efficiency of the education system was relatively low, partly because of the large number of students who repeated courses and the high dropout level. The number of school-aged children was expected to grow at an average annual rate of 4.3 percent by 1995, increasing the school-aged population by 50 percent. Unfortunately, teacher-training programs could not keep pace with these changes, and educational planners were in particular demand. The link between education and employment was also weak, exacerbated by the economic recession of the 1980s. Graduates, in effect, expected more than society could give them. As in many countries, academic institutions and personnel often annoy government officials with their outspoken criticism of national policies (see Discontent on Campus, ch. 1). A number of mechanisms are used to co-opt or intimidate dissident leaders, although a few of their criticisms have been received favorably and have produced policy changes. Some outspoken teachers have been offered government jobs, in effect to receive the brunt of criticism they have generated. Some students have been expelled from the university. The campus was closed down following antigovernment demonstrations in 1982, and campus organizations were banned. Secondary-school teachers who protested against the elimination of their housing benefits in 1983 found their professional organizations banned as well.

Health and Welfare

Economic progress since independence outpaced improvements in the general health status of the population, despite substantial improvements in health conditions. As in other areas, nationwide statistics mask sharp regional and socioeconomic disparities. In the mid-1980s, life expectancies ranged from fifty-six years in Abidjan to fifty years in rural areas of the south and thirty-nine years in rural areas of the north. The resulting overall national average of fifty-one years represented a marked improvement over that of thirty-nine in 1960.

Infant and child mortality rates remained high in rural areas, where access to potable water and waste disposal systems was limited and housing and dietary needs often remained unmet. An estimated 127 infants per 1,000 births died in their first year of life, a rate that fell steadily from 1960 to 1985. In 1987 one-half of all deaths were infants and children under the age of five. Infectious diseases—primarily malaria, gastrointestinal ailments, respiratory infections, measles, and tetanus—accounted for most illness and death in children. Unsanitary conditions and poor maternal health also contributed to infant deaths. Close spacing of births contributed to high rates of malnutrition in the first two years of life.

In 1985 the nation had a generally adequate food supply, averaging 115 percent of the minimum daily requirement, but seasonal and regional variations and socioeconomic inequalities contributed to widespread malnutrition in the north, in poorer sections of cities, and among immigrants.

Public health expenditures increased steadily during the 1980s, but the health care system was nonetheless unable to meet the health care needs of the majority of the population. Medical care for wealthy urban households was superior to that available to rural farm families, and the health care system retained its bias toward curing disease rather than preventing it. Chronic shortages of equipment, medicines, and health care personnel also contributed to overall poor service delivery, even where people had access to health care facilities. In many rural areas, health care remained a family matter, under the guidance of lineage elders and traditional healers.

Staffing policies in the health sector led to low ratios of doctors to patients and even more severe shortages of nurses and auxiliary health care personnel in the 1980s. In 1985 there were 6.5 doctors per 100,000 people, and 0.7 dentists, 10.9 midwives, 24.9 nurses, and 11.2 auxiliaries. For this same population, 158 hospital beds were available, 120 of them in maternity care centers. In the northeast, these ratios were much lower, and rural areas of the southwest also received less attention by medical planners.

Maternal Health Care (MHC) centers taught classes aimed at reducing maternal and infant mortality. The World Health Organization (WHO) and the United Nations Children's Emergency Fund (UNICEF) also assisted in programs to vaccinate children against poliomyelitis, diphtheria, tetanus, pertussis, tuberculosis, yellow fever, and measles, and to vaccinate pregnant women against tetanus.

In 1987 the government began to implement testing programs for antibodies to human immunodeficiency virus (HIV), which causes acquired immunodeficiency syndrome (AIDS). By the end of that year, it had reports of 250 AIDS cases nationwide, most in urban areas. Although this number was small in comparison with many nations of East Africa and Central Africa, it represented twice the number of reported AIDS cases one year earlier and posed a potentially serious health threat. The government neither repressed reports on the spread of HIV nor treated them lightly. With French medical and financial assistance, and in collaboration with WHO's Special Program on AIDS (SPA), it began to implement blood screening programs and to establish public information centers to meet immediate needs. By 1988, however, no medium-term program to prevent the spread of HIV was in place.

The Ministry of Public Health and Population, which bore nationwide responsibility for health care planning, lacked adequately trained personnel and information management systems, and it shared the urban bias found throughout much of the government in the 1980s. It sought private sector involvement in disease prevention and declared the improvement of health care standards a national priority. At the same time, historical, ethnic, socioeconomic, and political factors contributing to the nation's health problems continued to complicate policy making at the national level.

Social Programs

Social programs generally benefited the wealthy more than the poor, subsidizing those who had access to resources and an understanding of public services. Public housing, a high priority under successive development plans since 1960, was an example of this trend. Most available public housing was in Abidjan. It was generally of high quality, so even with subsidized rents, it was beyond the means of poorer families. The result was government assistance to relatively high-wage earners.

Some World Bank (see Glossary) programs were helping redress this imbalance by providing funding for low-income housing and low-cost transportation programs. World Bank assistance in housing in the late 1980s was also aimed at providing low-interest loans to enable families to purchase their own homes.

Social Problems

Through the 1980s, Côte d'Ivoire shared the concerns over poverty, unemployment, and crime that plagued developing and industrial countries alike. Human resource management was complicated by the large urban-rural ratio, however, and by population growth and economic recession. The cultural expectation of assistance through the extended family helped offset problems of unemployment, but high mobility within the work force resulted in more dispersed families, and this dispersal, in turn, contributed to rising problems of poverty and unemployment.

Poverty, population mobility, and ethnic and cultural diversity contributed to rising crime rates during the first two decades of independence. During the 1980s, white-collar crime—embezzlement, fraud, and misappropriation of funds—rose at a faster rate, and urban crimes such as robbery and theft generated widespread concern. In 1987 the president declared dishonesty and fraud a public disgrace and proclaimed his intention to wage a vigorous war against them. Drug abuse—primarily involving cocaine, marijuana, and heroin—was also declared a scourge against society, but the appropriate public response to these problems was not defined.

* * *

Ethnographic background reading on Akan, Mandé, and Voltaic societies is available in a variety of works by Meyer Fortes, R. S. Rattray, Charles Humana, Elliott Skinner, Kenneth Little, Helga Diallo, and Germaine Dieterlen. Alexander Alland, Jr.'s *When the Spider Danced* presents a personal account of ethnographic research among the Abron during the 1960s.

Michael A. Cohen's *Urban Policy and Political Conflict in Africa* focuses on urbanization and formation of the elite in the 1960s and early 1970s. Bastiaan A. den Tuinder, in *Ivory Coast: The Challenge of Success,* assesses data on sectoral progress during the 1970s. Jeanne Maddox Toungara's ''The Changing Status of Women in Côte d'Ivoire'' summarizes the history of changes in legislation regarding women in Ivoirian society.

Much of the more recent literature on Côte d'Ivoire describes the role of the president in crafting this complex nation-state and controlling the direction of social and political change. The years leading up to independence and the context of the evolution of the president's status as ''Le Vieux'' are analyzed in Aristide Zolberg's *One-Party Government in the Ivory Coast.* Claude E. Welch, Jr., in ''Côte d'Ivoire: Personal Rule and Civilian Control,'' assesses the president's role in maintaining the region's only long-standing civilian government.

Robert J. Mundt's *Historical Dictionary of the Ivory Coast* compiles a wide range of historical, political, and sociological data, presented in concise entries with an extensive bibliography. Philippe David's *La Côte d'Ivoire* presents an overview of Ivoirian society, including historical, economic, and sociological background reading. (For further information and complete citations, see Bibliography.)

Chapter 3. The Economy

Brass weights, container, and spoon for carrying and measuring gold dust

SINCE ACHIEVING INDEPENDENCE from France in 1960, Côte d'Ivoire's primary economic objective has been growth. During the 1960s, growth was accomplished by expanding and diversifying agricultural production, improving infrastructure, and developing import substitution industries. Implicit in this strategy was the emergence of an expanding domestic market to support budding consumer goods industries. Income redistribution and Ivoirianization (replacement of expatriates with Ivoirian workers) were made subordinate to growth. Although these goals were politically desirable, redistribution and Ivoirianization would be impossible without growth, according to policymakers. Using revenues generated from agricultural exports, the government financed improvements to infrastructure—roads, ports, railroads, power generation, and schools. To finance increased agricultural production and industrial development, the government turned to foreign investment and imported technology. Much of the manual labor was supplied by non-Ivoirian Africans.

Paramount in this planning was the maintenance of economic links to France that were almost as extensive as the preindependence ties. Before independence, French public and private capital helped to support the government, ensured the internal and external convertibility of the currency, financed most major commercial enterprises, and supported the country's banking and credit structure. French enterprises in Côte d'Ivoire were a major employer of Ivoirian labor, and France purchased—often at rates higher than market value—most of the country's exports. In addition, French managers held most of the key positions in business, and French advisers occupied important posts in many government ministries.

Côte d'Ivoire's ties to France grew even stronger after independence. Between 1960 and 1980, the total French population in Côte d'Ivoire nearly doubled, from about 30,000 to close to 60,000, forming the largest French expatriate community. In the mid-1980s, four out of five resident French had lived in Côte d'Ivoire for more than five years. French citizens filled technical and advisory positions in the government (albeit in diminishing numbers) and were also evident throughout the private sector. Until 1985 Côte d'Ivoire also had the highest number of French-controlled multinational businesses in all of Africa, had the largest percentage of French imports to and exports from Africa, and, along with Senegal, received the largest French aid package in Africa.

Economic development in Côte d'Ivoire has passed through three phases. During the first phase, from 1965 to 1975, the economy grew at a remarkable pace as coffee, cocoa, and timber exports increased. Surpluses from exports speeded growth in the secondary (industrial) and tertiary (services, administration, and defense) sectors. Gross domestic product (GDP—see Glossary) grew at an average annual rate of 7.9 percent in real terms, well ahead of the average annual population growth rate of approximately 4 percent.

During the second phase, from 1976 to 1980, external changes in the world economic system reverberated within Côte d'Ivoire. Coffee and cocoa prices peaked in the 1976–77 period as a result of poor harvests in Latin America, but two years later prices declined rapidly. GDP continued to grow at an average rate of 7.6 percent per year; within the period, however, the growth rate varied from 2 percent in 1979 to 11.5 percent one year later. The government, which had responded to the boom phase by vigorously expanding public investment, was by 1979 forced to rely on foreign borrowing to sustain growth. At the same time, the declining value of the United States dollar, the currency in which Côte d'Ivoire's loans were denominated, and rising prices for imported oil adversely affected the country's current accounts balance. By the end of the second phase, Côte d'Ivoire was at the brink of a financial crisis.

During the third phase, from 1981 to 1987, the economy deteriorated as terms of trade declined, interest rates increased, the prospects of new offshore oil development evaporated, and agricultural earnings dropped. Following a record 1985–86 cocoa harvest, the economy rebounded briefly; however, falling cocoa prices quickly eroded any gains the country had hoped to achieve, and by 1987 President Félix Houphouët-Boigny had halted further payments on foreign debt. Subsequently, Côte d'Ivoire was forced to adopt a structural adjustment program mandated by the International Monetary Fund (IMF—see Glossary) that limited imports, subsidized exports, and reduced government spending.

Growth and Structure of the Economy

By the end of the first decade of independence, the government's strategy for economic growth and development appeared remarkably successful (see table 2, Appendix). Agricultural output of cash crops expanded, and, as evidence of diversification, the relative importance of unprocessed coffee, cocoa, and timber diminished as that of bananas, cotton, rubber, palm oil, and sugar grew. Using revenues from commodity sales, the government upgraded roads, improved communications, and raised the educational level of the work force. Local factories were replacing some imports by producing a wide variety of light consumer goods.

During the 1970s, the government's economic objective of growth remained unchanged. Agriculture—coffee and cocoa in particular—remained the mainstay of the export economy and the largest component of GDP until it was overtaken by the service sector in 1978. But while agriculture provided about 75 percent of export earnings in 1965, that total had shrunk by 20 percent by 1975. Between 1965 and 1975, agriculture's share of GDP also declined by almost 20 percent. Industrial GDP, derived primarily from import substitution manufacturing and agricultural processing, increased by 275 percent from 1970 to 1975, while industry's share of export earnings increased from 20 percent in 1965 to 35 percent in 1975. The fastest-growing sector of the economy was services, which as a share of GDP increased by more than 325 percent from 1965 to 1975.

At the same time, problems that arose during the previous decade required adjustments. To reduce production costs of manufactured goods, the government encouraged local production of intermediate inputs, such as chemicals and textiles. The government also shifted some public investment from infrastructure to crop diversification and agricultural processing industries to improve export earnings. Meanwhile, work on such major projects as the Buyo hydroelectric generating station continued. Foreign donors, attracted by Côte d'Ivoire's stable political climate and profitable investment opportunities, provided capital for these endeavors. Until 1979, when coffee and cocoa prices plummeted and the cost of petroleum products rose sharply a second time, virtually every economic indicator was favorable.

Over the same twenty years, however, structural contradictions in Côte d'Ivoire's economic strategy became apparent and presaged the serious problems that became manifest in the 1980s. First, the emergence of a domestic market large enough to allow manufacturers of import substitutes to benefit from economies of scale required a wage for agricultural workers—the largest segment of the labor force—that was high enough to support mass consumption. But because the government relied on agricultural exports to finance improvements to infrastructure, commodity prices and wages could not be allowed to rise too high. Second, the government's focus on import substitution increased demand for intermediate inputs, the cost of which often exceeded that of the previously imported consumer goods. Moreover, Côte d'Ivoire's liberal investment code encouraged capital-intensive rather than labor-intensive industrial development. Consequently, industrial growth contributed little to the growth of an industrial labor force or a domestic market, and prices for consumer goods remained high, reflecting the high costs of production and protection. The investment code also permitted vast funds to leave Côte d'Ivoire in the form of tax-free profits, salary remittances, and repatriated capital. Decapitalization, or the outflow of capital, led to balance of payments problems and the need to export more commodities and limit agricultural wages. (As a result, the domestic market remained small, and consumer goods remained expensive.) By the start of the 1980s, as surpluses from commodity sales dwindled, the government continued to depend on foreign borrowing to stimulate the economy. Inexorably, the external debt and the burden of debt service grew.

In the 1980s, a combination of drought, low commodity prices, and rapidly rising debt costs exacerbated the structural weakness of the Ivoirian economy. Between 1977 and 1981, both cocoa and coffee prices fell on world markets, the current accounts balance dropped precipitously, and debt servicing costs rose, compelling the government to implement stabilization policies imposed by the IMF (see table 3, Appendix). The economy sagged even more when a drought during the 1983–84 growing season cut agricultural and hydroelectric output at the same time that rising interest rates on international markets increased the debt burden. No sector of the economy was untouched. Between 1981 and 1984, GDP from industry dropped by 33 percent, GDP from services dropped by 9 percent, and GDP from agriculture dropped by 12.2 percent.

Between 1984 and 1986, a surge in commodity prices and output, coupled with increased support from Western financial institutions, provided a momentary economic boost. The record 1985 cocoa crop of 580,000 tons, combined with improved prices for coffee and cotton, bolstered export earnings and confidence in the economy. Following both the 1984–85 and the 1985–86 growing seasons, the government again increased producer prices for cocoa and coffee, resumed hiring civil servants, and raised some salaries, all of which led to a rise in consumption. Food production also increased during this period, allowing food imports to drop. Similarly, a reduction in the cost of oil imports helped the country to attain a large commercial surplus by the end of 1986, thus considerably easing the balance of payments difficulties experienced earlier in the decade. These factors, combined with the rescheduling of foreign debt payments, gave the government some flexibility in handling its debt crisis and allowed it to begin paying its arrears to domestic creditors, including major construction and public works firms, supply companies, and local banks.

Market at Treichville, in Abidjan
Courtesy Eszti Votaw

The economic resurgence turned out to be short lived, however. In 1987 the economy again declined. Compared with the first six months of the previous year, sales of raw cocoa fell by 33 percent, and coffee exports plummeted by 62 percent. GDP declined by 5.8 per cent in real terms, reflecting the slide in local currency earnings from exports. The trade surplus fell by 49 percent, plunging the current account into deficit. Trade figures for the first half of 1987 revealed a 35 percent drop in the value of exports in comparison with the same period in 1986.

In May 1987, the government suspended payments on its massive foreign debt and appealed to official government lenders (the Paris Club—see Glossary) and commercial lenders (the London Club—see Glossary) to reschedule debt payments. The Paris Club acceded in December 1987; the London Club, in March 1988.

As negotiations were proceeding, lenders pressured the government to introduce fiscal reforms. In January 1988, the government implemented a series of revenue-raising measures, which extended the value-added tax to the wholesale and retail trades and increased import tariffs, stamp duties, and tobacco taxes. In addition, the government initiated programs to privatize most state enterprises and parastatals (companies under joint government and private ownership) and to give a "new orientation" to industry.

Privatization was not a new measure. In 1980 the state made divestment an official policy and offered for sale many state corporations and the state's shares in jointly owned enterprises. Because the response to divestment was sluggish, the government proposed innovative alternatives to outright denationalization, such as leasing arrangements and self-managing cooperatives. By 1987, however, only twenty-eight of the targeted enterprises (in agribusiness, trading and distribution, public works, and tourism) had been sold. Moreover, the state still accounted for 55 percent of direct investment in the country.

The structural adjustments required by the World Bank (see Glossary) in 1987 gave a new impetus to the divestment process. The government placed 103 industries in which it had holdings up for sale, although several companies considered to be of strategic importance to the country were later taken off the market. Included in this category were the Commodity Marketing and Price Control Board (Caisse de Stabilisation et de Soutien des Prix de Production Agricole—CSSPPA), the Petroleum Operations Company of Côte d'Ivoire (Pétrole de Côte d'Ivoire—PETROCI), the Ivoirian Maritime Transport Company (Société Ivoirienne de Transport Maritime—SITRAM), and the Ivoirian Mining Company (Société pour le Développement Minier de Côte d'Ivoire—SODEMI).

Divestment was a mixed success at best. Although Ivoirians took over more than half of the companies, those enterprises in which Ivoirians held a majority of the capital were very small—three-quarters were capitalized at less than CFA F50 million (for value of the CFA F—see Glossary)—and their rate of return was substantially lower than that of foreign-owned and state enterprises. In general, the larger the capital of an enterprise, the smaller the proportion owned by Ivoirians.

Role of Government

In spite of its reputation for having liberal, noninterventionist economic policies, the Ivoirian government played a pivotal role in the domestic economy. Acting primarily through the Ministry of Planning and the Ministry of Finance, the government directed fiscal and monetary strategies over the long term and intervened in the short term in response to changing market conditions. The Ministry of Planning was responsible for coordinating long-term development projects, while the Ministry of Finance was responsible for financing annual investment. The technical ministries, such as the Ministry of Mining, the Ministry of Trade, and the Ministry of Industry, were responsible for preparing and implementing projects. The Ministry of Planning played the central role. It mediated between the technical ministries and the public enterprises on the one hand and the Ministry of Finance and the government (in its role as the formulator of economic objectives) on the other hand. The Ministry of Finance translated the government's policy objectives into a set of long-term output and investment targets and an aggregate investment package. The Ministry of Planning and the technical ministries then used the guidelines to undertake those projects that were deemed feasible and would most contribute to achieving the plan's output and investment targets.

Beginning in 1960, the Ministry of Planning prepared a series of ten-year projections. Subsequently, these were replaced by a series of five-year plans that had built into them a three-year "rolling" program called the Loi-Programme. The five-year plans formulated the overall objectives, set priorities, and provided a macroeconomic framework for the country's development. The three-year overlapping Lois-Programmes examined individual projects, taking into account progress toward implementation, annual changes in costs, and political impact.

Public Investment

In addition to its planning role, the government was the largest single investor in the economy. Following independence, the government embarked on an ambitious capital spending program. Much of the capital for government intervention came from the CSSPPA, which fixed producer prices, operated a reserve price stabilization fund, and extracted profits for the state. Much of this investment went toward developing infrastructure and was one of the state's more positive economic contributions in the 1960s.

By the 1970s, although there was no official change of economic policy, the state intervened more directly in the economy, primarily through the creation of parastatals. This surge in the number of parastatals reflected the government's desire to stimulate growth in those areas where the private sector was considered insufficiently active, to create employment for Ivoirians, and to encourage Ivoirians to invest locally. In the case of agricultural parastatals, the state wanted to lessen income disparities between the north and the south, decrease food imports, provide rural employment, and diminish the importance of foreign investment in agriculture. In some instances, social or political objectives superseded the profit motive, as appears to have been the case with parastatals like the Bandama Valley Authority (Autorité de la Vallée du Bandama—AVB), which promoted regional development, and the Sugar Development Company (Société de Développement Sucrier—SODESUCRE), which was also responsible for creating jobs and building schools and medical clinics in the savanna region.

All of the parastatals enjoyed relative financial autonomy, although their technical and financial operations were in theory supervised by the government. In fact, there was often little supervision by, or coordination of activities with, other government agencies, perhaps reflecting the fact that top-level managers of some parastatals were often politically well connected. In many instances, the parastatals withheld or otherwise could not produce crucial financial data for planners. Given the absence of governmental oversight and the sometimes vague social and political objectives of the parastatals, they performed badly and in some cases—notably the housing sector—were rife with fraud.

In spite of these shortcomings—or perhaps because of them—the government support of parastatals steadily increased. By 1974 it amounted to more than half of the entire investment budget. Over the same fourteen years, the proportion of investment spending covered by net public savings fell to 37 percent. This imbalance forced the government to borrow extensively from foreign sources to maintain an even level of investment and growth. Between 1965 and 1975, foreign loans rose from 41 percent to 65 percent of investment in parastatals. Moreover, the outstanding debt figures of the public enterprises and the amount of foreign borrowing, which in theory should have been cleared by the National Amortization Fund (Caisse Autonome d'Amortissement—CAA), were not disclosed until an end-of-year report. This process effectively precluded government attempts to control parastatal finances.

Budget

Public spending was handled under two different budgets: the Ordinary Budget (Budget Ordinaire) for current government expenditures, which were generally covered by domestic revenues, and the Special Investment and Capital Equipment Budget (Budget Special d'Investissement et d'Equipement—BSIE), which partly depended on foreign investment. The BSIE had two parts: the BSIE-Treasury (BSIE-Trésor or BSIE–T), which was financed by surpluses from the Ordinary Budget, levies on business profits and farm incomes, and borrowing through bonds issued by the CAA; and the BSIE–CAA, which was funded by foreign borrowing.

The size of each budget reflected the state of the economy. The Ordinary Budget grew by an average of more than 20 percent from 1976 to 1980 and then by an average of about 11 percent per year in 1980, 1981, and 1982. By 1983, however, the deteriorating economy and consequent decline in tax receipts prompted the

Hotel at Abidjan
Courtesy Eszti Votaw

government to implement a series of austerity measures. Cuts were initially limited to the BSIE, which fell from CFA F277.6 billion in 1980 to CFA F239.1 billion in 1984 and then fell dramatically to 101.8 billion in 1985. In 1984 the government cut the Ordinary Budget for the first time, by 1.5 percent from the previous year. The government reduced the number of foreign technical assistants, froze civil service salaries, and sold one-quarter of the official fleet of 12,000 automobiles.

In 1986, after three years of severe austerity, higher commodity prices increased revenues and, in turn, allowed both budgets to expand. Budgeted expenses rose by 8.6 percent, with most of the increase in the BSIE, where allocations were increased by 13.7 percent. More than a third of these allocations went toward a road building plan cofinanced by the World Bank. Agricultural diversification was the second largest beneficiary. A 3.7 percent increase in the Ordinary Budget again permitted civil service promotions following a protracted wage and hiring freeze.

The period of budgetary expansion, however, was brief. In 1987 coffee and cocoa prices again dropped, resulting in a 5.2 percent cut in the 1987 BSIE and an additional 19.8 percent cut in the 1988 BSIE. For the second year in a row, the BSIE did not receive any funds from the CSSPPA, the agency that marketed the bulk of Côte d'Ivoire's coffee and cocoa. In 1987 the largest share of BSIE

101

funding, amounting to CFA F85.8 billion, came from multilateral donor agencies (CFA F44 billion). Bilateral creditors—including France, Japan, Britain, the United States, and the Federal Republic of Germany (West Germany)—provided CFA F16.2 billion, and commercial creditors provided CFA F25.6 billion. Meanwhile, domestically generated revenue for the BSIE was set to increase from the 1987 level of CFA F38.8 billion to CFA F 57.8 billion in 1988. The increase, however, represented only the inclusion of funds previously classified as extrabudgetary.

The 1987 overall budget increased by a modest 4.8 percent and the 1988 budget by 2.6 percent. These increases were primarily the result of an increase in revenue from taxes on income, imports, fuel, agricultural products, and municipality receipts. But because of an annual inflation rate of approximately 7 percent, it was expected that real spending in 1988 would fall. Debt rescheduling agreements did not affect the budget because the government considered debt service to be outside the main budget calculation.

Banking and Finance

Côte d'Ivoire's banking system developed during the colonial period as an extension of the French financial and banking systems. In 1962 Côte d'Ivoire, along with seven other francophone nations, became a member of the West African Monetary Union (Union Monétaire Ouest Africaine—UMOA). The UMOA established the Central Bank of West African States (Banque Centrale des Etats de l'Afrique de l'Ouest—BCEAO), which issued the African Financial Community (Communauté Financière Africaine) franc (CFA F), the unit of currency for the member states, and established policies governing interest rates. Also in 1962, France and the members of the UMOA signed an agreement that guaranteed the convertibility of the CFA F to French francs and established operations accounts for each country with the French treasury in order to centralize their reserves. The signatories also agreed to the free circulation of capital within the union. Since 1962 the UMOA has modified its system gradually to grant greater monetary autonomy to the African member states. For example, the UMOA reduced the share of French votes on the board of directors from one-third to one-seventh, transferred the headquarters of the BCEAO from Paris to Dakar, Senegal, and in 1975 introduced changes to increase the managerial presence of Africans in their national economies and to help the member states make better use of their resources.

Domestically, Côte d'Ivoire had the second most sophisticated banking system in sub-Saharan Africa, after South Africa. In 1988 it had twenty-one credit and loan banks (including fifteen commercial banks and six specialized credit banks), nine foreign bank offices with limited activity, sixteen registered credit or leasing institutions, and seven organizations similar to credit unions. More than half of bank ownership remained in foreign control: six of the fifteen commercial banks were branches of foreign banks (including three American institutions). Of the fifteen banks with some domestic ownership, Ivoirians (publicly or privately) owned no more than 48.4 percent.

In the late 1980s, the banking system was especially hard hit by the fall in cocoa earnings and the subsequent liquidity crisis. In 1987 the Ivoirian Bank for Construction and Public Works (Banque Ivoirienne de Construction et de Travaux Publics—BICT) and the National Savings and Loan Bank (Banque Nationale d'Epargne et de Crédit—BNEC) were closed by authorities. In early 1988, the National Agricultural Development Bank (Banque Nationale pour le Développement Agricole—BNDA), which provided credit to peasant farmers, and the Côte d'Ivoire Credit Bank (Crédit de la Côte d'Ivoire—CCI), an industrial development bank, suspended operations. In the case of the BNDA, a politically well connected borrower who owed the bank as much as US$78.9 million was unable to account for the funds he had borrowed.

Interest and Investment Policies

Ivoirian investment policies reflected the dominant position in the local economy of expatriate capital and management. For example, in the early 1970s Ivoirian rates of interest were considerably lower than those in European countries, thus encouraging foreign enterprises to borrow as much money as possible in Côte d'Ivoire and to keep their liquid funds abroad. At one time during this period, an estimated 70 percent of the credits extended by the Ivoirian banking system went to foreign-owned companies. With little domestic capital to draw on, the government was forced to borrow—mostly from abroad—to finance domestic programs. To stem the outflow of capital (without offending foreign interests), the government initiated a series of banking reforms that set limits on the balances that commercial banks could have in foreign exchange and increased interest rates to the level prevailing abroad. The measure also compelled foreign-owned enterprises to import foreign capital and to retain a larger portion of their profits for local investment.

There were few incentives to encourage the average Ivoirian or small-scale entrepreneur to save. Before 1973, deposits of less than CFA F200,000 (US$800) earned no interest at all, and large deposits earned interest well below rates in Europe. In January of that year, small deposits began to earn 2.5 percent a year; this rate was raised to 3.25 percent two years later. As a result, demand deposits, which increased by 16 percent from 1962 to 1972, rose 19 percent between 1973 and 1975. But by 1985, these highly mobile accounts were costing more to manage than they were worth to the banks, so the BCEAO suspended interest payments for two years.

Regulations governing credit allocations also discouraged local investment. Banks preferred high liquidity, which meant that short- and medium-term loans (those with a payback period of between one and five years) were granted only against short and medium-term funds, effectively barring loans to local businesses, which lacked the funds. Thus, prior to new BCEAO regulations in 1975, the majority of short- and medium-term credit went to foreigners.

Before 1975 and even afterward, instead of relying on commercial banks, small-scale farmers and business people relied on an informal parallel banking sector, the activities of which were not included in official statistics. The brokers who collected cash crops for export provided loans and sometimes imported goods for local farmers at what amounted to usurious interest rates. As much as half the country's savings may have circulated in the parallel banking system.

Efforts were made to rationalize the parallel system and exploit the accumulated savings. In 1968 the government established the National Agricultural Development Bank, a parastatal that helped small farmers who otherwise could obtain credit only from commodity brokers in the parallel system. (In fact, many loans—and certainly its largest loans—went to wealthy agroindustrialists and commodity exporters.) In 1975 the government set up the National Savings and Loan Bank to fund long-term mortgages from local savings.

The Stock Exchange

The Abidjan Stock Exchange (Bourse de Valeurs d'Abidjan), one of only four in Africa, was created in 1976 to encourage domestic investment and to provide Ivoirian industries with access to the international financial market. It was only partially successful. Of an estimated 700 companies in Côte d'Ivoire, the shares of only 25 were quoted on the exchange. Most investors in the quoted companies were foreign residents or businesses; in 1986 Ivoirians owned only 30 percent of the shares. Trading activity tended to be sluggish, particularly during the protracted recession in the early 1980s. For example, the value of shares traded fell from CFA F830 million in 1982 to CFA F400 million in 1984.

Labor

Most Ivoirians were members of a traditional agrarian society, and virtually all able-bodied adults worked. Just over one-third were subsistence farmers who raised little beyond their immediate needs. In 1982 the economically active population numbered approximately 4.3 million, of whom about 47 percent were women. Approximately 85 percent of this population engaged in farming, herding, fishing, or forestry, as opposed to nearly 90 percent in 1962. At independence, agriculture accounted for 45 percent of all wage earners; 40 percent were employed in industry, commerce, and services, and 15 percent were government employees. In 1960 unskilled workers constituted approximately 67 percent of the entire labor force; skilled workers and technicians, 19 percent; white-collar workers, 11 percent; and executive and managerial positions, 3 percent. In 1982 unskilled workers made up about 80 percent of the work force; skilled workers, 17 percent; and managerial and professional workers, 3 percent. According to a 1985 census, the largest employer was the government, which employed 110,670 people (not including the armed forces), or approximately 7 percent of the nonagricultural work force. Of these workers, 81,561 were in the civil service, and the rest were in state-owned companies.

In 1968 the government created the Office for the Promotion of Ivoirian Enterprise (Office de Promotion de l'Enterprise Ivoirienne—OPEI) to reduce—or appear to reduce—the country's dependence on foreign entrepreneurial expertise. The OPEI was to help develop or improve the efficiency of Ivoirian commercial, industrial, and agricultural enterprises by providing studies, statistics, administrative assistance, and training for local entrepreneurs. In fact, the OPEI focused only on small-scale entrepreneurs, such as bakers, carpenters, tailors, plumbers, and electricians. These efforts could not—and apparently were not intended to—produce the high-level managerial expertise that would reduce the country's dependence on expatriate initiative, skills, and technology.

Until the mid-1980s, non-Africans—mostly French—still dominated the managerial and professional cadres. In 1973 the government set up the National Commission on Ivoirianization to encourage the appointment of Ivoirians to managerial posts throughout the economy. Although Ivoirianization of management was the announced purpose of the commission, Ivoirianization was not to be implemented at the expense of efficiency. Consequently, most Ivoirianization programs in commerce and industry were voluntary and produced only modest results. According to official figures, in 1979 Ivoirians held only 23 percent of senior management positions and 44 percent of junior management posts in all private, public, and parastatal enterprises. By 1982 the percentage of Ivoirians in senior management positions had actually dropped slightly to 21 percent; for junior-level management posts, the percentage had risen to 52 percent. Among the country's 300 largest companies, Ivoirians still filled only 29 percent of top management posts, compared with 67.4 percent that were filled by non-Africans. The remaining 3.6 percent were filled by non-Ivoirian Africans. In addition, many Europeans worked as mechanics, technicians, and shop owners, underscoring Côte d'Ivoire's continued reliance on foreign initiative and skills.

The government also employed a large number of European teachers and technical experts known as *coopérants* (see Glossary). Most were recruited by the French Ministry of Cooperation, but others were hired directly by the Ivoirian government through private, usually French, firms on a contract basis. The Ivoirian government was responsible for 80 percent of the total cost of those hired under official cooperation agreements and for 100 percent of the cost of those hired under private contract. Pressures for Ivoirianization and the economic recession of the early 1980s prompted a gradual reduction in the number of *coopérants* from a peak of 4,000 in 1980 to 3,200 in 1984. Over the next two years, as economic conditions worsened and as more Ivoirian university graduates took over teaching jobs in secondary schools, this number fell by 1,000.

The privately recruited foreign experts were employed mainly as technical advisers in government ministries and in state enterprises. As part of a series of austerity measures, the IMF insisted that 585 of the 650 foreign experts on government payrolls be let go. Those foreign experts allowed to stay were in highly specialized areas, such as the petroleum sector and computer technology. Despite the IMF dictum, by the end of 1987 there were still 425 privately recruited foreign experts, costing the government CFA F11 billion annually. In November 1987, the government recommended that these experts be retained only if their presence was "indispensable in certain high technology areas not yet mastered by nationals."

Côte d'Ivoire also depended on foreigners for unskilled labor. Since the early twentieth century, poor migrants from Burkina Faso, Mali, and other parts of West Africa had worked in Côte d'Ivoire as agricultural and construction laborers. Because immigration has been largely uncontrolled, estimates of the number of immigrants have varied by as much as 100 percent, ranging from 1 million to 2 million, and accounted for 70 percent to 80 percent of the unskilled labor force in the rural sector. According to official figures for 1974 (the most recent year for which they were available in 1988), 81.8 percent of the salaried positions in the primary sector (agriculture and raw materials) were filled by non-Ivoirian Africans, while only 16.9 percent were filled by Ivoirians. The figures, however, were skewed somewhat by the fact that most Ivoirians in the primary sector were self-employed or were working for family members. The labor force shifted easily between regions and occupational sectors. Surveys have shown that half the migrant farm laborers changed their employment every two months, and even the more permanent wage earners moved freely from job to job in search of higher pay and more attractive working conditions. The greatest movement occurred between the traditional and the modern sectors of the economy, as farmers from subsistence areas took temporary wage employment to meet specific cash needs. This mobility contributed to the lack of training and skills and the low productivity among nonagricultural workers.

Wages and Income Distribution

For several reasons, it is difficult to compare rural incomes with urban incomes. Agricultural workers earned income predominantly from the production of goods, rather than from the sale of labor. Much of this production was not marketed, and cash crops that were marketed were sold at prices that were, in effect, taxed by the government because of its pricing policies (see Public Investment, this ch.). By contrast, urban incomes were pretax incomes, and unadjusted comparisons exaggerate the difference between the two. In addition, urban workers often benefited from supplementary nonmarket sources of income, such as subsidized housing, access to credit on favorable terms, and rental income.

According to Ministry of Planning figures for 1974 (the most recent figures available in 1988), the group of workers whose salaries fell in the bottom 40 percent in the private sector received about 14 of total salary payments; the middle 40 percent received about 33 percent; and the top 20 percent received about 53 percent. Figures for workers in the public and parastatal enterprises (excluding the civil service) were similar: the group of workers whose salaries fell in the bottom 40 percent received 12 percent, the middle 40 percent received 32 percent, and the top 20 percent received 56 percent. In both sectors, the highest salaries were paid to expatriates, and the lowest incomes went to non-Ivoirian Africans. For the civil service, the income distribution was considerably more balanced: the lowest 40 percent received 27 percent of income payments, and the top 20 percent received 35 percent. Regionally, incomes in the north lagged behind those in the south.

Salaries earned by non-Africans ranged from about twenty times the average African salary in the primary sector, to ten times the average in the secondary sector, to five times the average in the tertiary sector. In money terms, non-Africans usually received two to three times as much income as Africans in the same job classification; in addition, expatriates benefited from generous housing, travel, and educational allowances.

Since 1932 minimum wage and other worker compensation standards have been fixed. The Labor Code of 1952 established guaranteed minimum wages and working conditions, and the Advisory Labor Committee, composed of an equal number of employers and workers chosen by their representative bodies, was set up to recommend appropriate standards. The committee based its recommendations on the cost of living and the minimum subsistence requirements of various segments of the population. The committee then elaborated two minimum wage standards: the Guaranteed Minimum Agricultural Wage (Salaire Minimum Agricole Garanti—SMAG) and the Guaranteed Minimum Interprofessional Wage (Salaire Minimum Interprofessionnel Garanti—SMIG).

Minimum wages have increased faster for nonagricultural workers. The SMIG rose from CFA F40 per hour in 1962 to CFA F58 per hour in 1970 and increased an additional 58 percent to CFA F93 per hour by 1974. In 1982 the SMIG was raised to CFA F191.4 per hour. By contrast, the SMAG rose only 20 percent to CFA F25 per hour between 1970 and 1974. In 1982 the SMAG was CFA F30 per hour. Most workers received wages substantially higher than the legal minimum based on scales determined by collective bargaining agreements or, in the absence of such agreements, by the government.

The government also determined other work rules. In 1988 the maximum work period was 40 hours a week for nonagricultural labor and 2,400 hours a year for agricultural labor. By law, all employers carried worker's compensation insurance. The labor code regulated labor practices, recruitment, contracts, the employment of women and children, and general working conditions such as paid holidays, sick leave, and medical care. The code also provided for collective agreements between employees and trade unions and for special courts to settle labor disputes.

As in most developing countries, measuring employment and unemployment was difficult because relatively few people were employed in the modern or formal economy, in which enumerating workers is easier; in the traditional economy, the concept of unemployment was almost meaningless. It was also difficult to determine the percentage of the population that was active in the labor force. In spite of these methodological problems, the rate of unemployment in the early 1980s was calculated to be 9 percent, with the highest rates in the Abidjan area.

By the end of 1987, the national unemployment rate was estimated to be 11 percent; the rate in urban areas was as high as 30 percent. The actual number of unemployed persons was estimated to be 600,000, although only 86,000 were officially registered with the Employment Office of Côte d'Ivoire (Office de la Main d'Oeuvre de Côte d'Ivoire—OMOCI). Contributing to the high rates of unemployment were a sharp increase in the number of high school and university graduates with inappropriate skills, migration of young people from rural areas, a continued high rate of immigration from neighboring countries, and reduced recruitment levels in the public, parastatal, and private sectors. Significantly, these problems were becoming more acute because the economically active population was growing 4 percent a year and was expected to reach 7.5 million by 1992.

Labor Unions

In the 1980s, approximately 100,000 full-time workers, mostly professionals, civil servants, and teachers, belonged to unions (see Interest Groups, ch. 4). Virtually all unions were under the umbrella of the General Federation of Ivoirian Workers (Union Générale des Travailleurs de Côte d'Ivoire—UGTCI), which was tightly controlled by the party and, by extension, the government. Consequently, the leadership of the UGTCI invariably supported the government in its efforts to promote unity and development, often at the expense of labor. As a political force, the UGTCI exercised little clout.

Agriculture

Agriculture was the foundation of the economy and its main source of growth. In 1987 the agricultural sector contributed 35 percent of the country's GDP and 66 percent of its export revenues, provided employment for about two-thirds of the national work force, and generated substantial revenues despite the drop in coffee and cocoa prices. From 1965 to 1980, agricultural GDP grew by an average 4.6 percent per year. Growth of agricultural GDP from coffee, cocoa, and timber production, which totaled nearly 50 percent of Côte d'Ivoire's export revenues, averaged 7 percent a year from 1965 to 1980. Contributing to this impressive performance were an abundance of fertile land, cheap labor, the collective efforts of many farmers cultivating small plots, relatively favorable commodity prices, and a stable political environment.

Success in the 1960s and 1970s overshadowed major problems developing in the agricultural sector. By the late 1980s, despite efforts to diversify its crops, 55 percent of Côte d'Ivoire's export earnings still came from cocoa and coffee. Moreover, highly volatile world markets for both commodities caused sharp fluctuations in government revenues and made development planning difficult. In addition, Côte d'Ivoire was not yet self-sufficient in food production and imported substantial quantities of rice, wheat, fish, and red meat. Finally, despite an enormous increase in the volume of agricultural output since independence, there was little improvement in agricultural productivity. To achieve higher production figures, traditional farmers using traditional technologies simply cleared more and more land.

To overcome Côte d'Ivoire's excessive dependence on coffee and cocoa (the prices for which were set by consumers), on timber (the supply of which was nearly exhausted), and on imported food, the government in the mid-1970s embarked on a series of agricultural diversification and regional development projects with the hope of boosting agricultural production by 4 percent per year. The plan, estimated to cost CFA F100 billion per annum (with just over 50 percent coming from foreign lenders) would allow the country to become self-sufficient in food (with the exception of wheat) and expand the production of rubber, cotton, sugar, bananas, pineapples, and tropical oils.

In spite of these efforts, the agricultural sector appeared unable to adapt to changing conditions. Distortions in the system of incentives reduced the comparative advantage of alternative crops. The vast revenues collected by the CSSPPA were often spent on marginally profitable investments, like the costly sugar complexes or expensive land-clearing programs (see Diversification Crops, this ch.). Finally, some diversification crops, like coconut and palm oil, faced new threats as health-conscious consumers in the United States and Europe began turning away from tropical oils. Consequently, the future for Ivoirian agriculture remained cloudy.

Land Use

Resources

Of the total land area of more than 322,000 square kilometers, 52 percent was considered agricultural land, or slightly over 3.6 hectares per capita. Total land area fell into one of two distinct agricultural regions: the forest region (about 140,000 square kilometers) in the south and the drier savanna region (about 180,000 square kilometers) in the north, where economic growth has generally been slower (see Climate, ch. 2). The forest region, which had higher and more reliable rainfall and better soils, produced most export crops. Rainfall in the savanna averaged about two-thirds of that in the forest region and was unreliable from year to year. In addition, the soils were generally light and ranged from medium to poor quality. As a result, agricultural yields were low and opportunities for using labor-saving technology were limited.

The prevailing system of cultivation for both cereals and *féculents* (starchy foods) was known as shifting agriculture, or bush fallow. Fields were cultivated for three to four years, after which they were left fallow for periods of up to ten years to restore their fertility. To maximize their return on a given plot, farmers first cultivated a more exigent crop like yams, followed in subsequent years with less demanding crops like corn, and finally planted cassava, after which the plot was left untilled. In Côte d'Ivoire, as elsewhere in Africa, population pressures forced farmers to reduce the fallow period, leading to diminished soil fertility and productivity. The use of chemical fertilizers was not common; annual consumption of fertilizers in 1982 was 51,800 tons, or only 8.5 kilograms per hectare.

As in most of sub-Saharan Africa, farm labor was usually manual, without the aid of animals or mechanization. In 1982 there were 3,200 tractors and 40 harvester-threshers in the country, nearly all of which were on large private or government-owned plantations. Nearly all agriculture relied on natural rainfall or, in the case of paddy rice, rudimentary, gravity-fed irrigation systems. Under the 1976–78 development plan, the government constructed dams on the Bandama River at Taabo and on the Sassandra River at Buyo for irrigation.

Tenure

Land tenure systems differed among the various ethnic groups; nevertheless, most systems were based on the concept of communal ownership of land. At the same time, individual families were granted rights to cultivate a specific area (which included fallow areas), and these rights included some form of inheritance within the family. Unused lands reverted to the community. In 1902 the French introduced the concept that individuals or corporations could hold legal title to land with exclusive rights; this law, however, had little impact in the rural areas. After independence, Ivoirian law on landownership provided for surveys and registration of land, which then became the irrevocable property of the owner and his or her successors.

Cocoa

In 1988 Côte d'Ivoire led the world in cocoa production with more than 500,000 tons (see table 4, Appendix). Cocoa was grown mainly on small family-owned farms with labor supplied principally by immigrants from other African countries. Production growth averaged 6 percent to 7 percent a year throughout the 1965–74 period and accelerated as the plantings of the late 1970s and the early 1980s entered their prime. The total area of cocoa cultivation more than doubled from 1973 to 1983, from 611,000 hectares to 1,398,900 hectares.

In Côte d'Ivoire, cocoa became a cash crop only in 1912, when colonial authorities forced Africans to cultivate it. Cocoa, like coffee, was a forest crop; it required ample rainfall, partial shade, and shelter from wind, all of which occurred only in the southern forest zone (see fig. 9). Cacao trees produced pods, which grew on the trunk and older branches, beginning at four or five years, and continued producing for twenty to thirty years. The pods were harvested from June through August and from November through January, although some pods ripened throughout the year. After harvest, the beans and pulp were extracted from the pods and allowed to ferment for six or seven days and then dried. Yields averaged 220 kilograms per hectare. The bulk of the crop was produced on small plots of one or two hectares.

Côte d'Ivoire's success as a cocoa producer has been a mixed blessing. In September 1987, cocoa prices fell to their lowest levels since 1983. In December prices were even lower following forecasts that the world surplus for the 1987–88 season would be substantially higher than the previous season's, marking the fourth successive year of a world cocoa surplus. In September 1987, talks aimed at restoring the price support mechanisms of the International Cocoa Organization ended in failure when producers and consumers were unable to agree on the price level to be defended.

Coffee

Côte d'Ivoire ranked third in world coffee production after Brazil and Colombia. Introduced as a cash crop during the colonial period, coffee was cultivated throughout the forest zone, with the heaviest production in the denser forests of the east and along the margin of the forest moving westward from Dimbokro to Man. The bulk of the crop consisted of robusta varieties, which were more bitter and less expensive than arabica varieties and therefore were used in blends to reduce costs.

Coffee trees were started in nurseries. After about a year, before the rains in May, they were transplanted to permanent sites. After two years they were pruned to a maximum height of two meters to make harvesting easier, and they were kept pruned to improve yields. Trees began bearing at above five years and continued to produce for ten to twenty years. Trees flowered several times throughout the year; however, the main harvests took place in August and November through January. Yields averaged 250 kilograms per hectare, or about 25 percent of the yields in Colombia and Brazil, where trees received better care. Following the harvest, the berries were hulled, peeled, dried, and sorted before being shipped or processed locally.

Prior to independence, production grew at a rate of 10 percent per year. By the late 1950s, however, expansion slowed, and between 1965 and 1984 annual coffee production averaged 252,000 tons. By the mid-1980s, 60 percent of the coffee trees in the country were more than fifteen years old and producing well below average yields. Attempts by the government to encourage the planting of new coffee trees were largely unsuccessful, and production in the aging plantations continued to drop.

Timber

Timber exports ranked third in importance behind cocoa and coffee; but by 1980 this industry was declining because of overcutting. From 1965 to 1975, the period of peak timber exploitation, log and sawed wood exports contributed an average of 23 percent of foreign exchange earnings annually. In the early 1980s, timber exploitation averaged an annual 4 million cubic meters of logs and accounted for 9 percent of the agricultural GDP (see fig. 10). By contrast, in 1984 exports of logs and sawed wood had declined to 2.1 million cubic meters and represented only 12 percent of exports.

Overexploitation through the 1960s and mid-1970s almost depleted forest resources. Côte d'Ivoire's forest shrank from 15 million hectares in 1960 to less than 3 million in 1987. Deforestation continued at a rate of 300,000 to 500,000 hectares a year, while annual plantings averaged only 5,000 hectares. The government's response to this ecological disaster was halfhearted: in 1985 the government-owned Forest Development Company (Société pour le Développement des Forêts—SODEFOR) initiated an industrial reforestation program designed to produce some 6.6 million cubic meters of wood in thirty-five years. The SODEFOR program will have little impact on timber production through at least the year 2000, however, and until then, producers will continue to exploit

113

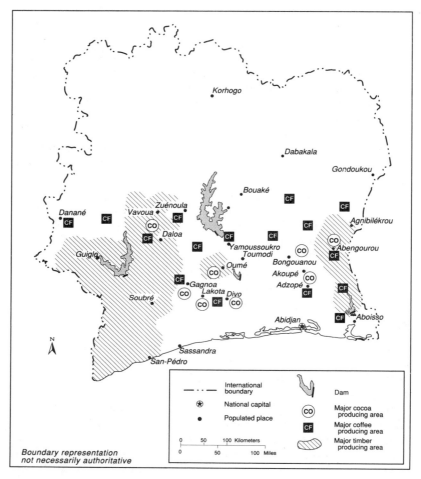

Source: Based on information from J.-N. Loucou, "Histoire," in Pierre Vennetier (ed.), *Atlas de la Côte d'Ivoire* (2d ed.), Paris, 1983, 39–45.

Figure 9. Cocoa, Coffee, and Timber Producing Areas

shrinking natural forests. As a follow-up on the SODEFOR program, the government declared 1988 "the year of the Ivoirian forest" and approved a CFA F1.3 billion tree-planting program to plant a total of 25,000 hectares. This represented only 0.2 percent of the forest land lost since 1960. Finally, the government announced a novel scheme to create agricultural belts around the remaining wooded areas, making those who were allocated plots responsible for policing the forests. Despite these gestures, the government insisted in 1985 that timber exports would cease only when the country's financial situation stabilized or when substitute exports could be found, neither of which had occurred by 1988.

Diversification Crops

In the mid-1970s, the government undertook major efforts to diversify export crops and end its dependence on cocoa and coffee. In the forest zone, diversification products were palm oil, coconut oil, and rubber, all of which enjoyed a comparative advantage on the international market. In the 1980s, Côte d'Ivoire had become the largest palm oil exporter in Africa, and the 1987 harvest of 215,000 tons made Côte d'Ivoire one of the world's largest producers. In 1985 an expansion program called for planting 65,000 additional hectares of oil palms and constructing four new industrial plantations. With some 15,000 hectares of new plantings each year, production was expected to continue its rise. At the same time, production costs in Côte d'Ivoire were high, perhaps reflecting the fact that individual holdings were small and often located on less productive land.

In 1987 Côte d'Ivoire's rubber production totaled 38,700 tons, and there were plans to increase production to 80,000 tons a year by 1990. This increase would place the country ahead of Liberia, then the largest African producer of natural rubber. The number of hectares under rubber cultivation increased sixfold from 1960 to 1984, from 7,243 to 43,634 hectares.

In the north, or savanna zone, cotton and sugar were the chief diversification crops. Cotton was first introduced during the colonial period by the French Textile Development Company (Compagnie Française de Développement des Textiles—CFDT), which at independence became the Ivoirian Textile Development Company (Compagnie Ivoirienne de Développement des Textiles—CIDT). Cotton became economically important only after independence. In 1965 there were some 12,000 hectares of cotton, and by 1979, there were 123,000 hectares. Production leveled off in the early 1980s but picked up again between 1981 and 1984. Cotton (fiber and cottonseed) production in 1986–87 set a new record of 213,506 tons, compared with the previous season's 190,000 tons and the country's previous record of 205,000 tons in 1984–85, making Côte d'Ivoire the third largest cotton producer in Africa, after Egypt and Sudan. Cotton fiber production over the same period amounted to 91,000 tons (1987), 75,000 ton (1986), and 88,000 tons (1985). Côte d'Ivoire exported about 80 percent of its crop.

115

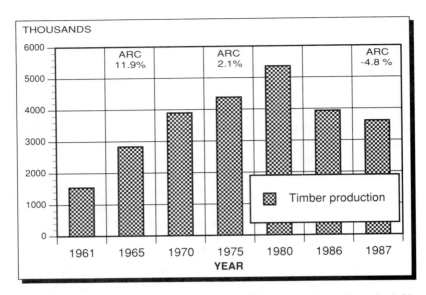

Source: Based on information from J.-N. Loucou, "Histoire," in Pierre Vennetier (ed.), *Atlas de la Côte d'Ivoire* (2d ed.), Paris, 1983, 52–55.

Figure 10. Timber Production, Selected Years, 1961–87

Côte d'Ivoire was Africa's eighth largest sugar producer, with a yield of nearly 144,000 tons in 1987, more than half of which was exported. Industrial sugar production began only in the early 1970s with the creation of SODESUCRE, a parastatal that constructed and operated six large industrial sugar refineries located at Ferkes-sédougou (Ferké I and Ferké II) and four smaller towns in the savanna region (By 1987 two of the factories had been closed.) In 1982 these complexes contributed about 3 percent of the agricultural GDP.

The colonial government introduced bananas for export in 1931, and by 1961 the fruit was the second largest earner of foreign exchange. The principal production areas lay between Aboisso and Divo. Exported varieties, which are larger and sweeter than native fruits, were harvested year round. French settlers owned the first plantations; by 1961 holdings by Africans amounted to about one-third of the 6,500 hectares under cultivation for export. By the mid-1980s, the fraction in land or in corporations held by foreigners dropped to less than 10 percent. Production for 1985 came to 163,000 tons, of which only 105,000 tons were exportable. In the mid-1980s, Côte d'Ivoire routinely fell short of its allotted export quota to Europe, in part because labor shortages adversely affected the quality of the fruit.

Pineapples have been raised commercially only since 1950. In 1961 fewer than 600 hectares were cultivated; Africans owned approximately one-half the area. By 1986, under the impetus of government encouragement and support, 438,000 hectares were under cultivation. Production amounted to approximately 250,000 tons, up from 195,000 tons a year earlier, of which 180,000 tons were exported as fresh fruit. The remainder of the harvest was canned locally. The major producing area was near Abidjan.

Food Crops

In 1987 the staple food crops made up about 38 percent of the value of agricultural production. The principal food crops in Côte d'Ivoire were the *féculents,* or starches (yams, plantains, cassava, and taro), which made up 76 percent of the value and 60 percent of the bulk of staples output. Gross production per annum amounted to approximately 4.5 million tons. Gross production of cereals (paddy rice, maize, sorghum, and millet) amounted to about 1 million tons per year; however, cereals, which occupied a larger cultivated area than did the *féculents,* had a higher total protein value. Food crop production increased by approximately 3.4 percent per annum between 1965 and 1984, with cereals having a slightly higher rate of growth. At the same time, food crop productivity per rural family increased by about 1 percent per year, well under the rate of population growth. This shortfall, along with a preference on the part of much of the population for imported rice and bread over indigenous foodstuffs, increased rice and wheat imports to a high of 590,000 tons in 1983, or about 40 percent of national cereals consumption. Cereal imports dropped to 150,000 tons in 1985 after prices for imported foodstuffs had increased, good rains had ended the drought, and the government had inaugurated a food self-sufficiency campaign. In 1987 imported cereals amounted to about 14 percent of the national diet, as compared with 20 percent earlier in the decade.

Measured by area cultivated and tonnage, yams were the leading food crop, especially in the region east of the Bandama River. A number of varieties of yams grew in Côte d'Ivoire, differing by size of tubers, moisture requirements, and length of growing season. Yams had stringent soil needs, however, and demanded far more labor to plant and harvest than did the other root crops. In addition, roughly one-quarter of the crop had to be reserved to seed the next crop. Seed yams were planted near the top of conical mounds, usually ⅔ to 1⅓ meters high and 1 to 1⅓ meters apart, and formed from finely cultivated soil. Usually other crops such as maize, beans, tomatoes, or peas were planted on the sides

117

of the mounds. Providing support for the yam vines (which could reach as high as seven meters) were either stakes or liana—long, climbing vines—which hung from dead, leafless trees purposely left standing in the yam fields in the forest zone. Depending on the variety, the yam tubers, which varied in weight from a kilogram or less to as much as forty kilograms, were ready for harvest after about eight months. The best yields in the Bouaké region were about 12.4 tons per hectare. In the more humid south, the yield was higher, and farther north it was lower. The heaviest yam-producing areas were around Bouaké, Séguéla, and Korhogo.

West of the Bandama River, rice was the principal food crop although rice cultivation was spreading across Côte d'Ivoire wherever conditions were suitable. Local farmers had cultivated a native variety of rice for centuries. In the twentieth century, however, French colonial administrators introduced more prolific Oriental species of both upland (dry) rice and paddy rice. Dry rice predominated, probably because it required less technology, matured more quickly, and could be interplanted with other crops. Dry rice matured in about three months and yielded about 560 kilograms per hectare, compared with a five- to six-month maturation period for wet rice and yields averaging 786 kilograms per hectare.

Among cereals, maize followed rice in tonnage harvested. It was planted throughout the country; however, except in the northwest where most maize was produced, it was subsidiary to other crops. Local varieties of maize matured in as little as two months, making it particularly suited to the north, where it could be planted after the first rains in May and harvested during the period when old yam stocks were depleted and the new yams were not yet mature. In the south, two crops per year were common. Because maize depletes the soil, farmers often interplanted it with other crops such as yams, beans, and gourds or cultivated it in fertilized household gardens. Yields, which were low by Western standards, averaged nearly 1.3 tons per hectare, reflecting the absence of both fertilizers and mechanized farming practices. As was true for other crops, insects, rodents, and, in the south, moisture, made maize storage difficult.

Other important food crops were plantains and cassava or manioc. The plantain, which is of the same genus as the banana, followed yams in annual tonnage harvested. Because it required sustained rainfall, production was limited to the south, where it was often interplanted with cacao. Plantains were raised from shoots removed from the base of a mature tree. The shoot formed a stalk (about three meters high) that bore a single cluster of fruit ready for harvest after twelve to fifteen months. After the plantains were harvested,

118

Log carriers waiting to unload at the port
Courtesy Robert Handloff

the stalk was cut off at ground level, and a new shoot was allowed to sprout. After five or six years, the old root system was removed, and a new tree was planted. Harvesting continued throughout the year; yields varied with soil conditions but averaged just under five tons per hectare.

Cassava, which served as a hedge against famine, was third in importance after yams and plantains. Cassava was also a root crop that was easy to cultivate, resisted pests and drought, and took little from the soil, yet still produced fair yields. Because cassava was propagated by stem cuttings, the entire crop could be used for food. The growing period was from six to fifteen months, but even after the roots matured, they could be left in the ground for several years without damage. In the south, where two plantings per year were common, cassava was often interplanted with other crops and held in reserve or planted as a final crop before a field was abandoned for fallow. In the north, only a single planting per year was possible. Estimates of yields ranged from about five tons to just under ten tons per hectare. These figures were unreliable, however, because roots were harvested only when needed.

Other food crops included taro (in the south) and varieties of millet and sorghum (in the north). Individual households raised garden vegetables, including okra, tomatoes, peanuts, and eggplant, in small plots near dwellings or interplanted among field crops.

119

Tropical fruit trees, both wild and domestic, produced sweet bananas, avocados, oranges, papayas, mangoes, coconuts, lemons, and limes. Oil palms and shea trees provided cooking oils.

Even in the best of years, Côte d'Ivoire imported vast quantities of wheat, rice, meat, and milk. To achieve food self-sufficiency, the agricultural recovery program proposed by the Council of Ministers sought to increase production of rice, maize, peanuts, and the newly introduced soybeans, all of which were grown primarily in the northern savanna zone. In addition, the government intended to revamp the Food Marketing Bureau (Office pour la Commercialisation des Produits Vivriers—OCPV) to streamline the marketing of such food crops as yams, plantains, and cassava. Finally, the Council of Ministers also inaugurated a project to achieve self-sufficiency in animal proteins.

Animal Husbandry

With some exceptions, tsetse fly infestation limited livestock production in savanna regions as did the absence of forage in the forest zone. Consequently, there were few pastoral groups in Côte d'Ivoire, and the country's livestock population was unable to meet domestic needs. In 1985 there were approximately 843,000 cattle, most of which were of the small, humpless N'dama breed. There were also 1.5 million sheep, 430,000 swine, 1.5 million goats, and 16 million poultry.

In 1987 the livestock sector contributed about 6 percent of agricultural output. About half of that total came from poultry and egg production, about one-quarter came from cattle, and the remainder came from sheep and goats. Although virtually all poultry consumed in Côte d'Ivoire was produced locally, domestic beef production met only about 40 percent of demand. The remainder entered as live cattle from Mali and Burkina Faso or as slaughtered meat from Western Europe, Argentina, or southern Africa. In the 1980s, the government sought to strengthen livestock production by providing education and training in modern animal husbandry and by introducing large-scale cattle fattening centers near Bouaké and Abidjan.

Fisheries

In 1987 combined fish production in Côte d'Ivoire was estimated to be worth CFA F15 billion, and its share in net agricultural value added was 1.6 percent. Contributing about equally to the total were the tuna industry; low-technology coastal and freshwater fishing, including a large smoked fish industry; and a fleet of privately owned trawling, sardine seining, and shrimping vessels. In the 1980s, canned fish was the country's seventh largest export commodity in revenue generated (behind cocoa, coffee, fuels and chemicals, timber, cotton, and palm oil), amounting to about 20,000 tons a year (see table 5, Appendix). Nevertheless, export revenues from fish exports only slightly exceeded foreign exchange payouts for the approximately 100,000 tons of frozen fish imported each year. The imports supplemented the canoe and fleet catches, which met about half of domestic demand.

Insofar as Ivoirian coastal waters had probably reached their maximum sustained yield in 1988, possibilities for growth in the fishing sector were limited without costly research and development, which the country could ill afford. The areas offering the greatest potential for growth were the tuna industry and domestic freshwater production in artificial lakes and ponds. After completion of the Kossou Dam on the Bandama River, freshwater catches increased (see Electricity, this ch.). Malian fishermen from the Niger River region moved into the area, set up fishing villages, and earned a comfortable livelihood from the carefully stocked lake.

Manufacturing

At independence, Côte d'Ivoire manufactured little more than timber by-products, textiles, and food processed from local agricultural products. Little was exported. The lack of an indigenous, skilled labor force, inexperienced management, and low domestic demand limited industrial growth.

At that time, there was little direct state involvement in manufacturing. Nearly all industrial companies were financed by private—mainly foreign—capital. On the strength of its growing and protected domestic market and, in the 1960s and 1970s, the development of regional markets under the aegis of the West African Economic Community (Communauté Economique de l'Afrique Occidentale—CEAO), Ivoirian industrialization flourished.

Following independence, light industry became one of the most rapidly growing sectors in the economy. Between 1960 and 1980, manufacturing grew at the rate of 13 percent per year, and its contribution to GDP rose from 4 percent in 1960 to 17 percent in 1984. The number of firms rose from 50 at independence to more than 600 in 1986. Expanding most rapidly were import substitution industries like textiles, shoes, construction materials (such as cement, plywood, lumber, ceramics, and sheet and corrugated metal), and industries processing local agricultural raw materials (such as palm oil, coffee, cocoa, and fruits).

Although agricultural processing plants used locally produced inputs, import substitution industries—as well as firms manufacturing or providing chemicals, plastics, fertilizers, and engineering services—imported their raw materials (50 percent of intermediate inputs were imported). In many instances, these costly intermediate inputs raised the price of completed products far above the price of comparable imported goods. Consequently, the government promoted and protected local industry by imposing tariffs and incentives.

The system of industrial tariffs and incentives, however, proved to be shortsighted. These measures avoided quantitative import restrictions and included a tariff schedule that protected all industrial activities, whether threatened by imports or not. By assigning tariffs according to the degree of processing and by exempting some inputs that could be produced locally and less expensively, the government discouraged domestic production of intermediate inputs.

Additional efforts to promote industry, and particularly small- and medium-scale enterprises, were equally inadequate. Management personnel often lacked skills and experience, political connections often influenced policy, and there was little coordination among state bureaucracies responsible for assisting the struggling firms. In response, the government promulgated a new investment code in 1984 (subsequently altered in 1985) by providing bonuses for exports and by reforming tariffs, which served to shelter elements of an already overprotected and inefficient industrial sector.

In 1987 the government adopted additional measures originally proposed by the United Nations Industrial Development Organization (UNIDO) to expand exports and make industry more efficient. This new policy proposed modernizing import substitution industries, manufacturing new products with high added value for export, and expanding the existing range of agriculture-based, export-oriented industries. The new exportable agricultural products were to include processed food (maize, cottonseed, fruits, vegetables, manioc, yams, and coconuts), textiles (spinning and weaving, ready-to-wear clothing, and hosiery), and wood (paper and cardboard). The new, nonagricultural exports were to include building materials, such as glass and ceramics; chemicals, such as fertilizers and pharmaceuticals; rubber; agricultural and cold storage machinery; and electronics, such as computers (see fig. 11). As part of the reform package, UNIDO also insisted that credit restrictions be eased, domestic savings potential be tapped, and funds held abroad by Ivoirians be repatriated. Under pressure from the World Bank, the government cut its levy on pretax bank transactions from 25 to 15 percent.

The process of modernizing import substitution industries and increasing exports included measures to reduce the high level of

customs protection accorded local industries and to extend export subsidies. In November 1987, the government began a five-year program to reduce import duties and surcharges progressively to an eventual 40 percent of value added for the entire industrial sector. In addition, the government extended export subsidies to the entire manufacturing sector in order to compensate for comparatively high local production costs in the agroindustrial sector (oils and fats, processed meat, fish, chocolate, fruits, and vegetables) and for such industrial goods as textiles, carpets, shoes, chemicals, cardboard, construction materials, and mechanical and electrical goods. As of early 1988, the reforms had not yet yielded the desired results, partly because export subsidies were granted on an ad hoc basis with no assurance that they would be renewed and partly because the reforms were financed from customs receipts, which, under the government's pledge to reduce tariff protection, were diminishing.

Energy

Electricity

In the late 1980s, electrical production in Côte d'Ivoire surpassed that of most other countries in sub-Saharan Africa. Its five hydroelectric stations and the large thermal station at Vridi provided electricity for the central and southern portions of the country, where most industrial activity took place. In addition, a number of smaller thermal facilities provided electricity for urban areas scattered throughout the country. The number of urban centers with electrical service increased rapidly from 292 in 1975 to 620 in 1984, with 740 predicted for 1990. In 1986 total generating capacity amounted to 1.08 gigawatts. The industrial sector consumed 1,026 gigawatt-hours of high-voltage electricity; the remaining capacity was consumed by more than 350,000 low-voltage subscribers.

After independence, Electrical Energy of Ivory Coast (Energie Electrique de Côte d'Ivoire—EECI), the Ivoirian power company, had sought to replace costly thermal units with hydroelectric power. The first two dams, Ayamé I and Ayamé II at Ayamé, began generating in 1962 and 1965, respectively. Following the rise of oil prices on the world market in the early 1970s, the government embarked upon a major program to tap its considerable hydroelectric potential. In 1973 the government commissioned a 176-megawatt hydroelectric facility on the Bandama River at Kossou. The Kossou Dam project was by far the most expensive of Côte d'Ivoire's hydroelectric facilities; construction cost billions of CFA francs, as did the relocation of 85,000 Baoulé farmers from the region that was to have been flooded (see Ethnic Groups and Languages, ch. 2). Lake Kossou (Lac de Kossou) was expected to cover a surface three times the size of Lake Geneva and to double the country's electrical generation. In fact, poor rainfall during the mid-1970s prevented Lake Kossou from filling to its maximum capacity, and Kossou's output was far less than anticipated. With the return of normal rainfall levels in 1979, hydroelectric power generation rose significantly and permitted a cutback in oil-fired thermal output.

A second dam, with a capacity of 210 megawatts, was constructed downriver at Taabo and was brought into production in 1979. In the west of the country on the Sassandra River, the 165-megawatt Buyo Dam was completed in 1980, bringing the country's total hydroelectric capacity to 600 megawatts. By 1982 about 90 percent of the country's electrical energy came from hydroelectric sources, thus reducing significantly the amount of fuel the country needed to import.

A serious drought in 1983 and 1984, however, nearly dried up the lakes behind all five dams. Turbines were shut down, and the country was obliged to rely once again on the thermal power produced by its original 210-megawatt facility at Vridi and to reactivate two smaller thermal units in the north and west of the country. Electrical production fell by 18.3 percent, causing blackouts in Abidjan and productivity losses amounting to 35 percent in the industrial sector.

To help alleviate the crisis, the government installed four thermal generators at Vridi, financed by the European Investment Bank and the Central Fund for Economic Cooperation (Caisse Centrale pour la Coopération Economique—CCCE). The four turbogenerators had a total capacity of 100 megawatts and were able to run on natural gas as well as fuel oil, enabling EECI to tap offshore gas sources as they became available. The government also agreed to purchase 178 gigawatt-hours of power from neighboring Ghana in 1983–84 and 322 gigawatt-hours in 1984–85. Good rains in 1984 replenished the lakes and allowed EECI to reactivate the hydroelectric generators; accordingly, thermal production decreased from 78.1 percent of the total in 1983–84 to 30.5 percent in 1984–85.

Other Energy Sources

In the rural areas, most of which were not serviced by electricity, wood, in both its natural state and as charcoal, and kerosene were the most important source of household energy. At the same time, the government encouraged small-scale attempts to exploit solar and wind energy. The French-owned Energy Management Agency used solar energy to power a community health clinic, and in the north of the country, wind-operated pumps raised subsurface water for drinking and irrigation.

Extractive Industries

Petroleum

By far the most important mineral in Côte d'Ivoire was petroleum. Petroleum was first discovered in the early 1970s on the continental shelf off the coast of Jacqueville, west of Abidjan. A short time later, a second field was discovered off Grand-Bassam, east of Abidjan. The discovery and development of the two fields coincided with the collapse of world cocoa and coffee prices in the late 1970s and was seen by many as the means by which the country could continue moving toward prosperity, although the fields, named Espoir and Bélier, were relatively small, geologically complex, and located in deep water. The Espoir field was developed by United States-based Phillips Petroleum. (PETROCI had a 10 percent share.) Espoir began operations in August 1982 with an output of 18,000 to 20,000 barrels per day (bpd—see Glossary). Because of technical problems, output declined the following year to 15,000 bpd. By 1988 production had fallen to 10,000 bpd.

The Bélier field, developed by Exxon, did not begin producing oil until 1980 because of technical difficulties. Output reached 10,000

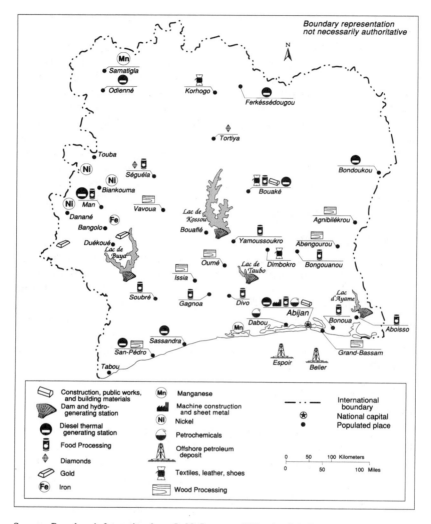

Source: Based on information from J.-N. Loucou, "Histoire," in Pierre Vennetier (ed.), *Atlas de la Côte d'Ivoire* (2d ed.), Paris, 1983, 56–58.

Figure 11. Economic Activity, 1983

bpd in 1981 and then fell to 6,000 bpd by 1986 in spite of a US$50 million investment by Exxon on a water injection program to maintain output and prolong the field's life.

Agip of Italy and Tenneco of the United States drilled exploratory wells elsewhere along the coast, but neither found sufficient reserves to continue exploration. By 1985, as world oil prices dropped and projected yields from Côte d'Ivoire's fields were reduced to more realistic levels, both Phillips and Exxon had halted exploratory and development drilling in their oil fields. Moreover, production in the existing fields failed to attain projected output, and the government's target of achieving self-sufficiency in oil production was never reached. Total oil production declined a further 5 percent in 1986 to less than 20,000 bpd, while national consumption exceeded 30,000 bpd. By the end of 1988, Exxon had halted production from the Bélier field and capped its wells.

In 1965 the Ivoirian Refining Company (Société Ivoirienne de Raffinage—SIR) completed construction on a refinery at Vridi with a capacity of 11,000 bpd per year. When petroleum prices surged in 1979, demand dropped substantially, and output fell to only 50 percent of capacity. Contracts with Chevron Oil of the United States to process crude oil from other African countries (primarily Nigeria) raised output to near capacity and, along with a financial recovery plan, led to a net improvement in the profitability of SIR. In 1986 capacity was increased to 50,000 bpd, making SIR the major source of refined petroleum products for West Africa. It also became Côte d'Ivoire's leading industrial plant and the third-ranking enterprise in French-speaking Africa, with revenues surpassing CFA F200 billion in 1986.

Natural Gas

The exploratory oil wells revealed large reserves of natural gas, some of which were associated with the oil fields. In 1987 estimates of the Espoir and Foxtrot gas reserves off the coast of Abidjan amounted to 3.5 billion cubic feet, or enough to produce 55 million cubic feet a day for twenty years. Apart from reducing the country's dependence on fuel oil, the government sought to use the gas to generate electricity—thus justifying its purchase of four large gas-powered turbines during the drought of 1983–84—and to produce fertilizer. In late 1987, the government and Phillips Petroleum were still trying to negotiate an acceptable price for the gas. Start-up costs for drilling two producer wells and constructing a sixty-kilometer gas pipeline to the thermal power station at Vridi were estimated at US$150 million in 1986.

Other Minerals

Although the subsoil of Côte d'Ivoire contained many other minerals, none existed in commercially exploitable amounts, given the high costs of extraction. Mining contributed only 1 percent of GDP in 1986.

During the precolonial era, gold was extracted from small shafts dug into the earth or from river and streambeds and was traded at the coast or across the Sahara Desert. Efforts under the colonial administration to exploit gold deposits at Kokoumbo in the center of the country and at small mines in the southeast proved unprofitable. In 1984 the state-owned SODEMI and a French mining company formed the Ity Mining Company (Société Minière d'Ity—SMI) to exploit a deposit discovered thirty years earlier at Ity near Danané. Total investment in this period was estimated at CFA F1.2 billion. The gold ore was of medium quality, with a ratio of gold to ore in the range of 8.5 grams per ton. Extraction was to begin in 1987, with output anticipated at 700 kilograms of gold metal during the first two years of operation. Ity estimated an additional investment of CFA F2.3 billion to expand output to 700 kilograms of gold metal a year. SODEMI also located gold deposits in the region of Issia and in the Lobo River bed, with anticipated annual yields of 100 kilograms and 25 kilograms, respectively.

In the mid-1970s, low-grade deposits (less than 50 percent) of iron ore estimated at 585 million tons were assayed at Bangolo near the Liberian border. A consortium representing Japanese, French, British, American, Dutch, and Ivoirian interests was formed to exploit the deposits; however, depressed world prices for iron ore forced the participants to postpone the project indefinitely.

Following World War II, diamond mining seemed promising, but by the mid-1980s expectations had waned. The Tortiya diamond mine, operating since 1948, peaked in 1972 when 260,000 carats were mined. In 1980, however, the mine was closed. The Bobi mine near Séguéla produced 270,000 carats per year until the late 1970s; it was closed in 1979. Remaining reserves for Tortiya were estimated at 450,000 carats; for Bobi, 150,000 carats.

Between 1960 and 1966, manganese mines in the region of Grand-Lahou on the coast yielded 180,000 tons of ore per year. In 1970, after world market prices had dropped and production costs had risen, the mines were closed. There were additional unexploited managanese deposits near Odienné. Côte d'Ivoire also had small deposits of colombo-tantalite, ilmenite, cobalt, copper, nickel, and bauxite.

Transportation and Communications

Following independence, the government invested heavily in infrastructure to transport the country's major export products. The relatively well-developed transport infrastructure was believed to be instrumental in the spectacular growth of the country's economy between 1960 and 1979. In 1986 the transport network

Dam on the Biya at Ayamé
Courtesy Eszti Votaw

included more than 53,736 kilometers of roads, of which some 3,765 kilometers were paved; 660 kilometers of railroads; two major seaports; 980 kilometers of navigable inland waterways (primarily lagoons because the country's rivers were not navigable); 3 international airports; 13 major domestic airfields; 17 smaller regional airfields; and 50 private airfields (see fig. 12).

Railroads

Construction on the Abidjan-Niger Railroad (Régie du Chemin de Fer Abidjan-Niger—RAN) began in 1905 and continued through 1954. The single, one-meter-gauge track extended northward from Abidjan through Ferkessédougou into Burkina Faso and terminated at Ouagadougou. Its total length, including the portion in Burkina Faso, was 1,180 kilometers. Through the early post-World War II period, the RAN contributed significantly to the development of agriculture and forestry in the southeast and central regions of the country. Following the opening of the Abidjan port in 1950 and the upgrading and expansion of the road network, the RAN became primarily a long-distance hauler. Except for points located directly on the rail route and for bulk transport, rail transport was no longer important to the south and to the center of the country. Nevertheless, the RAN was still considered crucial to economic development in the north; accordingly, new industries were situated along the rail line.

The RAN was also important to the landlocked countries to the north. At one time, it carried 90 percent of Burkina Faso's foreign trade and half of the 50 percent of Mali's foreign trade that passed (via Bobo Dioulasso in Burkina Faso) through the seaport of Abidjan.

In the 1980s, economic recession in Côte d'Ivoire and Burkina Faso, and political instability in the latter, confronted the RAN with financial and administrative problems, deteriorating equipment, and debt. These problems were caused in part because Burkina Faso did not pay its bills for five years, accumulating arrears amounting to CFA F17 billion. For political and economic reasons, the two countries agreed to liquidate the RAN and divide its assets, estimated in 1987 to be CFA F78 billion in rolling stock, railroad stations, buildings, and land.

Côte d'Ivoire had planned to construct a 350-kilometer railroad to link the port city of San-Pédro with iron ore deposits near Bongolo in the west-central region of the country. But because prices in the 1980s for iron ore were low, the government scrapped plans to exploit the deposits and build the railroad, which would have cost an estimated CFA F80 billion in 1986.

Roads

As the demand for Côte d'Ivoire's exports increased in the 1960s and 1970s, the government improved the road network dramatically. From 25,000 kilometers of roads in 1961, the network expanded by 1986 to 53,765 kilometers, of which 3,765 were paved, including 141 kilometers of divided highway. Paved roads linked Abidjan with all major population centers in the country, and although they constituted only 7 percent of the total road network, they carried approximately 70 percent of the traffic. Roads were the principal mode of domestic transport, carrying about 78 percent of interurban passenger traffic and 70 percent of freight traffic. In Abidjan, as elsewhere in the country, traffic growth was rapid, expanding 10 percent per year for passenger traffic and 7 percent per year for freight traffic from 1970 to 1980. In 1986 a daily average of 14,000 vehicles entered and left Abidjan, as opposed to an average of 4,800 vehicles in 1969.

A 1969 World Bank transportation survey strongly recommended improvements to the primary road network during the 1970s. Over the first five years of the plan, inadequate planning and a lack of overall policy coordination and evaluation resulted in gross overspending. Although 75 percent of the road projects originally proposed were implemented, they cost 123 percent more than the amount earmarked to pay for the entire program. Nevertheless, highway construction did not abate. In 1986 the World Bank approved a US$40 million loan as part of a US$230 million highway construction and improvement program, described as the "quickest way to inject money into the economy and affect all sectors." For the same year, the BSIE earmarked CFA F39.4 billion for highway construction and improvement.

Ports and Maritime Shipping

Côte d'Ivoire has no natural, sheltered deepwater harbors. Until 1950 all imports had to be offloaded at sea onto lighters that either crossed the surf and landed on a beach or, as at Grand-Bassam and Sassandra, unloaded at a wharf that extended beyond the surf. In 1950 the 2.7-kilometer Vridi Canal, which cut through the barrier island south of Abidjan, was completed, linking the Gulf of Guinea with the Ebrié Lagoon. Until port facilities at Abidjan were completed, lighters were still required to unload cargo, but by 1955 all port operations were handled at dockside.

By the 1970s, Abidjan was the largest port in West Africa. The amount of cargo handled grew from 5 million tons in 1970 to 9.5 million tons in 1986, a large proportion of which was containerized. Abidjan had 5,485 meters of quays representing 35 berths, 105,000 square meters of warehouse space, a quay with refrigeration installations for the fishing industry, and twelve specialized quays for bananas, fish, timber, cement, hydrocarbons, tankers, and roll-on roll-off cargo operations. In 1987 the government enlarged the Abidjan port, adding two new quays in Locodjo across the lagoon from the city.

To stimulate development in the southwest and reduce the cost of transporting raw materials to Abidjan, the government constructed a second deepwater port at San-Pédro. The San-Pédro project, which represented a major governmental effort to exploit the timber, cocoa, coffee, rubber, and palm oil production planned for the southwest and the iron ore mines farther north, included road building and development of an urban infrastructure. The port with two large quays began operating in 1971, but because the iron ore project was dropped and timber production for the region was less than the amount anticipated, the San-Pédro port handled far less than its planned capacity. In 1984 cargo amounted to approximately 1.3 million tons, or 14 percent of all maritime commerce. In 1984 Abidjan and San-Pédro handled a total of 9.7 million tons of cargo.

Côte d'Ivoire had two merchant marine companies flying the national flag: SITRAM and the Ivoirian Maritime Navigation

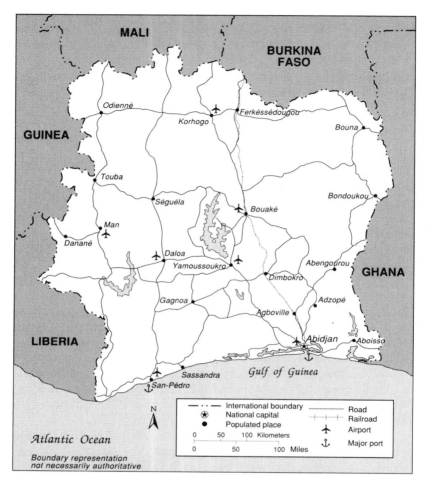

Source: Based on information from J.-N. Loucou, ''Histoire,'' in Pierre Vennetier (ed.),
   Atlas de la Côte d'Ivoire (2d ed.), Paris, 1983, 59–61.

Figure 12. Transportation System, 1988

Company (Société Ivoirienne de Navigation Maritime—
SIVOMAR), with a combined total of twenty cargo ships. The
former company was state owned; the latter was privately owned.

Air Transport

In the 1980s, the Abidjan-Port Bouët International Airport, situated on the outskirts of Abidjan, was one of the most active in Africa,
handling more than 1 million passengers each year. It had two

runways more than 3,000 meters in length and could handle all large carriers, as could the airports at Bouaké and Yamoussoukro. There were also thirty public airports serving the major towns and approximately fifty private airfields. Air Ivoire, the state airline, also known as Ivoirian Air Transport and Liaison (Groupement Aérien de Transport et de Liaison—GATL), handled air traffic within the country and also flew to neighboring countries. Air Afrique, a multinational consortium formed by ten francophone African countries and headquartered in Abidjan, was the major carrier for international traffic serving Côte d'Ivoire. Air Afrique's major competitors were Air France and the Air Transport Union (Union des Transports Aériens—UTA), a private French-owned carrier. Other carriers from Europe and the United States also provided regular service.

Telecommunications

Telecommunications, like so many other areas, reflected Côte d'Ivoire's colonial heritage. Thus, 251 telephone circuits linked Côte d'Ivoire with France, and 29 linked it with Senegal, the former colonial seat for French West Africa (Afrique Occidentale Française—OAF; see Glossary). No circuits linked Côte d'Ivoire directly with its immediate neighbors. An INTELSAT ground satellite station located east of Abidjan provided links to the United States, Europe, and other African countries. In addition, the government planned by 1990 to lay a submarine cable linking Côte d'Ivoire with Senegal, Guinea, Liberia, and Gambia.

In 1984 there were 87,700 installed telephone lines in the country, or 1.3 telephones per 100 people. Only 45 percent of the telephones were working at any one time because of technical problems, however, so actual users of telephone service numbered 59,247. In 1986 Abidjan had 67.9 percent of the total number of telephone lines in the country, or one telephone per 50 inhabitants compared with one telephone per 430 inhabitants in the interior of the country. At the end of 1986, outside of Abidjan 115 cities had telephone service, of which 44 were equipped with automatic installations. The government intended to construct a network of satellite earth stations in the interior in early 1990; the network would improve rural telephone service dramatically. Meanwhile, the military, government offices, and some businesses used radio communications, which were the responsibility of the National Telecommunications Bureau (Office National de Télécommunications—ONT).

As of the mid-1980s, ONT was beset with problems in spite of its new US$35 million headquarters. It suffered from traffic congestion, a poor call-completion rate (as few as 50 percent, 30 percent, and 20 percent for urban, interurban, and international call attempts, respectively); poor billing and collections (accounts receivable amounted to twelve months' receipts, or CFA F31 billion); an inadequate tariff structure; and lack of oversight. Moreover, the ONT often bought sophisticated technology that ended up increasing rather than reducing maintenance costs.

In 1982 the postal service handled 59,861,000 pieces of mail and 581,000 telegrams, or approximately 6 pieces per capita. There were 1,181 telex subscriber lines.

Foreign Trade and Commerce

At independence, Cote d'Ivoire had strong economic and political ties with France. In contrast with nearly all other former French colonies in Africa, the government of Côte d'Ivoire continued to cultivate these links into the late 1980s, some twenty years after France had suspended tariff preferences for major Ivoirian exports. By the 1980s, however, Côte d'Ivoire had found supplementary trading partners and sources of foreign investment, primarily among France's neighbors in the European Economic Community (EEC).

Between 1960 and 1974, the value of Côte d'Ivoire's exports to EEC countries more than doubled, while the value of its exports to France was halved. Although this trend continued into the 1980s, French exports to Côte d'Ivoire remained important because most of the Ivoirian import substitution industries were either linked to, or otherwise dependent on, French parent companies.

In 1986 Côte d'Ivoire's principal markets for exports were France and the United States, which together purchased approximately one-third of its total exports (see table 6, Appendix). West Germany was the third largest export market, having overtaken Italy in 1985. France, which provided one-third of Côte d'Ivoire's imports, was by far the largest supplier. The United States and the Netherlands each supplied about 5 percent of the country's imports.

After cocoa and coffee, Côte d'Ivoire's principal exports were timber and processed wood, cotton and textiles, sugar, rubber, palm oil, pineapple, and other agricultural and manufactured goods. Its principal imports were manufactured goods, food, petroleum products, machinery, and transport equipment.

Balance of Payments and Foreign Assistance

Between 1950 and 1975, Côte d'Ivoire had far fewer problems with its balance of payments than did most other African states

Crossing the Comoé River
Courtesy Robert Handloff

(see table 7, Appendix). Exports increased at a faster rate than the gross national product (GNP—see Glossary), with real expansion averaging 9 percent per year from 1962 to 1975. Until 1978 the balance of trade was invariably positive. Export earnings from coffee and cocoa rose consistently as production grew, and earnings surged when world market prices for coffee and cocoa increased. In the boom period from 1974 to 1977, export earnings soared, peaking in 1977 with a record trade surplus of almost CFA F100 billion.

In 1979 lower prices for coffee and cocoa, coupled with higher prices for imports, especially crude oil, sharply cut the trade surplus to what was then an unprecedented CFA F1.880 billion. In subsequent years, as the volume of exports rose (notwithstanding weaker coffee and cocoa prices) and as government-imposed austerity measures cut imports, trade surplus figures stabilized at about CFA F30 billion a year.

National Debt

To finance its development projects—given the paucity of domestic capital—Côte d'Ivoire borrowed substantial amounts abroad, especially during the mid-1970s. At that time, high prices for coffee and cocoa led Ivoirian planners to overestimate the potential of the economy and, consequently, undertake overly ambitious capital investment programs. By 1976 Côte d'Ivoire's high debt payments,

135

together with repatriated profits and foreign worker remittances, produced a negative net reserve position for the first time in its history, despite continuing trade surpluses.

Following the drought and recession of the early 1980s, external debt rose even more sharply, reaching US$9.8 billion in 1985—about triple the level of five years earlier and more than three-quarters of the annual GNP (see table 8, Appendix). By 1981 total debt service amounted to about US$1 billion. Between 1978 and 1983, the ratio of debt service to export earnings rose from 13 percent to 31 percent.

Since the early 1980s, Côte d'Ivoire had engaged in a series of foreign debt rescheduling exercises with both private and public creditors. Faced with falling commodity prices and recession, Côte d'Ivoire asked to reschedule its debt with Paris Club donors; the request was granted in May 1984. By the terms of the rescheduling agreement, all payments on principal and half the interest payments due that year would be spread over nine years, with a four-year grace period. The London Club of commercial creditors also rescheduled the US$775 million in interest and principal due in 1984 and US$420 million due in 1985. In addition, the country obtained new credits equivalent to US$176 million, contingent upon enactment of a retrenchment program approved by the IMF that limited government spending and foreign borrowing.

As economic conditions improved in early 1985, the government signaled its intent to assume its full debt service burden in 1986 rather than negotiate a second London Club rescheduling agreement. At World Bank and IMF urging, however, Côte d'Ivoire in August 1985 arranged a multiyear rescheduling package with its foreign creditors that would allow the country renewed access to commercial capital markets while phasing in debt rescheduling over the next five years. The IMF approved a US$66.2 million standby agreement loan that was followed in September by a US$30 million World Bank loan to finance technical assistance in support of an industrial reform program. Earlier, Côte d'Ivoire had adopted a World Bank industrial sector reform plan, resulting in strong World Bank support for the country in its negotiations with private and bilateral creditors. This multiyear debt rescheduling exercise was the first of its kind in Africa and was intended to allow the country to "grow out of" its debt crisis.

By 1987, when Côte d'Ivoire was to start payments on the first installment on the debt that it rescheduled in 1984 and that then totaled approximately US$8 billion, the economy had not improved. The continuing decline in coffee and cocoa prices, which Houphouët-Boigny blamed on American and European speculators, cut export

The Economy

earnings by an estimated CFA F180 billion. At the time, the IMF projected a US$811 million current accounts deficit for 1987. The IMF also projected debt servicing costs for 1988 of US$1.4 billion—roughly two-thirds of the national budget—as compared with the 1987 cost of US$1.5 billion. Payment was clearly out of reach. In May 1987, the government announced that it would suspend payment on its foreign debt.

The May 1987 decision to suspend foreign debt payments placed Côte d'Ivoire in the high-risk category for some trading partners and potential investors, even though the move was explained by Ivoirian officials as simply a political maneuver to win a fairer deal for Côte d'Ivoire and other African debtors. Nevertheless, by the end of 1987 the Paris Club, the IMF, and the government had negotiated a new economic recovery and structural adjustment program. The new package granted Côte d'Ivoire a six-year grace period and rescheduled all principal due in 1987–88 plus 80 percent of interest due (approximately US$500 million). Earlier, the World Bank had agreed to release the second US$150 million installment of a US$250 million structural adjustment loan originally approved by its board in mid-1986. Finally, disbursement of an IMF structural adjustment credit and a compensatory financing facility worth approximately US$235.8 million awaited the outcome of the London Club negotiations.

The IMF further warned the government that unless it lowered producer prices, it would face severe and persistent budget deficits for the foreseeable future. Although Houphouët-Boigny had declared that producer prices would not be reduced, CSSPPA officials conceded that some modification of producer prices was under consideration. The pricing formula being studied was similar to that applied in Cameroon, where prices reflected both the quality of a producer's crop and the previous year's commodity earnings.

For its part, the government reduced by 20 percent the 1988 capital spending budget from about CFA F179 billion in 1987 to CFA F144 billion to satisfy the IMF's recommendation for a more rigorous selection of investment projects. At the same time, the government rejected IMF demands to increase income taxes, limit family allowances, and cut guaranteed prices to farmers, claiming that such measures would jeopardize political and social stability.

Foreign Assistance

As a middle-income developing country, Côte d'Ivoire found it easier to borrow from private commercial sources than from multilateral and bilateral financial institutions, which lent primarily to the poorest countries. More than two-thirds of its foreign debt was owed to commercial lending agencies. Nevertheless, the government borrowed substantial sums from Paris Club donors. From 1981 to 1984, net official development assistance from Western countries and from multilateral agencies averaged US$136.4 million per year. This figure increased in the mid-1980s as multilateral donors, particularly the World Bank, financed the various structural readjustment programs. In 1986 the World Bank financed five programs amounting to US$340.1 million, and by the end of that year it had loaned Côte d'Ivoire about US$1.8 billion in a series of forty-nine operations, including three structural adjustment loans that totaled US$600 million. Other sources of multilateral aid in 1985 were the African Development Bank (US$124.4 million), the European Development Fund (US$15.5 million), and the Council of the Entente (Conseil de l'Entente; US$375 million).

France was the most important bilateral aid donor. French assistance was channeled through the CCCE and the Aid and Cooperation Fund (Fond d'Aide et de Coopération—FAC). After France, Canada and West Germany were the largest donors, providing US$7.7 million and US$8.7 million, respectively, in 1985.

Future of the Economy

The debt rescheduling and structural adjustment program negotiated in 1988 afforded Côte d'Ivoire a respite from burdensome debt repayment. Nevertheless, the country's economic future remained cloudy. Timber production, which at other times sustained the economy when coffee and cocoa prices were weak, was manifesting the stark effects of overcutting. Houphouët-Boigny's refusal to cut producer prices for cocoa guaranteed continuing high levels of production and low prices on world markets because Côte d'Ivoire was the world's leading cocoa producer. To diversify its economy, the country turned to other agricultural products like palm and coconut oils, tropical fruits, sugar, cotton, and rubber. In none of these products, however, did the country have as commanding position as it did with coffee or cocoa. Moreover, the market in tropical oils faced a potential threat as health-conscious consumers in the United States demanded substitutes thought to be lower in saturated fats than were palm and coconut oils. For many of the other diversification crops, particularly sugar, world supply already surpassed demand, and Côte d'Ivoire would be competing with other Third World tropical countries similarly seeking to diversify economies heretofore dependent on coffee and cocoa. Finally, although the retrenchments mandated by the IMF affected all income groups in Côte d'Ivoire, they most visibly affected the young and poor, giving rise to crime, drug problems, and other manifestations of social dislocation, all of which demanded additional expenditures from the government. In 1987 government revenue losses from customs fraud alone, especially in the textiles sector, were estimated at approximately CFA F200 billion (US$701 million) per year—or about one-third of the national budget. The path out of this downward spiral had yet to be discovered.

* * *

Because of its apparently remarkable performance, especially in comparison to the economies of nearly all other sub-Saharan African countries, the economy of Côte d'Ivoire has a rich bibliography. General reference works like Europa's *Africa South of the Sahara, African Contemporary Record,* and *Encyclopedia of the Third World* provide important guidance. Articles and monographs by scholars such as Samir Amin, Bonnie Campbell, Michael A. Cohen, Lawrence R. Alschuler, I. William Zartman, and Y.-A. Fauré provide insightful, relevant, and sometimes highly critical analyses of Ivoirian economic growth. More detailed information has appeared in publications of international development organizations like the World Bank and various agencies of the United Nations. Publications of the government of Côte d'Ivoire and its agencies are also helpful. Several periodicals provide current information, particularly on debt negotiations. These include *Africa Research Bulletin, Africa Economic Digest, Bulletin de l'Afrique noire, Marchés tropicaux et méditerranéens,* the Economist Intelligence Unit's *Country Report, West Africa,* and *Jeune Afrique.* (For further information and complete citations, see Bibliography.)

Chapter 4. Government and Politics

Akan chief with his official regalia

THE FIRST POSTINDEPENDENCE regimes of sub-Saharan Africa were characterized by some form of personal rule. In theory, such regimes would govern during the transition period following independence but preceding the full development of the governing institutions of the newly independent states. In reality, however, the leaders of the various independence movements, who subsequently had become government officials, often manipulated public resources, acquired vast wealth and status, and generally consolidated their hold on power. Where the transitional systems acquired legitimacy, as in Côte d'Ivoire, it was almost entirely the result of the ability of the leader-politician, in the absence of strong governing institutions, to provide adequate material and political rewards to a broader constituency.

In 1988 governance in Côte d'Ivoire remained the province of one man: President Félix Houphouët-Boigny, affectionately called *le vieux* (the old man). He had ruled since independence and had dominated Ivoirian politics since the stirrings of nationalism in the mid-1940s. From the onset of his tenure in 1960, debate was virtually suspended as Houphouët-Boigny subjected the polity to his paternalistic yet stern control. He wielded executive power as head of state, head of government, head of the ruling party, and commander in chief of the armed forces. In his role as head of government, he appointed his cabinet (Council of Ministers), named the chief justice of the Supreme Court, and selected the heads of all extragovernmental commissions and councils. As head of state, he formulated and conducted foreign policy. As head of the party, he set policy directions and appointed the entire membership of all policy-making boards. Although there were occasions when popular sentiment as expressed through party organs or the National Assembly forced the president to alter a policy decision, he was without question the dominant political force.

Houphouët-Boigny's charisma contributed to the myth of Houphouëtism, as his ruling style was labeled, enabling him to convert the skeptics and awe the faithful. In spite of his power, Houphouët-Boigny's style of rule was by choice paternalistic. Houphouët-Boigny became a transcendent symbol of unity to the disparate groups in Côte d'Ivoire, and his charismatic authority supplanted the traditional authority of the local chiefs. Although Houphouët-Boigny's hold on the national imagination was weakening by the late 1980s, many Ivoirians continued to reject out of hand any reports of the president's avarice or violations of trust.

To repay his supporters with adequate material rewards, Houphouët-Boigny developed economic policies that combined free enterprise and state capitalism with liberal foreign investment and continued economic dependence on France. Houphouët-Boigny's strategy for development also led to a broad gap in wealth and power between the urban elite—the rulers—and the rest of the population.

As a measure of Houphouët-Boigny's success, liberal economic theorists and conservative students of African politics cited Côte d'Ivoire as an economic and political miracle. Indeed, through 1979 Côte d'Ivoire posted one of the highest rates of economic growth among all developing countries, and the highest per capita gross domestic product (GDP—see Glossary) of any nonpetroleum-exporting African country. Coupled with the rapid rate of growth was a political stability unparalleled in sub-Saharan Africa. Unlike most of his counterparts in sub-Saharan Africa, Houphouët-Boigny resisted pressures to sever ties with the colonizing power (France) or to Africanize the bureaucracy, two steps that, when taken in other former colonies, usually meant reduced funds for investment and expanded opportunities for corruption. He also resisted pressure to subsidize large industrial projects with revenues from cash crops. Instead, he relied on foreign—mostly French—investment, technology, and support to develop the country's economic base and administrative infrastructure.

Under Houphouët-Boigny's administration, Côte d'Ivoire's foreign policy was consistently pro-Western. Its fundamental objective was to promote economic development at home by promising peace and security within West Africa. Côte d'Ivoire also maintained extensive economic and military ties with France, even though this meant bearing the neocolonialist label. Diplomatic relations with the United States, if less substantial, were also warm. For instance, Côte d'Ivoire was sub-Saharan Africa's staunchest supporter of the United States in the United Nations. Matching the strength of its support for the West was Côte d'Ivoire's distrust of the Soviet Union. Côte d'Ivoire did not establish diplomatic relations with the Soviet Union until 1967, severed them in early 1969 amid accusations of Soviet subversion, and did not reestablish them until 1986, as part of Houphouët-Boigny's quest for international stature. Houphouët-Boigny also broke with most other African leaders by attempting to establish a dialogue with South Africa and, in 1986, by reestablishing diplomatic relations, which had been broken following the October 1973 War, with Israel.

Mural honoring President Félix Houphouët-Boigny
Courtesy Eszti Votaw

Formal Power

The Constitution

On October 31, 1960, the National Assembly of Côte d'Ivoire adopted the Constitution establishing an independent republic. The 1960 Constitution calls for a strong, centralized presidential system with an independent judiciary and a national legislature.

As in much of the Ivoirian political system, French influence weighed heavily in the preparation of the Constitution. Houphouët-Boigny and its other authors had received much of their formal political education and experience in France, and Houphouët-Boigny himself had served in successive French governments in the 1950s. Not unexpectedly, the 1960 Constitution was largely taken (often verbatim) from the 1958 Constitution of the Fifth Republic of France. Like its French counterpart, the Ivoirian Constitution declares that all power derives from the people and is expressed through universal suffrage. It also mandates the separation of executive and legislative authority with limits on the power of the former.

In its preamble, the Constitution proclaims its dedication to liberal democratic principles and inalienable human rights as expressed in the 1789 Declaration of the Rights of Man and of the Citizen and the 1948 Universal Declaration of Human Rights. Under the

145

rubric "Of the State and Sovereignty," the initial articles of the Constitution describe the symbols of the state—the flag, the motto, and the national anthem—and name French the official language. Articles 3 through 7 delineate the fundamental rights and principles pertaining to Ivoirian citizenship: universal suffrage, popular sovereignty, and equality before the law. Significantly, in light of the government's subsequent coercive support of a single political party, Article 7 of the 1960 Constitution formally allows a multiparty system.

The first chapter of the Constitution directs that the government consist of executive, legislative, and judicial branches. The three subsequent chapters of the Constitution list the powers accruing to each. The Ivoirian Constitution provides for a strong executive, although it couches the language of power in democratic terms. For example, in keeping with the articulated principle of popular sovereignty, the Constitution provides that the National Assembly shall vote laws and consent to taxes but then limits the assembly's power by specifying exactly the matters on which the legislature may act. Matters constitutionally excluded from the legislature's purview automatically fall within that of the executive and are dealt with either by decree or by regulation. The Constitution also stipulates that the executive and the National Assembly share the power to initiate legislation, but the pertinent article appears in the chapter dealing with executive—not legislative —responsibilities. In fact, for most of Côte d'Ivoire's brief history as an independent republic, nearly all legislative programs have originated with the president and have been rubber-stamped by the assembly.

The Constitution also calls for a separate judiciary. As with the legislature, however, the Constitution makes the judiciary subordinate to the individual who guarantees its independence, that is, the president. The Constitution neither establishes nor protects a judiciary independent of or opposed to the government. The Constitution does provide for the Supreme Court and a subordinate court system; nevertheless, it does not stipulate the exact structure of the judiciary, a task that officially was to be done by the National Assembly. In fact, the assembly simply approved the president's plan.

The ninth chapter of the Constitution establishes the Economic and Social Council (Conseil Economique et Social), the purpose of which is to advise the president on matters pertaining to economic development and social change. The final two chapters provide procedures for amending and adopting the Constitution.

Civil Rights

The Constitution lists and defines protected civil rights in the initial articles and in a few brief references elsewhere. Like the

French Constitution, it promises equality before the law without respect to place of origin, race, sex, or religion. It also specifically mandates religious freedom and prohibits any manifestations of racial discrimination. The Constitution also guarantees freedom from arbitrary arrest and detention, the right to representation at a trial, and the principle of innocence until guilt is proven. However, the Constitution does not guarantee bail; thus, suspects are routinely incarcerated from the time of arrest until either acquitted in a trial or sentenced. The Constitution does not guarantee a free press or freedom of assembly, thereby virtually eliminating the means by which opposing political parties might develop. Otherwise, the Constitution leaves more explicit guarantees of individual liberties to the legislature.

In practice, the government generally respected the civil rights provisions of the Constitution, preferring co-optation instead of coercion to enforce its will. The United States Department of State described human rights as generally satisfactory, in contrast to conditions in most other sub-Saharan countries (see Human Rights, ch. 5). At the same time, the government was not timid about violating the spirit of the Constitution when dealing with political opponents. For example, youthful political opponents were routinely conscripted into the armed forces, which was one of Houphouët-Boigny's favorite ploys to silence opponents while still being able to boast of holding no political prisoners. Also, all local news media were state owned and therefore expected to support the government and its policies. In October 1986, in the face of a budding movement for a more independent press, Minister of Information Laurent Dona Fologo threatened to fire "black sheep" journalists who did not sufficiently assume the role of public servants. Although major European and American newspapers and magazines were generally available and interested Ivoirians routinely heard French radio broadcasts, government leaders did not hesitate to ban the circulation of a publication deemed offensive. In November 1987, for example, the Political Bureau of the Democratic Party of Côte d'Ivoire (Parti Démocratique de Côte d'Ivoire—PDCI) asked the government to ban the sale of *Jeune Afrique* following its allegations that Houphouët-Boigny was involved in the October 1987 coup in neighboring Burkina Faso.

The Executive

The executive branch was headed by the president and included cabinet ministers and their administrations. The Ivoirian Constitution augments presidential power by combining with it the functions of prime minister while subordinating the role of the National

147

Assembly. Under the Constitution, the president has authority to appoint and dismiss ministers, military officers, and members of the judiciary. The president promulgates laws and ensures their execution, negotiates and ratifies treaties (subject in some cases to the National Assembly's approval), and sets national policy.

As a coinitiator of laws, the president was able to exercise effective control over legislation. Moreover, constitutional mandates coupled with enabling legislation ratified by the National Assembly gave the president what amounted to government by decree. Bills were not always passed unanimously, but that was the practical effect.

The president is elected to a five-year term by universal suffrage and can be reelected indefinitely. To be elected, a candidate must be at least forty years old; other qualifications were fixed by legislation.

The Constitution also provides for the Council of Ministers, whose members are appointed by the president (see fig. 13). Although ministers served at the will of the president, he accorded them considerable freedom of action to propose policies and projects within their respective areas of competence. The proposals were then debated by the Council of Ministers.

In the 1980s, Houphouët-Boigny selected his ministers from the growing pool of younger, educated technocrats who had replaced the political militants of an earlier generation. Selected at least in part on the basis of merit, the new men came to government without independent constituencies and were therefore indebted to the president, which was consistent with Houphouët-Boigny's view that government in immature states should be personal rather than institutional. Government, then, became Houphouët-Boigny's administrative agency and not a forum for settling political differences.

The National Assembly

Under the Constitution, legislative responsibilities theoretically belong to a unicameral National Assembly (Assemblée Nationale). In 1985 it was enlarged from 147 to 175 members, who were known as deputies (*députés*). Qualifications for candidates to the Assembly were established by the government. Like the president, deputies were elected by universal suffrage within a constituency for five-year terms. Until 1980, Houphouët-Boigny had handpicked the deputies, who were automatically elected to the assembly as part of a single slate. Consequently, the National Assembly was a passive body that almost automatically consented to executive instructions. The assembly did have power to delay legislation by means of extended debate. Deputies, however, rarely challenged the president's policy decisions, and little debate occurred. Starting with the 1980 election, Houphouët-Boigny opened the process so that any qualified citizen could be a candidate. Moreover, the constitutional amendment of October 1985 stipulating that the president of the National Assembly would become interim president of the republic, should the presidency be vacated, conferred greater importance on the workings of the assembly.

Pursuant to the Constitution, each legislative term lasted five years, during which the National Assembly sat for two sessions per year. The first term began on the last Wednesday in April and lasted no more than three months. The second opened on the first Wednesday of October and ended on the third Friday in December. The president or a majority of the deputies could request an extraordinary session to consider a specific issue. Meetings of the assembly were open unless otherwise requested by the president or one-third of the deputies.

The National Assembly elected its own president, who served for the duration of the legislative term. In 1988 this position was second only to the president of the republic in the table of precedence. It was held by Henri Konan Bedié for the 1985–90 term. The assembly president's staff was also elected by the assembly. A member of this staff would preside over the National Assembly whenever the president of the assembly was not present.

Legislation was proposed within three standing committees: the Committee for General and Institutional Affairs, which covered interior matters, the civil service, information, national defense, foreign affairs, and justice; the Committee for Economic and Financial Affairs, which covered financial and economic affairs, planning, land, public works, mines, transportation, postal service, and telecommunications; and the Committee for Social and Cultural Affairs, which covered education, youth and sports, public health and population, labor, and social affairs. The assembly could also form special standing committees for specific purposes. Each committee presented to the full assembly legislative proposals pertaining to affairs within its area of expertise. Determining the legislative agenda was the responsibility of the president of the National Assembly, his staff, and the committee heads.

The Economic and Social Council

The Constitution also provides for the establishment of the Economic and Social Council, which advises the president on issues of an "economic or social character." In 1988 the council had forty-five members, all of whom were selected by the president for five-year terms from among those members of the elite most concerned

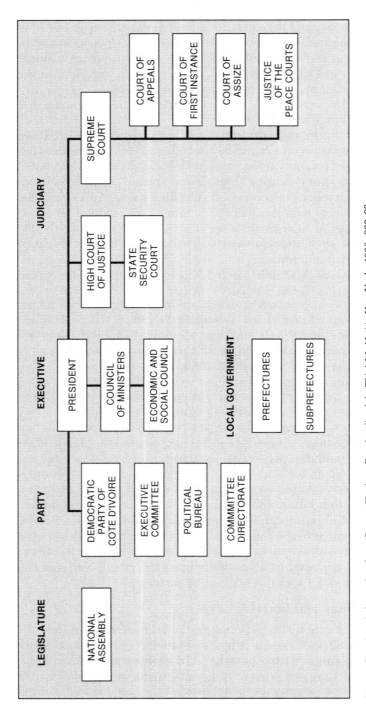

Source: Based on information from George Kurian, *Encyclopedia of the Third World*, 11, New York, 1986, 983–99.

Figure 13. Organization of the Ivoirian Government, 1986

with economic development and social change. By the late 1970s, membership included the leaders of the growing commercial and industrial sector. With the exception of its president, who was named by the president of the republic, the council elected officers and distributed its members among various standing committees with discrete areas of responsibility. In 1986 Houphouët-Boigny named Philippe Yacé to head the council. Although the president was obligated to consult with the council on all matters within its competence, the council could also offer unsolicited opinions pertaining to economic development on all laws, ordinances, and decrees. Moreover, on its own initiative, the council could direct the president's attention to any economic or social issue.

Judicial System

The 1960 Constitution entitles all Ivoirians to a fair public trial. That mandate was generally respected in urban areas; in rural villages, traditional institutions more commonly administered justice. Indigent defendants were also entitled to legal counsel by court-appointed attorneys. In practice, public defenders were often unavailable, and there was a vast difference between the representation accorded rich and poor clients. According to the Constitution, judges are subject only to the law, and the president, with the assistance of the Superior Council of Magistrates, is charged with ensuring the independence of the judiciary. Because the president of the republic controlled appointments to the courts, the judiciary seldom, if ever, opposed the president.

The judicial system bore the imprint of both the French legal and judicial traditions and, to a lesser extent, customary law. It consisted of two levels. The lower courts, all of which were created by presidential decree and exercised limited jurisdiction, included the courts of appeals, the courts of first instance, the courts of assize, and the justice of the peace courts. The five courts of first instance, which handled the bulk of trials, heard misdemeanor and minor criminal cases (with a maximum sentence of three months or less), juvenile cases, and civil cases. The courts consisted of a president, one or more vice-presidents, and one or more examining magistrates and trial judges, all of whom were appointed by the president of the republic. The courts were located in Abidjan, Bouaké, Daloa, Korhogo, and Man. Each had two or more delegated sections in larger towns within their respective jurisdictions. The courts of assize, which were paired with courts of first instance, handled only major criminal cases. At the lowest level were justice of the peace courts, presided over by justices of the peace who handled petty cases in civil, criminal, and customary law. The two courts of appeals, located in Abidjan and Bouaké, heard appeals from courts of first instance and courts of assize. The Abidjan court heard appeals from the Abidjan court of first instance and its delegated sections; the Bouaké court handled referrals from the other four courts of first instance.

The superior courts are mandated by the Constitution and have nationwide jurisdiction. They include the Supreme Court, the High Court of Justice and the State Security Court. The Supreme Court is separated into four sections handling, respectively, constitutionality of laws, administrative appeal, criminal appeal, and financial control of government services. The Constitution directs that the court include one president, three vice-presidents (one for each section except the constitutional), nine associate justices, one secretary general, and four secretaries. The Constitutional Section, which always met in closed session, reviewed laws that had been passed by the National Assembly but not yet promulgated. The section had fifteen days to complete its consideration of a bill. The president of the republic or the president of the assembly could forward requests for a constitutional review. The president of the republic could also submit government bills to the section for a constitutional hearing before they were submitted to the Council of Ministers. The Constitutional Section also supervised referenda as called for in the Constitution and ruled on the eligibility of candidates for the National Assembly. The president of the Supreme Court presided over sessions of the section, which also included the vice-presidents of the court and four persons noted for their juridical and administrative competence. These four could also be members of the court. Two of the four were appointed by the president of the assembly, and two were appointed by the president of the republic. The term of office was four years, and there was no provision for removal from office.

The Judicial Section was the highest court of appeals in criminal cases. The section consisted of one vice-president, four associate justices, and two secretaries. It was organized into civil and criminal divisions with three additional magistrates in each. The Administrative Section handled cases of alleged abuse of administrative power involving individuals in public administration. This section consisted of a vice-president and two associate judges. Unlike the judges in other sections, those in the administrative section were magistrates, but not necessarily members of the bench. Another section of the Supreme Court, the Audit and Control Section, monitored public expenditures and annually audited accounts of the state and its agencies. This section consisted of a vice-president, three associate justices, and one secretary.

The two other superior courts included the High Court of Justice and the State Security Court. The High Court of Justice was composed of members of the National Assembly who were elected to the court every five years, following each general election. The court was empowered to impeach the president of the republic for treason and to judge other members of the government for crimes or misdemeanors committed in the exercise of their official duties. Cases concerning crimes against state security were heard in the State Security Court.

All judges, as well as all employees of the Central Administration of the Ministry of Justice, comprised the professional judiciary. They were required to have obtained a bachelor of law degree and could not concurrently hold an elected office. A Superior Council of the Judiciary was responsible for assisting the president in the task of guaranteeing an independent judiciary. The council advised the president on nominations to the Supreme Court, on cases concerning judicial independence, and on disciplinary problems. It also advised the minister of justice on nominations to magistrate positions. The council's membership included members of the Constitutional Section of the Supreme Court and three magistrates, each appointed to two-year terms by the president from a list prepared by the minister of justice.

Local Government

As of 1987, the country was divided into forty-nine prefectures (see fig. 1). The prefectural administration, headed by a prefect (*préfet*), represented executive authority within the prefecture. Constitutionally, the prefects responded to the local interests of their respective constituents and directed and coordinated the administrative services represented in their respective constituencies. As representatives of each ministry within their prefectures, the prefects issued directives to the heads of services and ensured their compliance, presided over all state organizations and commissions within the prefecture, periodically met with service heads at the prefectural level, and acted as trustees for public enterprises and activities in the prefectures. Prefects also were responsible for maintaining public order and security in their respective prefectures. In that capacity, they supervised local police and oversaw the execution of laws, statutes, and executive orders. To deal with civil unrest or other emergencies, they were also empowered to issue binding orders or decrees, detain suspects for up to forty-eight hours, and request assistance from the armed forces (see Internal Security Organization and Forces, ch. 5).

The prefectural administration included a secretary general, a chief of cabinet, and two division chiefs, one of whom was responsible for administrative and general affairs such as elections, supervision of the police, administration of subprefectures (*sous-préfectures*), and civil affairs. The other division chief was responsible for economic, financial, and social affairs, including the budget, accounts, public works, health, education, and the supervision of markets and price controls. The secretary general, besides substituting for the prefect during the latter's absence, supervised and coordinated all departmental services. The chief of cabinet, in effect an administrative aide, was responsible for intradepartmental affairs (mail, inspection visits, and liaison with ministerial departments and personnel in Abidjan).

According to enabling legislation passed in 1961, the prefectures were to be decentralized, autonomous units competent to deal with local issues. Governing the prefecture was to be a general council whose members, representing local interests, were to be elected by slates for five-year terms by universal suffrage within the prefecture. The general council was to pass a budget and act on local issues. Its decisions were then to be passed on to the prefect for execution. In reality, as of 1988 the central government in Abidjan had not passed the enabling measures establishing the general councils; hence, the prefectures were exclusively administrative structures.

Every prefecture was segmented into subprefectures, each headed by a subprefect (*sous-préfet*). Subprefectures were the lowest administrative unit of government and the unit with which most people interacted. Unlike the prefectures, the subprefectures had neither autonomy nor deliberative responsibilities; their function was purely administrative. The subprefects acted under the delegated authority of the prefects but also had other responsibilities. First and foremost, the subprefect was responsible for maintaining public order and could, in emergencies, request aid from the prefect or the armed forces. The subprefect also submitted a public works and civil action program as well as a budget to the prefect. As an officer of the state, the subprefect supervised the census and elections within the subprefecture and officiated at civil ceremonies. He also monitored, albeit loosely, the behavior of chiefs of villages and cantons (see Glossary) within the boundaries of the subprefecture and represented the authority of the central government to local populations. Finally, the subprefect elicited from notables living within the subprefecture a list of grievances or suggestions that was passed on to the prefect.

Administration at the subprefecture level included a secretariat consisting of the various administrative services and divisions in the subprefecture. Assisting the subprefect was the Subprefectural Council, which replaced the council of notables, an artifact of the colonial era. This council was composed of the subprefect, the heads of public services represented in the subprefecture, local party officials, and twelve to sixteen private citizens, all residing in the subprefecture and known for their active participation in affairs pertaining to politics, commerce, and social change. The councils met twice yearly in open sessions under the direction of the subprefect. The council's responsibilities were solely consultative. At the first meeting of the year, the subprefect was obligated to present to the council the budget and accounts of the past year. By law the council had to be consulted on expenditures allocated to the subprefecture by the government or collected in the form of market, parking, or other fees. The council also submitted a program of public works or other public projects of local interest to be financed with the allocated funds.

The council had no decision-making authority and no direct political role. However, its opinions carried some weight. The citizen-members represented wealth and influence that often transcended the physical boundaries of the subprefecture. These citizens often understood the needs and customs of the local community better than the subprefect, who in most instances was not from the region.

Modern and traditional governance merged at the level of village and canton. Using criteria based on traditions, villages selected their own leaders, who were subsequently proposed to and formally invested by the prefect. The ceremony granted formal legitimacy to the village leader while at the same time confirming his status as subordinate to the subprefect. In the formal bureaucratic sector, village chiefs served simply as conduits between the subprefect and the villagers. Informally, village chiefs filled a multitude of roles, many of which paralleled the obligations and responsibilities of the modern bureaucratic administration. Under the colonial regime, groups of villages linked by common ethnicity and encompassing a relatively large area were designated a canton; this designation continued into the modern period. Canton chiefs, whose authority was also rooted in tradition, were selected according to traditional norms and formally appointed by the minister of interior. Because their responsibilities in the formal sector were never resolved, the canton chiefs remained largely symbolic figures.

By the 1980s, thirty-seven cities had been designated autonomous communities (*communes en plein exercice*), a legal status that dates from 1884 and applied originally to the Senegalese cities of Saint

155

Louis and Dakar. Governing structures in autonomous communities included a municipal council and a mayor. A council would be composed of eleven to thirty-seven members, depending on the population of the city. All were elected by universal suffrage and, until 1980, as part of a slate. In the 1985 elections, council members ran independently. The legal status of the municipal councils was ambiguous. According to law, they enjoyed broad powers which were to be exercised independently of the granting authority in Abidjan. For example, the enabling legislation of 1955 instructed the councils, through their deliberative processes, to "direct the affairs of the community," which included voting on budgets. In fact, most of the decisions taken by councils first had to be approved by the minister of interior, who could veto them. Moreover, the Council of Ministers could dissolve an excessively independent municipal council by a simple decree. Consequently, the council members routinely accepted guidelines proposed by authorities in Abidjan.

The councils also elected mayors, whose functions were identical to those of subprefects. Like the municipal councils, mayors routinely submitted to the authority of the minister of interior.

In practice, municipal administration was not an outgrowth of a preexisting social and political institution. The label "autonomous communities" was, instead, the creation of a state bureaucracy that was not inclined toward sharing power. Consequently, from 1956 until the late 1970s, councils shrank in size and importance as council members died. For example, the Abidjan council, which at one point consisted of thirty-seven members, had only seventeen in 1974. As the central government loosened its grip on politics prior to the 1985 elections, potential candidates saw the position of municipal council member as a first step toward higher political office, and interest in the institution grew. In the 1985 election, more than 840 candidates ran for 235 places on municipal councils.

Actual Power

The Party

The trappings of political power were concentrated in a single party, the PDCI, to which all adult citizens were required to belong. The principal goal of the party was stability, and compared with parties in other sub-Saharan states, it had achieved its objective. By and large, political conflict took place within constitutional bounds. To continue that tradition in the 1980s, the government expanded political participation and discouraged political—and especially ideological—competition. The party embraced what it defined as centrist policies, and although Ivoirian citizens did not enjoy democratic freedoms in the Western tradition, foreign observers considered Ivoirian society among the freest in Africa.

Party membership was synonymous with citizenship. At its inception and during the late stages of colonial rule, the party was a broad coalition, less nationalist than nativist, and calling itself populist, consultative, and representative. At that time, the PDCI enjoyed considerable grass-roots support, especially on issues pertaining to forced labor and the *indigénat* (see Glossary; Colonial Administration, ch. 1). After independence, however, the party came under increasingly tight presidential control. Instead of political mobilization, the government demanded of the citizenry what Philippe Yacé called "active acquiescence." The party leaders closest to the president, almost all of whom had been plantation owners, wielded great power in their home (ethnic) constituencies, where they were able to influence the distribution of patronage in the form of public and party offices, contracts, public works, and other benefits. This enabled them to increase their own wealth and further secure their positions in the political system. Over time, patronage supplanted political organization, and many local PDCI committees in rural areas withered.

In the 1980s, with the anticolonialist struggles long over and the era of Houphouët-Boigny and his fellow political militants waning, the party continued to lose its vitality. The party's dated preoccupation with unity deflected attention from the pressing issues in Côte d'Ivoire. Economic development demanded greater technological sophistication and gave rise to conflicts pitting cities against the rural periphery and young against old. Incrementally, technocrats and developmentalists with modern Western values replaced party militants in the government bureaucracy. The new elite did not challenge the militants, who continued to dole out party offices, nor did they insist that the government become more democratic or less authoritarian. The new elite simply had different concerns: government rather than the party and bureaucratic rationality rather than party mobilization.

Without the infusion of competing ideas, the party atrophied as a creative political force. To be sure, the governing elite remained members of the party; however, as the state became more complex and bureaucratized, the distinction between party and state blurred. The government and not the party assumed responsibility for national integration. By the late 1980s, the party served primarily as a sinecure for old party stalwarts, and the PDCI administration became a vehicle for self-advancement and the protection of narrow interests. That situation was not entirely true in the case of party activities at village levels where, reversing an earlier trend, the position of party secretary (the local party representative) became an openly contested electoral office. Increasingly, political neophytes viewed the office as an initial step to higher office, and so they invested resources in campaigns and tried to fulfill their campaign obligations.

Party Organization

In the late 1980s, power lay in the Political Bureau and Committee Directorate. Like the National Assembly, both were expanded in the mid-1980s in an attempt to broaden the PDCI's representation among educated people between the ages of thirty-five and forty-five. The Political Bureau was expanded from 35 to 58 members, and the Committee Directorate grew from 100 to 208.

The members of the Political Bureau included the cabinet ministers, plus other members of the political, military, and business elite. Heading the Political Bureau was a thirteen-member Executive Committee, which in 1980 replaced the party secretary general at the apex of the party. (The transition from a single leader to a committee in fact appeared to constitute a calculated rebuff to Philippe Yacé, who was PDCI secretary general at the time.) By the mid-1980s, the Executive Committee was composed exclusively of younger cabinet ministers, thereby excluding many long-time political allies of the president.

Major policy decisions affecting the party and state originated in the Political Bureau. (The Political Bureau would probably be responsible for nominating a successor should the president, as seemed to be the case in 1988, decline to do so prior to leaving office.) Political divisions and alliances within the Political Bureau thus assumed great importance. The most apparent division was a generational one pitting old party stalwarts such as Mathieu Ekra, Auguste Denise, Camille Alliali, and Philippe Yacé against ambitious young technocrats such as Henri Konan Bedié, Jean Jacques Bechio, Balla Keita, and Alphonse Djedje Mady. Within the second group were equally significant divisions between the aforementioned Young Turks and other well-educated specialists such as Laurent Dona Fologo and Donwahi Charles, who were known as team players.

The Committee Directorate represented a further attempt to incorporate—some would say co-opt—larger segments of the population, especially potential foci of opposition, into the political process. Another purpose of the directorate was to invigorate the

President Félix Houphouët-Boigny
Courtesy Embassy of Côte d'Ivoire, Washington

party by expanding its representation. Accordingly, the Committee Directorate included members of the judicial, executive, and legislative branches of the government, current and former military officers, leaders of government-backed unions, women, business leaders, and members of the professions, including university professors. It functioned by advising the president through a series of ad hoc committees addressing particular issues.

In the smaller cities, towns, and villages, the party official with whom most Ivoirians dealt was the local secretary general. As their principal task, all secretaries general sold party membership cards, the revenues from which funded local political operations. In larger constituencies, the secretary general served as a spokesperson and propagandist for the government by placing the symbols and slogans of governance before the voting public. In rural constituencies, the local secretary general settled disputes generally involving land tenure and land use.

Orientation Toward the Political System

Starting with independence, the Ivoirian polity experienced an unusual reorientation of political and moral values not found elsewhere in most of sub-Saharan Africa. Strong economic growth (at least through the mid-1970s) and relatively high rates of urbanization and literacy, in combination with a pervasive media, have exposed the polity to Western cultural values and the politics of consumption. In few other countries was materialism as open and avowed an ideology as in Côte d'Ivoire. Consequently, the salient divisions in the Ivoirian polity were economic rather than ethnic or religious. Stratification by class was congruent with the fundamental difference between rulers and ruled. In many instances, class differences also coincided with ethnic divisions, which tended to exaggerate the importance of ethnicity while permitting some observers to diminish the importance of class membership. This was no new phenomenon—the same stratification characterized most precolonial societies in Côte d'Ivoire. Nevertheless, the expanded opportunities for material consumption and the manifest extremes of wealth and poverty that subsequently emerged were new. Members of the elite translated the struggle for independence into a quest for privilege. They insisted that the interests of all Ivoirians were in harmony, a supposition that allowed them to rationalize the use of public policy on their behalf. For their part, the have-nots not only envied the elite for its material attainments but also knew how the elite, using the political system, attained them. So while rich and poor—the rulers and the ruled—nurtured vastly different expectations of the political system, they shared a clear understanding of its ultimate purpose.

Historically, the political elite included the wealthiest 10 percent of the plantation owners. By the late 1980s, however, with the bureaucratization of the state, the nature of the elite had changed markedly. Most often its members were high-level bureaucrats and party officials. Simultaneously, and as a direct consequence of their political connections, many held directorships in locally based corporations or were minority shareholders in multinational corporations. Characteristically, the businesses in which members of the elite invested required relatively small investments in comparison with anticipated returns. That situation was especially common in real estate, where investors typically sought a full return on investment within three years. Another industry favored by the elite was transportation. Finally, some members of the elite invested in agriculture, exporting bananas and pineapples, the prices of which, unlike the prices of coffee and cocoa, were not regulated by the government.

Significantly, the elite was not a true entrepreneurial class; that is, its members, with few exceptions, did not save and invest capital. Rather, they created a favorable environment for schemes initiated by foreigners and subsequently mediated (for a fee) among bureaucracy, business, and politicians. Instead of investing, the elite consumed. Its members sent their offspring to France for at least part of their education. They became accustomed to imported food, clothing, and high-technology consumer goods. Perhaps most important, the elite nurtured—and in turn sought—legitimacy in an ethos that openly elevated materialism to the level of political and moral ideology. According to one observer, the elite became, in effect, a class that could not afford to lose power.

To sustain its position of privilege, the elite formulated a political strategy based on limited participation and the politics of co-optation to vent the pressures linked to rapid change. Thus, with independence the government banned any opposition political parties or voices, incorporated nearly all unions into the party, and handpicked National Assembly candidates who then ran on a slate presented to voters who either cast a ''yea'' ballot or did not vote. Even after the government permitted contested elections for the assembly, the party, acting as surrogate for the government, passed on the acceptability of all candidates. Similarly, the indigenous private sector was unable to compete with the vast resources that the elite-dominated public sector could marshall and effectively was excluded from participating in economic transformation.

Appreciative of the importance of political stability, the government ostensibly compromised by permitting small changes for the sake of order. Nevertheless, none of the demands for change, which in the past may have included pay raises, better working conditions, scholarship aid, or improved relations between groups, required a substantial change in governing institutions or procedures, and they were generally co-opted by Houphouët-Boigny's expressions of concern and the appointment of a commission to study the problem. Finally, the government bought compliance from its more articulate and therefore more serious critics by offering them resources such as land, licenses, forestry rights, or positions in the party and government.

Counterpoised to the modern elite were the peasantry, students, middle- and lower-level civil servants, and a growing urban underclass. Because of explicit public policy decisions, few members of that group benefited directly from Côte d'Ivoire's vaunted economic growth. This group was no less politicized than the elite, but it lacked avenues of expression. Accordingly, this underclass responded to restrictions either by refusing to participate in the political process or by challenging public policy. Nonparticipation was generally a rural phenomenon, and in some areas less than 40 percent of eligible voters cast ballots in the 1985 elections, in which Houphouët-Boigny boasted of having received more than 99 percent of the vote. Challenges to public policy took the form of riots against unemployment, student protests, and demonstrations against high prices, shrinking subsidies, land confiscation, foreigners, and high taxes (see Internal Dissent and Further Consolidation of Power, ch. 1; Internal Security, ch. 5). The government customarily responded to conflict with force followed by a demand for loyalty to the ruling regime. Groups demonstrating their political support received benefits in the form of clinics, schools, investment in infrastructure, markets, and other public facilities. Conversely, those withholding support were simply denied any resources for economic development.

Interest Groups and National Politics
Political Issues

The party-government in the mid-1980s most closely resembled an old-fashioned political machine. Although it called itself a one-party democracy, Côte d'Ivoire was not a political democracy in the Western sense. There was no institutionalized opposition, although by the 1980s National Assembly elections were being contested. As under the French, civil liberties remained limited.

Although Côte d'Ivoire appeared to be a country of laws, those laws were tailored to suit a set of rulers who could easily alter the laws at their discretion.

By the end of the 1980s, the Ivoirian political system was facing serious problems. Because the structure, form, tone, and policies of the government were the personal creations of the president, who was said to be in his late eighties, the succession question had substantial implications. Moreover, no candidate enjoyed the charisma or stature of Houphouët-Boigny. In 1988 rivals seeking to succeed Houphouët-Boigny barely maintained any pretense of unity. No plausible candidate—with the possible exception of Yacé—had the experience or preparation necessary to assume the office.

By the late 1980s, two decades of rapid economic growth followed by serious economic setbacks had transformed social mores and altered civil society. Students and teachers were protesting the continuing control of government by a small number of party leaders for the benefit of a privileged class of landowners and bureaucrats. Corruption in the business community was becoming embarrassingly obvious, particularly among textile importers. Uncontrolled urbanization had weakened family ties and had prompted sharp increases in unemployment, underemployment, drug use, and violent crime. (see Crime and Punishment, ch. 5). On a different plane, economic austerity had abruptly curtailed the rising expectations of the middle class and pitted ethnic groups against one another in the competition for scarce resources.

Economic austerity also exacerbated tensions between Ivoirians and resident foreign nationals. Students and members of the political elite expressed resentment over the continuing presence of French nationals in important government positions. Ivoirian wage laborers resented competition from immigrants from Côte d'Ivoire's poorer neighbors. Dramatic increases in violent crime were attributed to Ghanaians and business corruption to the Lebanese.

Perhaps more important, the governing institutions created by Houphouët-Boigny to mediate conflict were weak and unresponsive. That was especially true of the state-owned media, which carefully managed information by releasing only what it deemed harmless. Consequently, rumors often passed for news on the streets of Abidjan.

Single-Party Democracy

Since independence, Ivoirian leaders had insisted that the PDCI have no opposition, although Article 7 of the Ivoirian Constitution specifically guarantees freedom of expression to "parties and political groups'' as long as they respect the principles of ''democracy and national sovereignty.'' At one time, some political leaders had argued for a legal—but constrained—opposition to generate enthusiasm for elections and to vent political pressures that might otherwise threaten the position of the governing elite. A recognized opposition, it was argued, would also provide Côte d'Ivoire with some of the forms—as opposed to the pretenses already in place—of democracy. However, the ruling elite and even some dissidents continued to believe that a single-party system was best for a developing country like Côte d'Ivoire, where class and regional cleavages threatened unity.

Houphouët-Boigny himself had always considered forging a national constituency out of Côte d'Ivoire's more than sixty ethnic groups to be his greatest responsibility if his economic agenda was to be achieved. If unchecked, he said, rivalry among ethnic groups or geographical regions would erode nationalism and dissipate valuable resources that would be better spent on economic development. Left unstated was the concern that this rivalry also would threaten the ruling elite's control over crucial aspects of political life. National unity therefore came to mean party unity. There was room for opposition, Houphouët-Boigny insisted, but only within the party. Thus, in the early years of independence Houphouët-Boigny promulgated laws that severely sanctioned individuals who published, disseminated, divulged, or reproduced false news or documents that, in good or bad faith, ''undermined'' the morale of the population, discredited political institutions, or led others to disobey laws. With virtually all avenues for criticism closed, platitudes replaced political debate.

Although generally successful at co-opting political foes, Houphouët-Boigny was not averse to bullying his opponents when he felt they threatened stability. He stated on several occasions that if forced to choose between disorder and injustice, he would not hesitate to choose injustice. He added that ''When there is disorder, the lives of people and a regime are at stake, but an injustice can always be corrected.'' Nonetheless, he resorted to force only rarely (see Consolidation of Power, ch. 1). Côte d'Ivoire had no preventive detention laws and, by its own definition, no political prisoners, although the army, under instructions from Houphouët-Boigny, commonly conscripted political foes into the military for what he called ''judicious training.''

Succession

By early 1988, Houphouët-Boigny had given no indication of when he might resign. However, there were increasingly clear signs that his control, like his health, was slipping. To avoid the kind of damaging and embarrassing circumstances that surrounded the political demise of Tunisian leader Habib Bourguiba, who in 1987 was declared unfit to govern, senior members of the PDCI pressed Houphouët-Boigny to step down. In early 1988, observers reported that Houphouët-Boigny might heed their advice to retire by year's end, although he intended to remain as head of the PDCI. Presumably, he would then be able to lend his authority to his successor and thereby prevent an acrimonious struggle among potential contenders in the presidential election that, according to the Constitution, would shortly follow.

Article 11 of the Ivoirian Constitution, amended on October 12, 1985, states that if the office of the presidency is vacated by death, resignation, or incapacitation as attested by the Supreme Court, the functions of the president shall be performed on a provisional basis by the president of the National Assembly. After at least forty-five but no more than sixty days, elections will determine the new leader, who may also have been the provisional president. As president of the Assembly, Henri Konan Bedié appeared to have an advantage over his potential rivals, including Yacé. At the same time, Yacé appeared to have a larger following in the PDCI Political Bureau, where the ultimate decision would be made if there was to be a single, unanimous choice by the party. Much of Yacé's popularity derived from his years of faithful service to state and party. As younger Ivoirians replaced older party stalwarts in the government and party, Yacé's support would diminish and that of Bedié, his chief rival, would grow.

By mid-1988 Houphouët-Boigny had avoided naming or even suggesting a successor, reportedly believing that were he to do so, party loyalty would split between the heir apparent and other candidates, his own power would shrink, and the successor he selected would immediately become the target of political criticism. Consequently, the president allowed the political process to take its course, which led to a standoff between Bedié and Yacé, the two leading candidates. Houphouët-Boigny's decision to allow politics to determine the choice also demonstrated his belief that the Ivoirian polity was sufficiently mature to pursue its own interests without recklessly endangering the system.

Meanwhile, the succession debate continued. Many Ivoirians stressed the importance of choosing a member of a minority ethnic group as a compromise acceptable to the Baoulé, Bété, Krou, Sénoufo, and Mandé groups (see Ethnic Groups and Languages, ch. 2). Others stressed the importance of choosing an elder statesman, thus avoiding a possible crisis of confidence should a younger,

165

less experienced leader be named. Still others insisted that choosing a young, educated technocrat was the only way to resolve the country's daunting economic and social problems.

Equity Issues and Ethnic Tensions

Houphouët-Boigny inherited the political apparatus of the nation-state but by 1988 had not yet forged bonds uniting citizens of diverse ethnicity to one another or to their leaders. Houphouët-Boigny had dealt with ethnic conflict by denouncing ethnocentrism as a legitimate issue and by the time-tested strategy of co-opting the leadership of potentially dissident ethnic groups by incorporating them in the party or governmental bureaucracy. Thus, for example, from the mid-1970s the Sénoufo in the north were overrepresented in the army, and southern peoples were overrepresented in the police and National Gendarmerie (Gendarmerie Nationale). Meanwhile, Houphouët-Boigny invariably appointed as his minister of defense a member of the Baoulé, who were also overrepresented in the National Security Police (Sûreté Nationale), and appointed a Bété chief of staff of the army.

Ivoirianization

From time to time, the replacement of French workers with Ivoirians became a political issue. Popular resentment of the French presence, particularly as the competence of Ivoirians increased, emerged periodically in the form of student strikes and anonymous political tracts. Especially irksome to many Ivoirians were the highly paid French counterparts to Ivoirian cabinet ministers; however, in the late 1980s most of the approximately 30,000 French workers were in the private sector, where they held the majority of all jobs requiring postsecondary education. Some also worked in middle-level white-collar and blue-collar jobs. There were, for example, French citizens working at tasks for which their qualifications in no way distinguished them from Ivoirian employees but who nonetheless received substantially higher salaries. Throughout the country, there were French mechanics, foremen, plantation owners, storekeepers, clerical workers, and supervisors. French women filled many of the top secretarial positions and thus became special targets of nationalist resentment (see The French, this ch.).

Most controversial in the 1980s was Houphouët-Boigny's appointment of Antoine Cesareo to head a newly created superagency to control government waste. Cesareo was a French national with a reputation as an incorruptible and efficient public servant. The Public Works Authority (Direction et Contrôle des Grands Travaux—DCGTX), which Cesareo headed under the direct control

of Houphouët-Boigny, supervised virtually all government contracts and construction projects. By 1987 Cesareo claimed that he had overseen some US$3.3 billion in contracts and, by avoiding delays and overruns, had saved the Ivoirian government US$2.6 billion. However, he also irritated many within the Ivoirian political establishment, one of whom anonymously pointed out that Côte d'Ivoire was the only country in Africa to accord a foreigner a stranglehold over local finances.

Government Responses

As serious as these challenges appeared, processes were in place to lessen their impact. For example, the political system loosened perceptibly as opponents of Houphouët-Boigny were co-opted and as the ruling elite's interests in the status quo became more deeply entrenched. By the late 1980s, there were mechanisms—if only rudimentary—for publicly registering disagreement. In 1980, for the first time, Houphouët-Boigny permitted open elections to the National Assembly. Voters promptly replaced sixty-three of the ninety incumbents seeking reelection. In 1985 open elections were expanded to include local party and municipal offices as well as assembly seats. (That time, voters rejected 90 of 117 candidates seeking reelection to the National Assembly.) Other avenues for expressing dissent also opened. In 1987 the state began broadcasting

167

two controversial and popular shows: one featured political debate, albeit over carefully limited questions; and the other, political satire. Observers construed those measures as part of a continuing if cautious process leading to a more mature, democratic political culture. Moreover, the government appeared at least to have the support of important opinion makers. In contrast to the populations of all of its West African neighbors who, in a mid-1970s poll taken of its readers by *Jeune Afrique,* preferred an ambiguous socialism for their economic future, almost 50 percent of the magazine's Ivoirian readers—who were probably on the left of the political spectrum—favored an equally ambiguous capitalism.

Interest Groups

Labor

In the 1980s, approximately 100,000 full-time workers in the regulated sectors belonged to trade unions. Union membership was highest among white-collar workers, professionals, civil servants, and teachers. All unions except the National Union of Secondary School Teachers of Côte d'Ivoire (Syndicat National des Enseignants du Secondaire de Côte d'Ivoire—SYNESCI) were part of a government-controlled federation, the General Federation of Ivoirian Workers (Union Générale des Travailleurs de Côte d'Ivoire— UGTCI), which counted approximately 190 affiliates. Its secretary general from its founding until 1984 was Joseph Coffie, a veteran of the PDCI and trusted companion of President Houphouët-Boigny. In 1988 the secretary general was Hyacinthe Adiko Niamkey.

From its inception, the UGTCI saw itself as a participant in development rather than a combatant on behalf of labor. In that role, the UGTCI supported government efforts to promote unity and development, justifying its stance as helping to continue the struggle for independence. The UGTCI did not object to the state's development policies, and its leaders participated in government policy debates, thereby becoming, in effect, instruments of economic development.

Not surprisingly, the UGTCI exercised little political or economic clout. Strikes were legal, but principals first had to complete a lengthy process of negotiation, during which any work stoppage was illegal. Moreover, demands on its members by UGTCI leadership seeking more efficient production counted more than workers' complaints. At the same time, the UGTCI exercised a modicum of autonomy in protests over wages and the pace of Ivoirianization. In response, the guaranteed urban minimum wage had been raised several times since the mid-1970s. However, wages were not keeping pace with inflation.

Wildcat strikes or other unsanctioned job actions were not much more productive. In dealing with job actions, the government first exploited the media to gain sympathy for its position and then confronted strike leaders with overwhelming force. Usually the government softened its position by rehiring most of the workers previously dismissed and by compromising on peripheral matters. Underlying problems remained unresolved or were settled in accordance with government intentions. In 1985, after 16,892 parastatal workers, many of whom were highly paid professionals, staged a job action to protest deep wage cuts, the government threatened to fire all workers who refused to honor the government's deadline and to replace them with unemployed university graduates. Eventually the government fired 342 holdouts. At other times, the government dissolved the refractory union, thus depriving any strike of legitimacy and the union of any recourse.

Military

The Ivoirian armed forces consisted of three services, all small and lightly equipped (see Constitutional, Legal, and Administrative Structure, ch. 5). With the exception of military training exercises and a small, regional revolt in 1970, as of mid-1988 the military had remained in its barracks. It played no role in domestic peacekeeping, in the drive for modernization, or in mobilizing the population. Unlike its counterpart in neighboring states, the Ivoirian officer corps viewed itself as a distinct profession under civilian control. The presence of a French battalion based near Port Bouët reinforced the importance of maintaining professional norms of service. Moreover, Houphouët-Boigny kept military salaries attractive and named officers to high positions in the PDCI, in effect assimilating the military elite. Greater contact between the civilian elite and military officers led to social integration and completed the co-optation of the military. With a solid stake in the "Ivoirian miracle," the senior officer corps had little interest in altering the status quo. With the passage of time, psychological inertia further institutionalized civilian control, and the civil bureaucracy gained experience, expertise, and confidence.

Many events had the potential to precipitate future military intervention in domestic politics. These would include a stalemate in the Political Bureau of the PDCI over a successor to Houphouët-Boigny, the emergence of an incompetent administration, extreme economic austerity coupled with a declining franc, and widespread

169

unrest led or supported by students, unions, or the urban unemployed. As an institution with an untainted past, the military could, in any of these cases, be called upon to lead a movement promising a return to stability and greater access to economic resources for less favored groups. Nevertheless, given the broadening base of the party, the politics of co-optation, the as yet inchoate class struggle, and the division of peacekeeping responsibility among the Sûreté Nationale and the armed forces, most observers agreed that government control over the military would probably continue.

The French

Côte d'Ivoire's ties to France had grown stronger since independence in 1960. Although the number of French advisers continued to shrink, between 1960 and 1980 the total French population in Côte d'Ivoire nearly doubled, from about 30,000 to close to 60,000, forming the largest French expatriate community. By 1988, as Côte d'Ivoire's economy continued to contract, about half of the French either returned to France or moved elsewhere in Africa. In the mid-1980s, four out of five resident French had lived in Côte d'Ivoire for more than five years. French citizens filled technical and advisory positions in the government, albeit in diminishing numbers, but were also evident throughout the private sector. Until 1985 Côte d'Ivoire also had the highest number of teaching and nonteaching French *coopérants* (see Glossary) in Africa, the highest number of students in French universities, the highest number of French multinationals in all of Africa, the largest percentage of French imports and exports in Africa, the highest number of nonroutine French diplomatic visitors of all African countries, and, with Senegal, was the recipient of the largest French aid package in Africa. Côte d'Ivoire also hosted the highest average number of visits by the French head of state per year.

On a formal level, a series of agreements and treaties have ensured the continuation and extension of French influence in diplomatic, military, legal, commercial, monetary, political, and cultural affairs, although most of these agreements were modified over the years to accommodate the sensitivities and growing political sophistication of Ivoirians. Perhaps most significant for the future were joint defense treaties and the permanent basing of the French marine battalion at Port Bouët. Although it had never interceded in Ivoirian politics, the battalion's presence provided an implicit warning against political or military action that might create instability and jeopardize French interests. The colonial heritage and contemporary realities suggested that France would remain Côte d'Ivoire's principal commercial partner, albeit in increasing competition with other states.

The Levantine Community

In the late 1980s, reportedly 60,000 to 120,000 Lebanese and Syrians lived in Côte d'Ivoire, although some observers gave a figure as high as 300,000. Many descended from families that had been established in Côte d'Ivoire for more than a century. Along with the French, they were the most easily identifiable foreign group. They generally resided in enclaves, married within their community, and resisted integration. At the same time, many held Ivoirian citizenship. Although they were concentrated in Abidjan, there was a Lebanese or Syrian family or two in virtually every community of more than 5,000 people. Some members of the Levantine community were Christian; of the Muslims, most were Shia. Significantly, the waves of Lebanese émigrés who arrived in Côte d'Ivoire after the Lebanese civil war began in 1975 brought with them the same political beliefs that divided groups in Lebanon. As of the mid-1980s, violence among Lebanese had not erupted in Côte d'Ivoire; nevertheless, the government considered sectarian violence a distinct possibility.

The Arab community was known for its entrepreneurial skills and had long played a leading role in certain intermediate sectors of the economy, especially commerce. The Arabs dominated in areas such as textiles, shoes, petroleum distribution, and coffee and cocoa brokering. The Lebanese had also invested heavily in urban real estate and were among the first to develop hotels and restaurants in previously less accessible areas of the interior. For the most part, Houphouët-Boigny ardently defended the presence of the Lebanese community, citing its contributions to the Ivoirian economy. The Lebanese community, in turn, sought to assure the Ivoirian leadership of its loyalty and its commitment to national goals by public declarations and by charitable contributions in support of cultural and sporting events.

The jump in the Levantine population since 1975, coupled with its growing domination of commerce, made it a target of increasing protest. In the mid-1980s, Houphouët-Boigny began issuing warnings to merchants—unmistakably Lebanese—who were allegedly guilty of customs fraud and monopolistic practices. Thus, the unconditional welcome that the Lebanese community had enjoyed appeared to be wearing out.

Students and Intellectuals

Student radicalism has had a long history in francophone Africa. It originated in post-World War II France, where most students from the colonies studied. Students favored independence long before Houphouët-Boigny and the PDCI lobbied for it, and neither the president nor the party escaped student criticism. In 1988 students were generally concerned with scholarships, student aid, and housing, although they were also the most outspoken group in the nation on the issues of succession, Ivoirianization, and one-party democracy.

The PDCI sought to control student dissent by co-optation or outright repression. It placed the Movement of Primary and Secondary School Students of Côte d'Ivoire (Mouvement des Etudiants et Elèves de Côte d'Ivoire—MEECI), the official student organization, under the umbrella of the PDCI, and, when necessary, the government impressed student leaders into the army. Typically, however, the government followed repression with clemency, and then sought to co-opt student leaders. In 1988 no fewer than four former MEECI presidents were members of the PDCI Executive Committee.

In the 1980s, Laurent Gbagbo gained recognition as the intellectual leader of an incipient movement seeking a more open political system. A historian living in exile, Gbagbo was Côte d'Ivoire's best known opposition figure. In two books, which were banned in Côte d'Ivoire, Gbagbo attacked the PDCI regime as conspiratorial, opportunistic, and corrupt. He was involved in disturbances at the National University of Côte d'Ivoire (formerly the University of Abidjan) in 1982, after which he fled to Paris. There he founded an opposition party, the Ivoirian People's Front (Front Populaire Ivoirien—FPI), which called for a multiparty democracy. Although the FPI had no formal membership, it gained a small following in Abidjan among students, intellectuals, civil servants, and some unions.

Foreign Relations

Houphouët-Boigny treated foreign policy as his personal domain. Following independence, his long-term foreign policy objective had been to enhance economic development and political stability in Côte d'Ivoire. That objective was manifested in foreign policies that sought, first, to maintain an organic relationship with France, Côte d'Ivoire's principal and most consistent donor and, second, to control the regional environment in order to guarantee access to cheap labor from Mali and Burkina Faso.

Although Côte d'Ivoire eschewed close links with the Soviet Union and its allies, Ivoirian policymakers were nominally disposed toward treating all foreign powers equally. One former minister of foreign affairs insisted that Côte d'Ivoire was the foe of no ideology or any regime. Nevertheless, Côte d'Ivoire had no diplomatic ties with the Soviet Union from 1969, when relations with Moscow were severed, until February 1986. Only a month earlier, the cabinet had approved a measure to reestablish ties with Czechoslovakia, Hungary, Albania, the German Democratic Republic (East Germany), and the People's Democratic Republic of Korea (North Korea). Relations with Romania and Poland had already been reestablished several years earlier.

Closer to its borders, Côte d'Ivoire alternatively befriended or attempted to isolate the rulers of the five states that surrounded it: Liberia, Guinea, Mali, Burkina Faso, and Ghana. Recognizing that "the oasis never encroaches upon the desert," Houphouët-Boigny sought to cultivate mutually beneficial ties with these five states, while allowing economic and political differences to persist. Military leaders in the neighboring states allowed their nationals to enter the Ivoirian labor pool, which eased a serious unemployment problem in their respective countries. Through the Council of the Entente (Conseil de l'Entente), in which Côte d'Ivoire is by far the dominant power and largest contributor, the Ivoirians aided Burkina Faso, Niger, Benin, and Togo. Houphouët-Boigny also scored a diplomatic triumph in 1985 when he brokered a peace agreement ending the border conflict between Burkina Faso and Mali. Houphouët-Boigny also facilitated Guinea's return to the franc zone.

Foreign Relations and the Council of the Entente

The Council of the Entente was established on May 29, 1959, by the heads of state of Côte d'Ivoire, Upper Volta (present-day Burkina Faso), Dahomey (present-day Benin), and Niger. (Togo became a member in 1966.) Ostensibly, the Council of the Entente coordinated the regulations and statutes of member states governing finance, justice, labor, public service, health, and communications. The Council of the Entente also initiated steps toward forming a customs union, integrating development plans, and creating a development fund, the Solidarity Fund (later known as the Loan Guaranty Fund). Each member state was to contribute 10 percent of government revenues to the fund. Côte d'Ivoire, the leader of the Council of the Entente and by far the wealthiest member state, was to receive only a small portion of the redistributed funds; other members were entitled to larger shares. In fact, by 1988 Côte d'Ivoire had never touched its share.

The Council of the Entente helped Houphouët-Boigny achieve his long-term regional foreign policy objectives. First, by allying himself with three desperately poor countries that could be expected to maintain close ties with France for years to come, he built a broader base to counter Senegal's attempts to isolate Côte d'Ivoire and reestablish some sort of federation of West African francophone states that would presumably be centered at Dakar. The demise of the Mali Federation in 1960 appeared to vindicate Houphouët-Boigny's strategy (see Reform and the French Community, ch. 1). He subsequently enlisted the Council of the Entente states to isolate the government of Ghana, which had supported a massive anti-government protest in the Sanwi area of Côte d'Ivoire and was linked to a plot to overthrow Niger's President Hamani Diori. After Ghana's President Kwame Nkrumah was ousted in a 1966 coup, Houphouët-Boigny sought diplomatic support from the Council of the Entente states in his feud with President Ahmed Sekou Touré of Guinea. Sekou Touré routinely accused Houphouët-Boigny of harboring Guinean exiles; he also threatened to send troops across Côte d'Ivoire to Ghana to restore Nkrumah, by then a refugee in Guinea, to power.

By the mid-1980s, populist and nationalist sentiments surging within the Council of the Entente member states threatened Côte d'Ivoire's staid leadership of the alliance. Togo, which was surrounded by radical states, remained a staunch ally; however, Burkina Faso and Benin increasingly criticized Houphouët-Boigny's conservativism and strengthened their ties with Libya and Ghana. As a result, the Council of the Entente's value as an instrument of Ivoirian foreign policy diminished.

Relations with Ghana, Burkina Faso, Guinea, and Mali

The tone of Ivoirian-Ghanaian relations had varied widely since independence. Côte d'Ivoire regarded the government of Flight Lieutenant Jerry Rawlings, who overthrew a civilian regime in 1983, with a mixture of disdain, contempt, and wariness. Relations with Ghana declined in the mid-1980s after Rawlings and Burkina Faso's leader Thomas Sankara appeared to ally themselves with Libyan leader Muammar al Qadhafi. In November 1987, Ghana condemned Côte d'Ivoire for granting landing rights to South African military and commercial aircraft, championing the Zionist cause in Africa, undermining Organization of African Unity (OAU) resolutions, isolating Burkina Faso in West African councils, and permitting Abidjan to become a haven for hostile South African, Israeli, and Western intelligence services. At the same time, the two states worked together harmoniously to end smuggling in both directions across their common border.

Relations with Burkina Faso, a traditional source of agricultural labor, were historically cordial, but they degenerated sharply in the wake of the coup that brought Thomas Sankara to power in

August 1983. Sankara soon made common cause with the Raw-lings government in Ghana, further raising suspicions in Abidjan. Following Libyan deliveries of military equipment to Burkina Faso, Ivoirian authorities investigated alleged arms trafficking between Burkina Faso and Côte d'Ivoire.

Tensions between Côte d'Ivoire and Burkina Faso increased sharply in early 1985 following the alleged mistreatment of Bur-kinabé immigrants in Côte d'Ivoire and the assassination of a prominent Burkinabé businessman in Abidjan. In September 1985, hours before Sankara was to arrive in Côte d'Ivoire for a Council of the Entente summit meeting, a bomb exploded in a hotel room he was to occupy. Sankara blamed forces in Côte d'Ivoire, although no one claimed responsibility and no one was arrested. In defi-ance of other Council of the Entente members, Sankara refused to sign the summit communiqué, rejected the expansion of the En-tente charter to include security cooperation, indirectly accused Côte d'Ivoire and Togo of victimizing resident Burkinabé and shelter-ing opponents to his regime, and called for the creation of an inter-nationalist and populist "Revolutionary Entente Council." Two years later, in October 1987, Sankara was killed during a coup led by his second in command, Captain Blaise Compaoré. Compaoré immediately reassured Côte d'Ivoire that he wanted warmer rela-tions and later pledged to strengthen ties with the Council of the Entente countries. For its part, Côte d'Ivoire reaffirmed its "readi-ness to engage in trustworthy, brotherly, and lasting cooperation with this neighboring and brotherly country."

Following Guinea's abrupt break with and estrangement from France in 1958, Sekou Touré adopted a socialist domestic policy, supported Nkrumah's pan-African ideology, and sought close re-lations with communist, socialist, and radical Third World states. Not unexpectedly, ties with Abidjan became strained. Following Sekou Touré's death in 1984 and the advent of a moderate, re-formist military regime in Conakry, Ivoirian relations with Guinea improved considerably.

Ivoirian relations with Mali and Liberia, although far from warm, were decidedly less confrontational than those with Guinea, Bur-kina Faso, and Ghana. Abidjan and Bamako maintained a rela-tively stable relationship that varied between cordial and correct, despite Mali's flirtations with Marxism in the 1960s and 1970s. Likewise, the peculiar conservatism of the Liberian regimes both before and after the April 1980 coup posed no inherent threat to Côte d'Ivoire. However, the unexpected and shockingly bloody Liberian coup greatly alarmed Abidjan and prompted fears of a coup plot in Côte d'Ivoire.

Relations with Other African States

Côte d'Ivoire maintained diplomatic relations with all the states of West Africa and nearly all francophone countries on the continent. It supported—and was most strongly supported by—the most conservative of African francophone countries, such as Zaire, Gabon, and Niger. Nigeria, which had vast oil deposits and the largest population in Africa, presented a special challenge to Ivoirian leaders, who feared the radical Marxism and militant Islam that stirred different segments of the Nigerian polity. Consequently, in the late 1960s and early 1970s Houphouët-Boigny adopted policies intended to weaken Nigeria. Côte d'Ivoire supported Biafra in the Nigerian Civil War (1966–70), and in 1973, with its francophone neighbors, organized the Economic Community of West Africa (Communauté Economique de l'Afrique Occidentale—CEAO) to counter the Nigerian-led Economic Community of West African States (ECOWAS).

Côte d'Ivoire's policy toward South Africa contrasted sharply with the antiapartheid stance common across the continent. In keeping with his antirevolutionary fervor, Houphouët-Boigny insisted that opening a dialogue with South Africa was far more effective than posturing and calls for sanctions. In 1970 he sponsored an exchange of visits at the ministerial level. Although trade with South Africa was officially banned in Côte d'Ivoire, some South African produce was freely available in Ivoirian markets. In late 1987, Côte d'Ivoire further distanced itself from its African counterparts by granting South African Airways landing rights for flights between Johannesburg and Europe. Again, Houphouët-Boigny justified the decision as a positive effort to pressure South Africa.

Relations with France

Time and again, the president has reminded fellow Ivoirians that their closest and best friend was France and that France made daily sacrifices for Côte d'Ivoire by offering protected markets and military assistance. He insisted that France maintained troops near Abidjan as a favor to ensure Côte d'Ivoire's security without impinging on its larger development plans.

A treaty of cooperation (the Franco-Ivoirian Technical Military Assistance Accord—Accord d'Assistance Militaire Technique) signed on April 24, 1961, outlined the salient aspects of Franco-Ivoirian ties. It provided for the exchange of ambassadors between the two countries, named the French ambassador to Abidjan the dean of the diplomatic corps, and reserved a ''privileged position'' among diplomats in Paris for the Ivoirian ambassador. The treaty also called for regular consultations between the two countries on foreign policy matters. France agreed to protect and represent Ivoirian interests in any country or international organization where there was no Ivoirian representation. Additional cooperation agreements signed at the same time covered economic matters, education, civil aviation, judicial affairs, telecommunications, and technical and military assistance.

The French government agreed to continue providing aid to Côte d'Ivoire for a period of five years, with a provision for five-year extensions. By encouraging such long-range commitments, the agreement enhanced French economic influence in Côte d'Ivoire.

Concomitantly, Houphouët-Boigny began implementing policies that diverged albeit in several minor respects from French policy. In 1972 he had Côte d'Ivoire vote against admitting China to the United Nations, and until 1985, in contradistinction to France, he labeled China and the Soviet Union as threats to Africa. In the Middle East, Côte d'Ivoire had been a staunch supporter of Israel since 1967, although during much of this time France regularly took positions more favorable to the Arabs.

Houphouët-Boigny's reliance on French private investment and government loans, coupled with his devotion to French culture, determined his stand on virtually every foreign policy issue. In the early 1960s, for example, he urged negotiations to resolve the Algerian Revolution and, unlike many of his African counterparts, refused to condemn France as the responsible party and refused to provide Algeria with any material assistance. Meanwhile, Houphouët-Boigny also supported French nuclear testing in the Sahara. Houphouët-Boigny also defended French military intervention in Africa.

Relations with the United States

Relations between Washington and Abidjan were cordial if less intimate than the ties with Paris. Through the mid-1980s, Côte d'Ivoire was Africa's most loyal supporter of the United States in the United Nations General Assembly. It supported the larger United States agenda on Chad, the Western Sahara, southern Africa, and Israel. The government strongly approved of moves by the United States against Libyan head of state Qadhafi, especially in light of rumors that Libyans in Burkina Faso were recruiting and training agents to infiltrate Côte d'Ivoire. United States secretary of state George Shultz visited Abidjan in 1986 following Houphouët-Boigny's visit to Washington in 1983.

The United States continued to be Côte d'Ivoire's leading trading partner after France. Foreign policymakers in Washington continued to point to Côte d'Ivoire as an exemplar of successful capitalism, even as Côte d'Ivoire's debt mounted out of control. While enjoying a favorable image in the United States, Houphouët-Boigny has indirectly criticized the United States by attacking the system of international trade, which the United States supported unequivocally, but which Houphouët-Boigny claimed was responsible for his country's economic ills.

Relations with the Soviet Union and China

Since independence, Houphouët-Boigny has considered the Soviet Union and China malevolent influences throughout the Third World. Côte d'Ivoire did not establish diplomatic relations with Moscow until 1967, and then severed them in 1969 following allegations of direct Soviet support for a 1968 student protest at the National University of Côte d'Ivoire. The two countries did not restore ties until February 1986, by which time Houphouët-Boigny had embraced a more active foreign policy reflecting a more pragmatic view of the Soviet Union and his quest for greater international recognition.

Houphouët-Boigny was even more outspoken in his criticism of China. He voiced fears of an "invasion" by the Chinese and their subsequent colonization of Africa. He was especially concerned that Africans would see the problems of development in China as analogous to those of Africa, and China's solutions as appropriate to sub-Saharan Africa. Accordingly, Côte d'Ivoire did not normalize relations with China until 1983, becoming one of the last African countries to do so.

Relations with Israel

From the early 1960s, Houphouët-Boigny openly admired Israel's application of technology to economic development. In 1962 the two countries signed a cooperation agreement and exchanged ambassadors. For its part, Israel provided aid, primarily in the form of technical expertise, to the Ivoirian military and to the agricultural, tourism, and banking sectors.

In spite of the close ties between the two countries, Houphouët-Boigny supported the OAU decision to sever ties with Israel following the October 1973 War. Nonetheless, the two countries maintained close if informal links that enabled Israel to continue to participate in the Ivoirian economy. In February 1986, Houphouët-Boigny announced the long-awaited resumption of diplomatic relations. Moreover, the Ivoirian embassy was again to be located in Jerusalem, in defiance of a 1980 United Nations (UN) Security Council resolution calling on all countries to withdraw their embassies from that city. The PDCI, presumably with Houphouët-Boigny's authorization, however, subsequently voted to honor the UN resolution and moved the embassy to Tel Aviv.

In its diplomacy at the UN and other multinational forums, Côte d'Ivoire remained firmly committed to the West. That commitment did not change through 1988—nor was it expected to—especially since the Ivoirian economy required continuing support from Western sources of funding. Nor were there expected to be significant foreign policy changes under a successor to the aging Houphouët-Boigny, since the consensus among the elite on domestic and foreign policy issues was holding, even as the political maneuvering and skirmishing among possible replacements intensified.

* * *

Because of its regional importance, its close identification with the West, and its spectacular economic growth through the 1960s and 1970s, the literature on government and politics in Côte d'Ivoire is rich and accessible. The principal sources of background material for this study include the following texts: *One-Party Government in the Ivory Coast* by Aristide R. Zolberg; *The Political Economy of Ivory Coast,* edited by I. William Zartman and Christopher Delgado; *Etat et bourgeoisie en Côte d'Ivoire,* edited by Y. A. Fauré and J.-F. Médard; and Michael A. Cohen's *Urban Policy and Political Conflict in Africa.* Especially useful for their critical perspective are Marcel Amondji's *Côte d'Ivoire: Le PDCI et la vie politique de 1944 à 1985* and Laurent Gbagbo's *Côte d'Ivoire: Pour une alternative démocratique,* as well as several articles by Bonnie Campbell. Two small but valuable texts on Ivoirian political institutions are Albert Aggrey's *Guide des institutions politiques et administratives* and Hugues Tay's *L'Administration ivoirienne.* Sources for contemporary reportage include *Africa South of the Sahara, Africa Contemporary Record,* the *Country Reports* published by the Economist Intelligence Unit, and the periodicals *Africa Confidential, Africa Research Bulletin, Fraternité matin, Jeune Afrique,* and *Marchés tropicaux et méditerranéens.* (For further information and complete citations, see Bibliography.)

Chapter 5. National Security

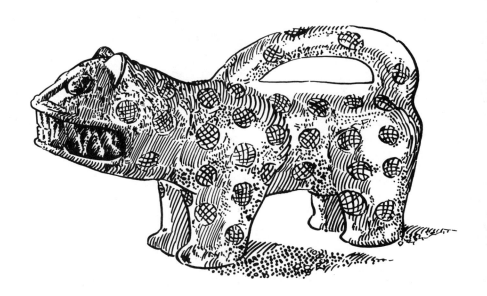

Gold leaf over wooden sculpture of a leopard, a symbol of power among the Akan

ITS ADMIRERS HAVE lauded Côte d'Ivoire's international security policy as moderate, pragmatic, flexible, realistic, conservative, and responsible; its critics have derided it as reactionary and neocolonialist. Its principal objective, according to President Félix Houphouët-Boigny, was to maintain regional peace and security in order to promote economic development at home. Diplomacy—rather than the threat of military intervention—was the vehicle he employed to achieve this objective.

Côte d'Ivoire does not have a long or distinguished national military history. Even after the country gained independence in 1960, the Ivoirian military continued to rely on French advisers, troops, and military aid. The military structure and the culture of French colonial rule remained virtually intact in the nascent Ivoirian nation, preserved by Houphouët-Boigny's deliberate reliance on the former colonial power for security guarantees and assistance. Consequently, the Franco-Ivoirian relationship had a profound impact on the organization, mission, matériel, and political behavior of the armed forces. Whereas at least half of the countries in Africa were under military rule in the mid-1980s, and all but a few had experienced at least one successful military coup d'état, the Ivoirian army was notably quiescent. The armed forces of Côte d'Ivoire were not actively involved in the independence movement. They had not fought in any foreign wars, executed any coups, or had to defend the country from external aggression. In early 1988, they remained a relatively small, lightly armed, and politically mute force, heavily influenced by French doctrine, equipment, and advisers.

In the late 1980s, the central mission of the Ivoirian armed forces was self-defense. The military was not prepared by doctrine or available resources for offensive operations. The armed forces had modest overland mobility, some light weaponry, and limited armor and air defense capabilities; the navy was suited only for coastal defense missions; and the air force, with its small fleet of aircraft, could carry out only token air defense, interdiction, transport, and support operations. The air force had no helicopters for tactical mobility or attack. With the establishment in 1984 of a radar network linking Bouaké and Yamoussoukro, some territorial surveillance was possible, but the military had no long-range ground or maritime surveillance capability.

These limited resources were consistent with the national defense policy and mission and appeared adequate and appropriate in the context of Côte d'Ivoire's regional security needs. Côte d'Ivoire had a larger military establishment than any of its immediate neighbors. Although in 1987 the armies of Ghana and Guinea—with 9,000 and 8,500 troops, respectively—were technically larger than Côte d'Ivoire's armed forces, their equipment was neither numerically nor qualitatively superior. Until the mid-1980s, Ghana had a substantially larger navy (numbering 1,200 personnel), but it had no offensive capability. Only the Malian air force, with twenty-seven combat aircraft, posed a potential threat.

Armed Forces

In the 1980s, the Ivoirian armed forces had a dual mission: to defend the nation from attack and internal subversion and to participate in the socioeconomic development of the country. They had no overt political role, although it was understood that they were to support the regime. To avoid diverting resources from national economic development, Houphouët-Boigny kept the armed forces relatively small and lightly armed. Compensating for the limited capacity of the armed forces was a strategic doctrine that relied on external military support from France. The government consciously sought to avoid conflicts or arms races with its neighbors and eschewed pan-African defense missions.

Early Development

Côte d'Ivoire's armed forces developed from the colonial military forces organized by France after the formal establishment of the colony in 1893. Although Côte d'Ivoire was a separate colony, France set up a regional military command structure for all of French West Africa (Afrique Occidentale Française—AOF; see Glossary). The command headquarters was located at Dakar, Senegal, and Côte d'Ivoire was integrated into a regional defense structure. Its African forces were organized into regiments of Senegalese Irregulars (Tirailleurs Sénégalais), whose name revealed the centralized character of the colonial administration and the subordinate status of the vast expanses of the AOF beyond the Senegalese hinterland. This externalization and regionalization of Ivoirian defense persisted after independence in the form of the Council of the Entente (Conseil de l'Entente), the security of whose member states continued to be guaranteed by France.

Between 1908 and 1912, when four-year conscription was introduced by the governor general of the AOF, the number of Africans serving in the Tirailleurs Sénégalais grew from 13,600 to 22,600. At the outbreak of World War I in August 1914, of the nearly 31,000 black troops under French arms, about half were deployed outside of the AOF and French Equatorial Africa (Afrique Equatoriale Française—AEF), underpinning French imperialism in Morocco, Algeria, and Madagascar. During World War I, about 164,000 black soldiers were recruited into the AOF for service in Europe and elsewhere.

In Côte d'Ivoire, pacification and conscription continued even as France was fighting for its survival. Between October 1914 and February 1916, approximately 13,500 Ivoirians were trained for military service. All told, about 20,000 Ivoirian soldiers fought for France during the war. Many others resisted recruitment, which was widely regarded as the heaviest of the colonial exactions. A major wartime revolt had to be put down by force. The colony suffered a sharp decrease in its standard of living because of the various war-related levies.

During World War II, France again called upon its colonies to fulfill manpower levies. Before France fell in 1940, over 100,000 men had been recruited from French West Africa alone, including 30,000 from Côte d'Ivoire. After the armistice, the Vichy government increased the size of its peacetime army by recruiting an additional 50,000 Africans, while another 100,000 Africans served under the Free French between 1943 and 1945. Thus, over 200,000 Africans fought on behalf of France during the war.

Although the Vichy government further intensified the burdens of colonialism, in the aftermath of the war the colonial regime was gradually dismantled to make way for independent nations. By 1950 the essential defense and internal security apparatus that would be bequeathed to Côte d'Ivoire after independence was in place. Defense was entrusted to a single army battalion with four companies: three were based at Bouaké, and the fourth was at Man, with an armored reconnaissance unit at Abidjan. Internal security was the responsibility of the National Security Police (Sûreté Nationale). This division of the Ministry of Internal Security copied French organization and had a headquarters element, four mobile brigades, a security service, and a central, colonial police force. These units were reinforced by a local constabulary (*gardes cercles*) organized by the army and a local detachment of the regional gendarmerie. During the 1950s, administrative powers devolved to the colonies of the AOF. Defense and foreign affairs remained the responsibility of the colonial authorities. Even at independence in 1960, no provision was made for an Ivoirian national armed force.

Not until after the April 1961 Franco-Ivoirian Technical Military Assistance Accord (Accord d'Assistance Militaire Technique), more than a year after independence, was a national army formed from indigenous members of the French colonial marines. These troops formed a single, undermanned battalion and used equipment donated by France. By the end of 1962, the armed forces had expanded rapidly to about 5,000 soldiers organized into four battalions. For the new military establishment, independence was more formal than functional: French influence remained paramount, delaying the emergence of an autonomous Ivoirian identity.

Constitutional, Legal, and Administrative Structure

Like its French model, the Côte d'Ivoire Constitution of 1960 provides for a highly centralized form of government that vests enormous power in the office of the president, particularly in the areas of national sovereignty, independence, territorial integrity, and military and security affairs (see The Constitution, ch. 4). Article 17 empowers the president to appoint the civil and military officers of the state, and Article 18 designates the president commander in chief of the armed forces. The president is authorized by Article 19 to take ''such exceptional measures as are required'' to deal with serious and immediate threats to national independence, territorial integrity, or the execution of international commitments. The National Assembly (Assemblée Nationale) is empowered to pass laws regarding martial law, states of emergency, and the principles of national defense organization (Article 41) and to declare war (Article 42). The Council of Ministers, over which the president presides, is authorized by Article 43 to declare martial law, which may be extended beyond two weeks only by the National Assembly.

In 1988 three main interministerial councils and advisory bodies were concerned with coordinating the various departments and soliciting technical advice in matters of defense. Chaired by the president, the Defense Committee consisted of the ministers concerned with defense policy and the chief of staff; it met to make government decisions in defense matters. The High Defense Council, which included the inspector general and chief of staff of the armed forces and the commandant of the National Gendarmerie (Gendarmerie Nationale), provided technical military advice, justifications, and recommendations to the Defense Committee. The High Committee on Intelligence, which was under the authority of the president, guided and coordinated record keeping, documentation, and intelligence services.

Defense organization had both central and regional components. At the national level, the president was the supreme authority. As commander in chief of the armed forces, the president directed and coordinated defense policy. The president was assisted in this by the minister of defense and by other ministers as required.

The minister of defense had two distinct but related functions: assisting the president in all defense matters and executing military policy. In the exercise of these functions, the minister of defense had direct authority over the chief of staff of the armed forces, who also served as commander of all the armed forces, and the inspector general of the armed forces, who was responsible for central administration (see fig. 14).

There has been remarkable continuity in the senior civilian and military defense posts. Jean Konan Banny served as minister of defense in the early 1960s, until he was implicated in a 1963 coup plot. His successor, Kouadio M'Bahia Blé, served as minister of defense for more than seventeen years, from September 1963 to February 1981, before the pardoned and politically rehabilitated Banny returned to the post. The first chief of staff, Brigadier General Thomas D'Anquin Wattara (who in August 1966 became the first Ivoirian general), held that post between 1961 and 1974. Wattara's successors, however, have had shorter tenures. In November 1987, President Houphouët-Boigny replaced the most senior army officers with new men; Brigadier General Félix Ory succeeded Major General Bertin Zézé Baroan as chief of staff, and Brigadier Joseph Ballou replaced retiring Major General Ibrahim Coulibaly as inspector general. In December 1987, the Ministry of Defense absorbed the Ministry of Maritime Affairs, and Banny became minister of defense and maritime affairs.

By decree in November 1963, the minister of defense was empowered to carry out government policy in military matters; to establish and oversee the National Service (Service Civique), an organization in which young men and women participated in the economic development of the country, especially in the rural areas; to review the organization of the armed forces, the National Gendarmerie, and the National Service and to present plans to the president as required; to administer and evaluate the mobilization and use of the armed forces and military requirements; to oversee veterans affairs; to prepare and execute budgets and programs for the ministry; and to present to the president or the Defense Committee all proposals for international negotiation concerning defense matters.

In 1984 the ministry's headquarters staff was budgeted for 529 billets (including 31 French technical assistance personnel). Most of the billets were allocated as follows: the cabinet received 46; the Central Administrative Services, 244; the Armed Forces of Côte d'Ivoire (Force Armée Nationale de Côte d'Ivoire—FANCI), 116;

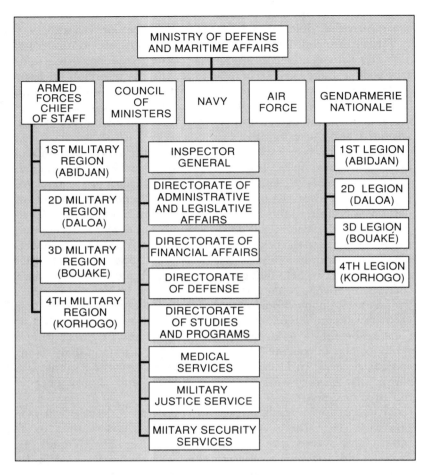

Source: Based on information from Côte Ivoire, Ministère de l'Information, *Annuaire Administratif, 1985;* and United States, Department of the Army, Abidjan Report, No. 6 851 5020 85, November 21, 1985.

Figure 14. Organization of Ivoirian Defense Forces, 1988

the Ivoirian Air Force (Force Aérienne de Côte d'Ivoire—FACI), 81; and the Presidential Guard and Militia (Garde Présidentielle et Milice—GPM), 7.

Since May 1972, local defense organization has been based on a territorial division of responsibility between the civilian prefectures (*préfectures*) under the minister of interior and the military regions under the minister of defense. This arrangement superseded a system of departmental commands. The minister of interior, supported as required by the minister of defense, was responsible for civil defense. Initially, three military regions were established with headquarters, at Abidjan, Daloa, and Bouaké. In July 1984, the country was reorganized into four military regions. The fourth region was centered at Korhogo in order to provide better defense coverage in the sparsely populated but politically sensitive northern territories. In each prefecture, the prefect (*préfet*) was responsible for all nonmilitary matters having a bearing on defense (see Local Government, ch. 4). On the regional level, the military commandant was specifically charged with defense responsibilities. This system required close cooperation and coordination between the regional military commanders and the civilian prefects. Each military garrison was under a commanding officer, who represented the regional commandant and whose functions were prescribed by decree in December 1971.

The military regions provided active-duty forces and an administrative structure for civilian and military defense planning. Each region comprised between six and twelve prefectures under a territorial commander who reported to the minister of defense through the chief of staff of the armed forces. The regions provided liaison service for the local political and administrative authorities, prepared plans for the protection of sensitive military and civilian assets in the region, coordinated regional and local military and civilian defense measures, maintained operational readiness, and conducted military exercises as required. The regional military commands did not have any organic logistical resources but rather drew on central support services.

Defense Mission and National Policy

In 1987 the armed forces consisted of about 14,920 regular and paramilitary personnel, organized into FANCI, the navy, FACI, the National Gendarmerie, the Presidential Guard and Militia, and the Military Fire Brigade. Although the National Gendarmerie was an integral part of the Ministry of Defense and Maritime Affairs, its mission related more to internal security than to external defense (see Internal Security, this ch.).

The effective strength of the army was about 3,000 troops during the early 1970s. It increased to 4,000 during the mid-1970s, and to more than 8,000 by the early 1980s, before declining steadily to about 5,500 by 1987. FANCI was equipped lightly and almost exclusively with French matériel, much of which was delivered during 1980 and 1981, when the army experienced its greatest expansion (see table 9, Appendix).

Headquarters elements included a general staff, headquarters and logistics companies, commissariat service, and matériel service. The main combat elements were the four infantry battalions of three companies each, stationed in the four military regions. The First Battalion at Port Bouët near Abidjan included two infantry companies, a paratroop company, and an air defense unit. An armored battalion with two squadrons also was stationed in the Abidjan region, along with the Military Preparatory Technical Academy (Ecole Militaire Préparatoire Technique—EMPT) at Bingerville. The Second Battalion at Daloa consisted of three infantry companies. In the Third Military Region at Bouaké was the Third Battalion, consisting of three infantry companies, a heavy weapons/artillery battery, an antiaircraft artillery battalion, an engineering battalion with a combat engineer company, two construction companies, and a training company. The Fourth Military Region at Korhogo was still being established, and in 1986 a new command battalion and a dog-handling center were reported to have been formed.

Until December 1987, the Ivoirian navy (Marine Nationale) was part of the Ministry of Maritime Affairs, which was also responsible for the merchant marine. In July 1974, Captain Lamine Fadika became the first Ivoirian minister of maritime affairs, replacing an expatriate. In December 1987, Fadika was removed from office, and the ministry was incorporated into the Ministry of Defense and Maritime Affairs under Banny.

The navy's mission was limited to coastal and river patrols and harbor defense, and its primary emphasis was on protecting the environment and fighting fires. The ministry planned to restructure the navy into two coastal patrol squadrons as additional fast attack craft were acquired. Naval headquarters were at the main naval base at Locodjo, near Abidjan; smaller bases were at Sassandra, San-Pédro, and Tabou, all on the southwestern coast. The navy expanded from about 200 personnel in 1970, to 400 in 1980, to about 700 in the late 1980s, maintaining a ratio of officers to enlisted men of 1 to 10. It had a small but versatile force of warships, auxiliaries, and service craft. Most of these were French craft, commissioned in the late 1970s (see table 10, Appendix). The navy was also reported to have a commando group and one light transport aircraft. The independent merchant marine fleet consisted of more than sixty vessels, including three tankers.

FACI was basically a military transportation and liaison service rather than a combat force. This mission was reflected in FACI's official name, Ivoirian Air Transport and Liaison (Groupement Aérien de Transport et de Liaison—GATL). Like FANCI, FACI was an independent service arm of the Ministry of Defense and Maritime Affairs. In 1988 Colonel Abdoulaye Coulibaly was

President Houphouët-Boigny inspecting the troops
Courtesy Embassy of Côte d'Ivoire, Washington

the FACI commander, having assumed that post from a French officer in 1974. FACI had only about 200 personnel through the 1970s. It then entered a period of expansion, reaching an estimated strength of 930 in the mid-1980s. Organizationally, FACI consisted of a headquarters staff with operational, technical, and general services sections and also various field activities and air bases.

FACI's one small combat aircraft squadron consisted of six French Dassault-Breguet light attack/trainer Alpha Jets, obtained during 1980 and 1981. The squadron was stationed at the Bouaké air base, which opened in December 1980. Some of FACI's original light transport planes, including three Fokker F–27s and four F–28s, were transferred in 1979 to the national airline, Air Ivoire, and several old transports (three C–47s, five MH–1521 Broussard light transports, and one Mystère 20) have been retired from service. In 1987, in addition to the Alpha Jets, FACI's aircraft consisted of twenty fixed-wing aircraft and eleven helicopters used for training, light transport, ferrying of dignitaries, and communications and utility missions. Pilots received training on French Aérospatiale Rallye 160 and Rallye 235 aircraft, two Reims Aviation/ Cessna 150Hs, and six Beech F33C Bonanzas (see table 10, Appendix).

FACI operated from a number of strategically situated air bases. Port Bouët near Abidjan was the main base for FACI, along with the First Military Region/FANCI Battalion, the paratroop

191

company, and the air defense forces. Other major bases were in the southwest at Daloa (the headquarters of the Second Military Region/FANCI Battalion) and in the populous central savanna at Bouaké (site of the Third Military Region/FANCI Battalion), which included a heavy weapons battery, an antiaircraft artillery battalion, and the engineering battalion. Yamoussoukro, Sassandra, San-Pédro, Tabou, Man, Séguéla, Odienné, and Korhogo also had airfields.

The remaining component of the armed forces having a combat mission was the GPM. President Houphouët-Boigny formed the GPM to serve as a paramilitary counterweight to FANCI after the 1963 military coup plot and to provide personal protection to the president. In 1986 the militia was estimated to have had 1,500 personnel; the Presidential Guard, 1,100. GPM members were recruited largely from the National Gendarmerie and were organized into two units, one based in Abidjan and the other at Yamoussoukro.

Recruitment and Conditions of Service

According to the Constitution, the burden of national defense is shared by all citizens of Côte d'Ivoire. As of June 1961, military service for all male citizens was required by law. Although nominally compulsory, military service in fact was not universal. The small size of the armed forces and the large number of volunteers made conscription virtually unnecessary. In general, conscription seemed to have been reserved for a handful of troublesome students and striking workers.

In the late 1980s, Côte d'Ivoire's population included at least 2.5 million males aged fifteen to forty-nine, of whom about 1.3 million were believed to be fit for military service. Active service varied from one to two years and normally included both military and civic training. Active service also could be spent in National Service work or working for state enterprises. The period for reserve service was twenty-three years. In general, all Ivoirian citizens could be required to perform certain duties in the national interest under the rubric of military service. The National Service was designed particularly with this purpose in mind, and it was primarily to this organization that young women were called to serve.

The pay, living conditions, and benefits available in the armed forces were relatively attractive and compared favorably with alternative employment opportunities; however, they were not lavish. The government attempted to strike a prudent balance by providing institutional support and emoluments sufficient to sustain satisfaction and loyalty without transforming the military into an unduly privileged elite. Nonetheless, some senior officers unethically profited from their temporary assignments to state enterprises, although corruption was not as widespread as in many other African countries. To some extent, military and security personnel were exempt from "salary alignments" and the impact of austerity measures introduced in the early 1980s.

Officers were recruited through the Military Academy (Ecole des Forces Armées—EFA) at Bouaké or by promotion from the ranks of noncommissioned officers (NCOs). Career NCOs were recruited from among those who had at least five years' active service. Promotions for officers were almost exclusively by merit selection. Officers were generally retired when they attained the age limit for their grade. The highest rank in the navy was admiral; in FANCI and FACI, it was general (see fig. 15; fig. 16). All military personnel were subject to obligations, regulations, and disciplinary rules prescribed by government decree. Career military personnel were prohibited from striking or joining trade unions; were obliged to serve both day and night; and were required to obtain authorization to marry, travel outside their garrisons, express their opinions publicly, or join outside associations.

Military justice was enforced by both administrative and judicial means, depending on the severity of the offense. The military courts had jurisdiction over members of the armed forces who were accused of crimes unrelated to any other offenses within the jurisdiction of any other court, crimes committed while carrying out military duties or while conducting operations to maintain peace and public order, or crimes committed inside the military establishment or against the security of the state. Unlike the civil and criminal court system, the military justice system had no court of appeals. The Supreme Court occasionally has been asked to review and set aside a military tribunal's verdict and to order a retrial (see Judical System, ch. 4).

Training

Before independence, military training was conducted almost exclusively by French personnel either on the job or at institutions in France, Senegal, and Côte d'Ivoire. Most training was based on informal arrangements. Only a few officers and NCOs were sent to France for advanced professional and technical training. Since independence, as it has acquired the necessary expertise, Côte d'Ivoire has assumed responsibility for training its own armed forces. In November 1961, France transferred the EMPT located at Bingerville to the new Ivoirian government. At that time, the school taught only specialized technical subjects, such as communications and automotive mechanics. Because the new government intended to use the military as a means to promote the ethos of national service and to teach skills relevant to national development,

IVORY COAST RANK	SOUS-LIEUTENANT	LIEUTENANT	CAPITAINE	COMMANDANT	LIEUTENANT COLONEL	COLONEL	GENERAL DE BRIGADE	GENERAL DE DIVISION	GENERAL DE CORPS D'ARMEE	GENERAL D'ARMEE
ARMY 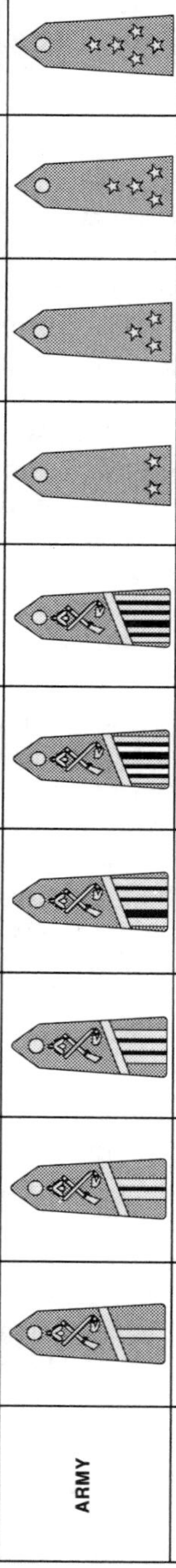										
U.S. RANK TITLES	2D LIEUTENANT	1ST LIEUTENANT	CAPTAIN	MAJOR	LIEUTENANT COLONEL	COLONEL	BRIGADIER GENERAL	MAJOR GENERAL	LIEUTENANT GENERAL	GENERAL
IVORY COAST RANK	SOUS-LIEUTENANT	LIEUTENANT	CAPITAINE	COMMANDANT	LIEUTENANT COMMANDANT	COLONEL	GENERAL DE BRIGADE AERIENNE	GENERAL DE DIVISION AERIENNE	GENERAL DE CORPS D'ARMEE AERIENNE	GENERAL D'ARMEE AERIENNE
AIR FORCE 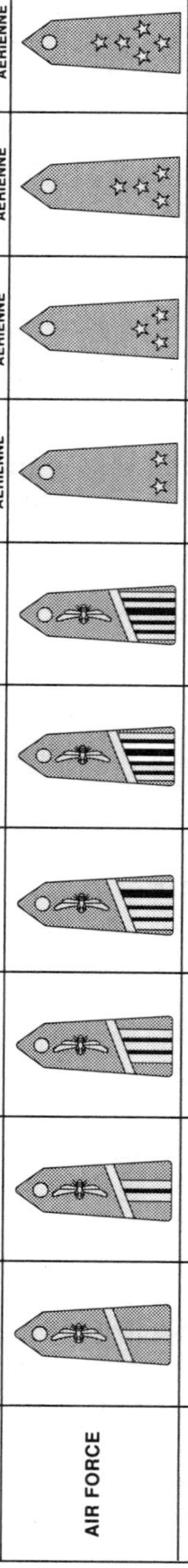										
U.S. RANK TITLES	2D LIEUTENANT	1ST LIEUTENANT	CAPTAIN	MAJOR	LIEUTENANT COLONEL	COLONEL	BRIGADIER GENERAL	MAJOR GENERAL	LIEUTENANT GENERAL	GENERAL
IVORY COAST RANK	ENSEIGNE DE VAISSEAU 2E CLASSE	ENSEIGNE DE VAISSEAU 1RE CLASSE	LIEUTENANT DE VAISSEAU	CAPITAINE DE CORVETTE	CAPITAINE DE FREGATE	CAPITAINE DE VAISSEAU	CONTRE-AMIRAL	VICE-AMIRAL/VICE-AMIRAL D'ESCADRE	AMIRAL	
NAVY 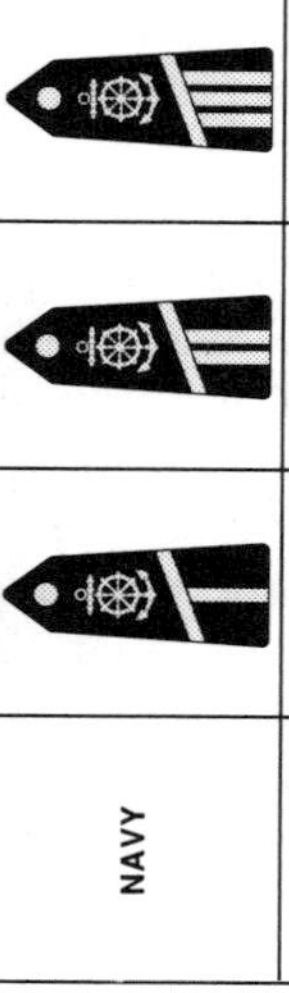				INSIGNIA NOT KNOWN	INSIGNIA NOT KNOWN	INSIGNIA NOT KNOWN	INSIGNIA NOT KNOWN	INSIGNIA NOT KNOWN	INSIGNIA NOT KNOWN	
U.S. RANK TITLES	ENSIGN	LIEUTENANT JUNIOR GRADE	LIEUTENANT	LIEUTENANT COMMANDER	COMMANDER	CAPTAIN	COMMODORE ADMIRAL	REAR ADMIRAL	VICE ADMIRAL	

Figure 15. Officer Ranks and Insignia, 1988

		SOLDAT DE 2EME CLASSE	SOLDAT DE 1ERE CLASSE	CAPORAL	CAPORAL-CHEF	SERGENT	SERGENT-CHEF	ADJUDANT	ADJUDANT-CHEF
ARMY	IVORY COAST RANK	SOLDAT DE 2EME CLASSE	SOLDAT DE 1ERE CLASSE	CAPORAL	CAPORAL-CHEF	SERGENT	SERGENT-CHEF	ADJUDANT	ADJUDANT-CHEF
	U.S. RANK TITLES	BASIC PRIVATE	PRIVATE	PRIVATE 1ST CLASS	CORPORAL	SERGEANT	STAFF SERGEANT	SERGEANT MAJOR	COMMAND SERGEANT MAJOR
AIR FORCE	IVORY COAST RANK	SOLDAT DE 2EME CLASSE	SOLDAT DE 1ERE CLASSE	CAPORAL	CAPORAL-CHEF	SERGENT	SERGENT-CHEF	ADJUDANT	ADJUDANT-CHEF
	U.S. RANK TITLES	AIRMAN BASIC	AIRMAN	AIRMAN 1ST CLASS	SERGEANT	STAFF SERGEANT	TECHNICAL SERGEANT	SENIOR MASTER SERGEANT	CHIEF MASTER SERGEANT
NAVY	IVORY COAST RANK	MATELOT	MATELOT BREVET	QUARTIER-MAITRE DE 2EME CLASSE	QUARTIER-MAITRE DE 1ERE CLASSE	SECOND MAITRE	MAITRE	PREMIER MAITRE	MAITRE PRINCIPAL
	U.S. RANK TITLES	SEAMAN RECRUIT	SEAMAN APPRENTICE	SEAMAN	PETTY OFFICER 3D CLASS	PETTY OFFICER 2D CLASS	PETTY OFFICER 1ST CLASS	SENIOR CHIEF PETTY OFFICER	FLEET FORCE MASTER CHIEF PETTY OFFICER

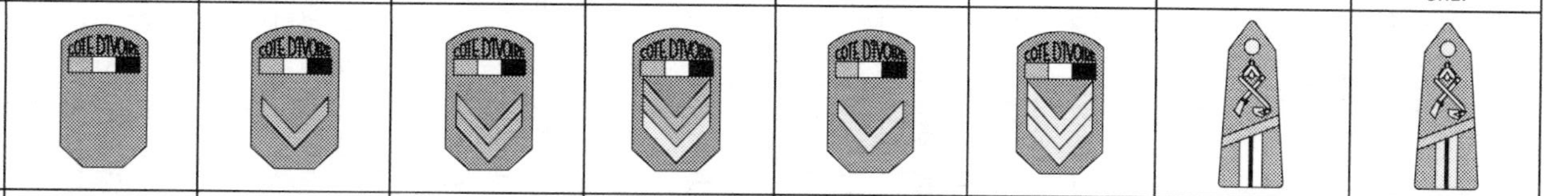

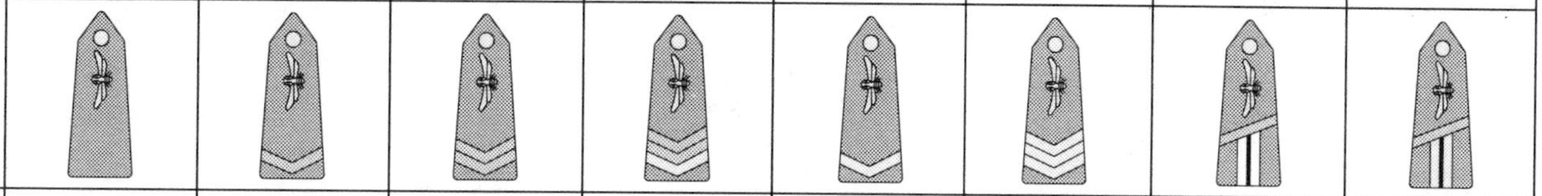

Figure 16. Enlisted Ranks and Insignia, 1988

the programs were immediately expanded to include agricultural and construction skills.

Since assuming control of the EMPT at Bingerville, FANCI gradually expanded the curriculum. Students entered the academy after their first year of secondary education and remained there throughout secondary school (see Education, ch. 2). Students took military training and academic courses simultaneously throughout the program. Initially, the curriculum stressed technical and vocational subjects, but by 1988 it was expanding to include courses in the humanities and social sciences so that graduates would qualify for entrance into universities in Côte d'Ivoire and Europe. Students were admitted to the school following a competitive examination, and graduates could either enter FANCI with a commission or proceed to college. About 86 percent of those admitted completed the program and graduated. In addition to training Ivoirian students, the Bingerville academy also accepted pupils from other francophone African countries, such as Niger, Burkina Faso, Gabon, Senegal, and Central African Republic. The school had a French commandant and employed both military and civilian faculty, including a sizable number of French instructors. In 1982 the school was reported to have almost 500 students, more than 40 French civilian professors, and several French military instructors.

In July 1963, FANCI established its own school, the EFA, at Bouaké. The EFA subsequently became a regional military training center serving francophone West Africa. It also was headed by a French commandant. The EFA selected officer and NCO candidates between the ages of eighteen and twenty-five by competitive written and oral examinations administered annually; officer candidates had to hold a baccalaureate degree. By 1983, the twentieth anniversary of the EFA, 251 Ivoirian officers and 48 officers from Gabon, 38 from Togo, 32 from Senegal, 20 from Central African Republic, 15 from Niger, 7 from Burkina Faso, and 6 from Chad had received commissions from the school.

Until 1983 all training for FACI pilots was provided in France in a four-year program of instruction. Following a 1982 Franco-Ivoirian agreement, however, a basic pilots' training school was opened at the Bouaké air base in April 1983. France provided the aircraft, operating budget, and matériel for the one-year program. By 1986 enrollees also included non-Ivoirians. Ivoirian students were selected by FACI, and the training was conducted by the French aircraft manufacturer Aérospatiale. The program included 140 hours of training. Graduates were awarded a pilot's license and went to France for further flight training in transports or jets, depending on their aptitude. Officer candidates had to meet advanced mathematics qualifications, and NCOs were required to have completed the equivalent of one year of postsecondary education. On the basis of the selection examination, candidates were divided into three groups for specialized duties. Candidates who scored the highest could become pilots; those who scored in the middle group could become mechanics or communications technicians; and those who scored in the lowest category could be trained for other occupations. Mechanics, communications technicians, and most other specialists were trained in Côte d'Ivoire. Because of its small size and the specialized technical expertise required, FACI recruited for officers and NCO candidates through selective examinations given only once a year.

The Ministry of Maritime Affairs had also operated a number of training institutions for Ivoirian and West African naval and merchant marine personnel. These schools were transferred to the Ministry of Defense and Maritime Affairs in December 1987. In 1975 plans were unveiled for a regional 1,500-student naval/merchant marine academy in Abidjan to serve the needs of the Economic Community of West African States (ECOWAS) and other inter-African organizations to which Côte d'Ivoire belonged. By 1983 several training facilities were in operation, including the Merchant Marine Training Academy, the Academy of Oceanographic Sciences and Technology, the Regional Maritime Instruction Center, and the Center for Antipollution Control. These regional training institutions and others were supported by the United Nations, the European Development Fund, and other international organizations. Several countries, particularly France and Japan, also provided aid. France supplied most of Côte d'Ivoire's naval craft as well as maritime training; Japan furnished the Navy's only training ship, trained Ivoirian naval officers, contributed more than US$500,000 toward the construction of the Abidjan Naval Academy, and participated in the phased expansion of the Naval Academy and the Abidjan port facilities.

Foreign Influences

France has been the dominant foreign influence on Ivoirian security concerns. France maintained its position through several institutional and informal arrangements. The most important was the mutual defense pact of the Entente Agreement of 1959. By this agreement, French forces guaranteed internal and external security of the Council of the Entente members. This relationship was strengthened by the supplementary quadripartite military accords of April 24, 1961, among France, Côte d'Ivoire, Niger, and

Dahomey (present-day Benin). In addition, the Franco-Ivoirian Technical Military Assistance Accord of 1961 reaffirmed France's position as the chief supplier of military aid, training, and equipment. These agreements secured for France a virtual monopoly of external military assistance to Council of the Entente countries, legitimized the continued presence of French armed forces on their soil, and served as justification for occasional direct military interventions. Thus, the national military forces of francophone Africa, together with the French forces stationed among them and France's rapid deployment forces (*forces d'intervention*), formed a transcontinental defense network that served both local security needs and French global interests. Although the level of French military assistance to Africa (and to Côte d'Ivoire in particular) declined in the 1980s, France's paramount position was not challenged by other foreign powers or by Ivoirian demands for autonomy. Indeed, since the 1970s France had consolidated its position as the leading Western arms supplier to Africa, where it was second only to the Soviet Union.

The Franco-Ivoirian Technical Military Assistance Accord of 1961 encompassed four categories of assistance. Three categories involved French contributions to Ivoirian defense, and the fourth dealt with joint military operations. First, France provided technical assistance personnel (*coopérants*—see Glossary) to headquarters and field commands. The agreement for the continued provision of these *coopérants* (who served as administrators, advisers, and in operational capacities) was reviewed and renewed every two years. In 1985 about 1,000 French military officers and NCOs provided technical military assistance to twenty African countries; 78 were assigned to Côte d'Ivoire, a decrease from a peak of 110 in 1981.

Second, France provided military equipment and training for the Ivoirian armed forces under renewable three-year agreements. Equipment and matériel were either donated or sold on favorable terms, and military training was furnished as grant aid. In 1985 France provided about US$2.1 million in direct military aid to Côte d'Ivoire. French military detachments sometimes undertook special projects in the country; for example, for eight months in 1984 and 1985 a vehicle and equipment repair team serviced Ivoirian equipment in Bouaké. In the early 1980s, France also subsidized approximately 200 Ivoirian officers and NCOs annually attending French military academies.

Third, a joint agreement allowed France to station troops in the country. These forces, represented in 1988 by the 400-man Forty-third Marine Infantry Battalion situated near Abidjan, served as tangible evidence of France's security commitment to respond to

Armed Forces color guard
Courtesy Ellen Perna Smith

any major crisis occurring in Côte d'Ivoire or in France's mutual security partners. This battalion could intervene upon request or direction, either alone or in conjunction with similar units stationed in Senegal, Niger, and Gabon, with rapid reinforcements by French rapid deployment forces.

Finally, the two countries participated in joint military exercises held each year and large-scale maneuvers held every two or three years. In the 1980s, these exercises became increasingly sophisticated and politically significant. At the operational level, they strengthened cooperation and coordination between French and Ivoirian forces. At the political level, they were a cogent symbol of the special relationship the two countries shared.

Apart from these formal accords, France also sought to bolster its influence with its former African colonies through visits, exchanges, conferences, and other meetings that promoted a continuing "defense dialogue." For example, the French Ministry of Defense conducted the biennial meetings of the Institute of Higher Studies for National Defense (Institut des Hautes Etudes de Défense Nationale—IHEDN) in Paris for key military and civilian leaders from francophone African countries. The conferences emphasized defense ties and military cooperation, the strategic significance of Africa in the global defense environment, and the importance of Franco-African solidarity. Participants also visited major French military and National Gendarmerie installations for briefings and demonstrations of French rapid deployment forces and the latest equipment.

Other industrialized countries also have furnished military assistance and equipment to Côte d'Ivoire. Japan provided a training ship, training, and naval technical assistance. The Netherlands, Sweden, Britain, and the United States furnished support aircraft, small naval craft, military utility trucks, jeeps, and mortars. In addition, FANCI procured assault rifles from Switzerland, and the police bought pistols from the Federal Republic of Germany (West Germany).

In the late 1980s, the military relationship between the United States and Côte d'Ivoire was becoming more important. Between 1967 and 1986, eighty-five Ivoirian trainees received military instruction under the United States International Military Education and Training (IMET) program. The program, which expanded sharply with the signing of a new IMET agreement in 1983, provided training in such areas as infantry and airborne skills, intelligence, and marine environmental science, thereby promoting professional relationships among military personnel. The value of training services increased to US$411,000 during fiscal years (FY— see Glossary) 1984 to 1986, covering six to ten Ivoirian military students per year.

Government-to-government sales of defense equipment and services, though relatively small, have also expanded. In FY 1986, the United States signed military sales agreements valued at US$500,000, of which US$25,000 was classified as foreign military sales and US$475,000 as foreign military construction sales. In 1985 the United States initiated the African Civic Action Program, which included a Coastal Security Program to help West African littoral states patrol and defend their Exclusive Economic Zones (EEZs) against treaty violations, illegal fishing, and smuggling. The African Civic Action Program also strengthened regional cooperation in search and rescue, pollution control, and training operations, all of which coincided with the Ivoirian navy's primary missions. By 1987 the United States had furnished some communications and navigation equipment to Côte d'Ivoire under the terms of the program.

Role of the Armed Forces in Society

Unlike the military in many other African and Third World states, the Ivoirian armed forces maintained a relatively low profile. According to a 1984 United States Arms Control and Disarmament Agency (ACDA) survey of 144 countries, Côte d'Ivoire ranked one hundred and second in military expenditure, ninety-first in the size of its armed forces, ninety-sixth in arms imports, one hundred and twenty-fourth in military expenditure as a percentage of the gross national product (GNP—see Glossary), one hundred and twenty-eighth in military expenditure as a percentage of the government budget, one hundred and eighteenth in military expenditure per capita, one hundred and sixth in military expenditure relative to the size of the armed forces, one hundred and thirteenth in the ratio of armed forces to total population, and seventy-ninth in the ratio of arms imports to total imports.

The Military in National Perspective

From 1976 to 1985, Ivoirian military expenditures averaged less than 2 percent of GNP and ranged between 4 and 6 percent of the government's budget. As measured in constant 1983 United States dollars, the country's arms imports multiplied sevenfold from about US$15 million a year during 1976 and 1977 to between US$90 and US$130 million per year from 1978 to 1981, when Côte d'Ivoire acquired several costly ships and aircraft. Expenditures then declined abruptly to an annual average of only US$22 million from 1982 to 1985, a period of austerity for the country (see Growth and Structure of the Economy, ch. 3). At least a portion of Côte d'Ivoire's arms imports from France was furnished on a grant basis during this period.

The government's operating budget for FY 1986 amounted to CFA F433.62 billion (for value of CFA F—see Glossary), of which CFA F31.3 billion (7.2 percent) was allocated to the Ministry of Defense. Although this represented almost an 11 percent increase from the ministry's 1985 budget, defense allocations were still a distant second to the budget of the Ministry of National Education and Scientific Research. Personnel costs absorbed about two-thirds of the defense budget, while materials and operating expenses each absorbed about one-fifth of the budget. In addition, for FY 1986 the Ministry of Maritime Affairs received CFA F1.1 billion (a substantial reduction from CFA F3.8 billion in 1985), bringing the total defense operating budget for 1986 to CFA F32.4 billion.

National Service and Veterans Groups

Given the top priority it has assigned to socioeconomic development, the government has regarded the armed forces as an instrument of nation building as well as national defense. In fact, in the 1960s it entertained the somewhat naive hope that the armed forces would become self-sufficient rather than a drain on the economy, and for that reason the National Service enjoyed strong presidential

201

backing. Until 1983 the Ministry of Defense was known as the Ministry of Defense and National Service, signifying its dual role of protector and nation builder. Initially, the National Service drafted its recruits, but recruitment soon became voluntary to make it more attractive.

The National Service program sought to train soldiers as farmers, halt migration to cities, teach useful skills, and provide a general education along with military training. (Within a short time, however, the military training was abandoned, although the National Service remained under the Ministry of Defense, was funded within the army's budget, and practiced military discipline.) National Service trainees, under the supervision of Israeli military and agricultural technicians, established the National Service Center at Bouaké in 1964. The National Service Center, which coordinated programs in the Bouaké area, also processed agricultural produce and provided materials, seeds, and machinery to regional centers. Various regional centers experimented with mechanized agriculture and poultry, egg, and livestock production. Plans called for transplanting National Service volunteers to villages where they were to serve as agents of change. The government, through the National Service program, created "Progressive Villages" as demonstration projects, which, upon attaining economic independence, were to be transferred to the Ministry of Agriculture. The government also transformed some existing villages into "Villages under Supervision," which cultivated certain experimental crops like tobacco, rice, and cotton.

By the mid-1960s, the National Service had expanded into other areas. The Company of Pioneers, also supported by Israeli technical assistance and led by officers and NCOs detailed from the army, undertook national construction and other projects. A Women's Corps was set up, with Israeli women officers as advisers.

In 1964 the National Service Center at Bouaké opened with 330 fifteen- to eighteen-year-old women trainees. Regular recruits attended a one-year course of instruction, and instructors attended for two years. The curriculum included French-language training, home economics, hygiene and nutrition, child care, animal husbandry, and poultry raising. After completing their service, the trainees, with government help, were expected to settle in villages and assist local women; however, only about two-thirds of the trainees completed the program, and the impact they had in villages was probably negligible.

The National Service program was as misconceived as it was ambitious. Two years were insufficient to turn raw recruits into proficient soldiers and farmers, and the government made no provisions to keep trainees on the farm once they had finished their course. Consequently, in 1983 the government transferred the National Service from the Ministry of Defense to the Ministry of Rural Development. This transfer recognized that the primary mission of the National Service was development rather than defense and permitted the Ministry of Defense to concentrate on its more conventional military responsibilities.

Veterans were not prominent in Côte d'Ivoire's independence movement and have not been a major force in the country's social and political life. The relatively small size of the armed forces and the correspondingly small career service corps, coupled with the limited role of the military in public affairs, has contributed to their quiescence. Veterans of the colonial armed forces have received generous pensions, as have military personnel who have retired from the national armed forces. The National Veterans Administration Office has been subsidized by the Ministry of Defense and Maritime Affairs.

Internal Security

According to many observers, Côte d'Ivoire has had one of the most stable political systems in Africa. As of 1988, President Houphouët-Boigny had been the dominant national figure for more than forty years. He was the country's founding father and its first and only president. In 1988 political violence was relatively rare in Côte d'Ivoire. Since independence, there have been few political prisoners, no executions of political opponents, and no officially sanctioned disappearances or abductions. At the same time, there were numerous indications of political instability. Since the 1970s, the Ivoirian polity has experienced several crises (see Economic and Political Issues of the Late 1970s and 1980s, ch.1).

Domestic Security

After the alleged coup attempts in 1962 and 1963, Houphouët-Boigny disarmed, disbanded, and reorganized the army; took over the defense and interior portfolios; formed a party militia composed predominantly of ethnic Baoulé kinsmen to maintain order in Abidjan; overhauled the State Security Court; and, for his personal protection, established a Presidential Guard separate from the army. Nevertheless, Houphouët-Boigny considered the army to be the cornerstone of Ivoirian internal security.

Following the 1973 alleged coup attempt in Côte d'Ivoire and the April 1974 military coup in Niger that ousted President Hamani Diori, a lifelong friend and regional political ally, Houphouët-Boigny ceded a larger political role to the armed forces to give them a formal stake in the regime. In June 1974, he removed the French commander of the FACI and the French commandant of the military academy at Bingerville, replacing them with Ivoirian officers. A month later, he brought military officers into the cabinet for the first time. Houphoüet-Boigny also promoted several senior army officers and appointed ten officers as prefects.

At same time, the new minister of interior, Mathieu Ekra, undertook organizational reforms and made new appointments in the territorial administration and police forces. By the end of 1974, a new ethnic balance had emerged among the security forces. Northerners controlled higher positions in the army; the demographically preponderant Baoulé dominated the National Security Police; and southerners were a plurality in the police and National Gendarmerie.

In the 1980s, as political upheavals became more frequent, Houphouët-Boigny repeatedly changed his government. In February 1981, in the wake of the 1980 coup and assassination attempts, he enlarged the cabinet from twenty-five to thirty-six ministers, bringing in Banny as minister of defense and Léon Konan Koffi, who had a reputation for being tough, as minister of interior. (Ironically, Banny had been the minister of defense who was arrested and sentenced to death for his role in the 1963 coup plot but later given presidential amnesty. Kouadio M'Bahia Blé, who replaced Banny after the 1963 incident, kept that post until Banny took it back from him in 1981.) In late 1985, several senior military officers were appointed to leadership posts in the Democratic Party of Côte d'Ivoire (Parti Démocratique de Côte d'Ivoire—PDCI), furthering the process of political co-optation that began in the mid-1970s.

Several other groups, including political exiles, labor unions, teachers, and university students, at times posed a threat to civil order; however, none of these groups was likely to topple the government (see Interest Groups, ch. 4). Secondary-school teachers in particular became especially outspoken during the mid-1980s. In April 1983, the National Union of Secondary School Teachers of Côte d'Ivoire (Syndicat National des Enseignants du Secondaire de Côte d'Ivoire—SYNESCI) staged a two-week strike to protest an 80 percent reduction in the teachers' housing allowance. The government responded by threatening to conscript union leaders, dissolve the union, expel teachers from their houses, and close all secondary schools. In July 1987, SYNESCI's leaders (who had also called the 1983 strike) were ousted by a progovernment faction during irregular rump proceedings of the union's congress, while uniformed police and plainclothes officers surrounded the union headquarters. The new union officials immediately pledged their loyalty to the government and charged their predecessors with misappropriation of union property and funds. Thirteen of the ousted unionists were arrested, and in late October the eleven males were sent to the army base in Séguéla. According to Minister of Education Balla Keita (who had taken over the newly consolidated ministry in the midst of the 1983 SYNESCI strike with instructions to break it), the detainees were ''well-known agents of international subversion'' who had been ''sent to the army for national service and civic and moral education in the supreme interest of the country.'' Significantly, SYNESCI—which was one of the last unions independent of the government—appeared finally to have fallen under government influence.

University students have also been a continuing source of antigovernment protest, much to the chagrin of a government that has invested up to 40 percent of the national budget in education. In 1969 police and soldiers occupied and closed the University of Abidjan (present-day National University of Côte d'Ivoire), arrested dozens of students, and detained them at Akouédo after they protested the government's attempt to place their newly formed Movement of Ivoirian Primary and Secondary School Students (Mouvement des Etudiants et des Elèves de Côte d'Ivoire— MEECI) under the PDCI. In February 1982, the government again closed the university after both students and faculty protested the government's banning of Professor Laurent Gbagbo's speech on political freedom. In 1985 police broke up a violent demonstration by students protesting wholesale reduction in scholarship aid.

Alien migrant labor also represented a potential security threat. Côte d'Ivoire's relatively robust economy made the country a magnet for migrant labor. In 1988 at least 2 million foreign Africans in the country—about half of them Burkinabé—(residents of Burkina Faso) comprised about one-fifth, and perhaps much more, of the population of Côte d'Ivoire. Most aliens were agricultural laborers or unemployed urban squatters, politically helpless and economically deprived migrants who turned to crime.

Foreigners who were more industrious often became scapegoats for the wrath of hard-strapped Ivoirians, who saw these outsiders taking jobs that they themselves had allegedly been denied. In April 1980, for example, hundreds of Mauritanians were taken under protective custody, and some 1,500 others took refuge in the Mauritanian embassy in Abidjan after days of rioting and fighting with Ivoirians. More serious incidents directed against Burkinabé occurred during xenophobic riots in 1985, leading Burkina Faso to recall its ambassador from Abidjan.

Human Rights

Côte d'Ivoire has a mixed record of human rights observance. The *World Handbook of Political and Social Indicators* ranked the country ninety-sixth on political rights and ninety-second on civil rights out of 144 nations. Freedom House has consistently rated Côte d'Ivoire low on its scale of political rights and civil liberties; nonetheless, in 1980 it elevated the country from the status of "not free" to "partly free." This rating put Côte d'Ivoire in the same category as Transkei (part of South Africa) and ranked it freer than Guinea but less free than Senegal. *The World Human Rights Guide* rated the country as "poor," while the United States Department of State's *Country Reports on Human Rights Practices for 1987* officially characterized human rights conditions in Côte d'Ivoire as "generally satisfactory."

Côte d'Ivoire was a signatory to a number of international human rights conventions, including the Slavery Convention of 1926, the Supplementary Convention on the Abolition of Slavery of 1956, the Geneva Conventions of 1949 Relative to the Treatment of Prisoners of War and Civilians in Time of War, and the Protocol Relating to the Status of Refugees of 1967. It had not yet signed the 1953 Convention on the Political Rights of Women, the Convention on the Prevention and Punishment of the Crime of Genocide of 1948, or the International Covenants on Civil and Political Rights and on Economic, Social and Cultural Rights of 1966.

Internal Security Organization and Forces

Responsibility for internal security in Côte d'Ivoire was shared by three ministries in a coordinated, multilayered pattern adapted from the French colonial system. The Ministry of Interior was responsible primarily for territorial and local administration and included local police forces; the Ministry of Internal Security was charged with state security and national police functions; and the Ministry of Defense and Maritime Affairs (primarily through the National Gendarmerie) provided paramilitary forces throughout the country in coordination with the respective regional and local authorities.

The Ministry of Interior, as chartered by decrees of January 1961 and May 1962, had broad regulatory functions. As part of its security-related responsibilities, it regulated public associations, gun control, access to public buildings, emigration and immigration, foreign propaganda, foreign visitors, and passport controls. It also directed the National Security Police, supervised traditional chieftaincies, and administered territorial subdivisions.

Although the National Security Police was transferred to the Ministry of Internal Security in 1976, the other functions of Ministry of Interior have remained essentially intact. In February 1981, Léon Konan Koffi replaced Alexis Thierry-Lebbe as minister of interior. As of 1985, its constituent elements included the minister's cabinet and six directorates covering territorial administration, local communities, financial affairs, personnel and manpower programs, the National Printing Office, and the National Archives. It had a staff of about 4,900 and an operating budget of CFA F13.3 billion, or 3.2 percent of the government's budget.

Territorial administration remained the ministry's most important function pertaining to public order and internal security. The prefects and subprefects executed government policies and represented the interests of the local population (see Local Government, ch. 4). Each prefecture and municipality also was responsible for maintaining order; executing government laws, regulations, and policies; and administrating the police. Moreover, the prefects and subprefects were empowered to call upon the armed forces if needed and to requisition persons and property in matters of public safety. Prefects were authorized to detain for forty-eight hours anyone apprehended for crimes and offenses involving state security.

The Ministry of Internal Security was established as part of a governmental reorganization in March 1976 to consolidate the national police and state security functions that had formerly been assigned to the Ministry of Interior. In November 1983, Brigadier General Oumar N'Daw, who had been the high commander of the National Gendarmerie for nine years, succeeded Colonel Gaston Ouassenan Koné, who served as minister of internal security from 1976 to 1983. In 1985 the ministry was reorganized into the following groups: the minister's cabinet; eight directorates (National Security Police, Regional Security, Inspector General of Police Services, Materials, Financial Affairs, Personnel, Police Economics and Finances, and Judicial Affairs); the National Police Academy, and an intelligence service. In 1985 the ministry had a staff of about 5,600, and its operating budget of CFA F11.7 billion (or 2.8 percent of the government's budget) represented a 5.8 percent increase over its 1984 operating budget.

The National Security Police was an investigative bureau and national police force with a strength of about 5,300 in 1987. It enforced law and order and provided special police services. The various directorates of the National Security Police were responsible for public security, internal and cross-frontier traffic, counterespionage, intelligence, criminal investigation, narcotics and drug control, and the administration of sixteen national police districts.

In larger towns and cities, the National Security Police cooperated with the municipal police forces; in the smaller communities and rural areas, it worked with the local police and the National Gendarmerie. The ministry's Regional Security Directorate included three separate divisions grouping the commissariats for subprefects and major urban centers and the Frontier Police. The Special Police, Frontier Police, and the Abidjan Port Police were grouped under the Central Commissariat.

The National Security Police Public Security Directorate consisted of the uniformed national police and the Companies for the Security of the Republic (Compagnies Républicaines de Sécurité—CRS), which were at the immediate disposal of the minister of internal security for deployment throughout the country. In emergencies, prefects could call upon the minister to use any CRS in his or her jurisdiction. The CRS were most frequently used to handle certain kinds of local emergencies and rescue operations. They also cooperated with the local National Gendarmerie forces and the Frontier Police. The Intelligence Directorate was responsible for collecting intelligence on security-related political, economic, and social events (such as industrial strikes and antigovernment demonstrations). The Counterespionage Directorate was responsible for protecting the state against treason and espionage. The Criminal Investigation Directorate coordinated and directed crime-fighting efforts, maintained the central files, and served as liaison with international police through the International Criminal Police Organization (Interpol).

Before independence and until the National Police Academy (Ecole Nationale de Police) was opened in 1967, police training consisted of a six-month course given at the Federal School in Dakar, Senegal. By 1988 about 6,000 police officers had been trained at the National Police Academy; in the 1980s, the academy annually graduated about 450 officers, who were then assigned to the Police Forces of the Ministry of Internal Security. Like its military counterparts, the National Police Academy also served as a regional training center for francophone Africa and has graduated officers from Burkina Faso, Cameroon, Central African Republic, Chad, Congo, Niger, and Senegal.

The academy's basic course of study varied from six months to two years (depending on the student's rank) and included forensic medicine, judicial procedure, criminal investigation, criminology and criminal psychology, police administration, computer technology, and communications. Admission was by direct recruitment or entrance examinations. Candidates for commissioner were required to have credits toward a law degree to gain entrance and to complete their law degree in order to graduate. Candidates who failed to obtain the law degree within two years were admitted to the police officer corps. Commissioners also were recruited from among police officers who fulfilled length-of-service requirements set by police ordinance. Police officer candidates, who also underwent a two-year training program, could be admitted directly to the academy with a bachelor's degree or were recruited by examination from among police officers with three years' service. Finally, police officers were recruited from among qualified Ivoirian nationals who had completed elementary school.

The third pillar of internal security, the National Gendarmerie, consisted of a headquarters staff, four legions (corresponding to the four military regions) and a professional training academy, the Gendarmerie School (Ecole de Gendarmerie). This national constabulary force was formed in October 1960, replacing the Guard of the Republic that had been established in 1958. In 1988 Colonel Koffi Botty was the high commander of the National Gendarmerie, having replaced Brigadier General N'daw in 1983. The National Gendarmerie was responsible for defending rural areas and maintaining domestic order, thereby complementing the conventional tactical capabilities of the regional military commands. Its effective strength of 1,500 in the late 1960s doubled to 3,000 in the early 1970s, and in 1987 it was estimated at 4,500. The headquarters included an intelligence bureau; administrative and training center; bureaus of logistics, personnel, and budget planning; and a security and foreign liaison division.

The four National Gendarmerie legions each had a general staff, detached companies that were deployed in and around the major towns and population centers in their respective prefectures, and a small number of mobile squads for rapid reaction and general support.

Before 1960 auxiliaries and auxiliary students trained in Dakar. In 1960 an officer instruction center was created in Abidjan. In 1961 the National Gendarmerie set up its own academy, the Gendarmerie School, in Abidjan. The school trained NCOs (recruited from among the police and other qualified persons) and constables (recruited from among qualified students). The training period lasted about eleven months, at the end of which graduating constables received a police aptitude certificate. NCOs received an equivalent diploma. Students received instruction in both police techniques and military training. The academy also offered eight-week in-service training courses for NCOs and motorcycle police. The academy has graduated a large number of NCOs but only a few officers. The 1983 graduating class included about

250 NCOs and 8 officers, bringing the academy's total number of graduates to 77 officers and 6,062 NCOs, which included 113 Burkinabé NCOs who underwent training between 1967 and 1969.

Crime and Punishment

The Constitution of Côte d'Ivoire establishes a legal basis for the Ivoirian criminal justice system. The right to a fair public trial is guaranteed by law, and that right generally was respected in urban areas. In rural areas, traditional justice often substituted for formal criminal law. By law, defendants are entitled to legal counsel, and the court is supposed to appoint lawyers for the indigent; however, attorneys were often not available.

Criminal Justice System

The Ivoirian penal code prohibited official violence without legitimate justification; nevertheless, suspects (particularly foreign Africans) were routinely subjected to rough treatment when detained or arrested by the National Gendarmerie or National Security Police. The penal code also allowed the police or investigative magistrates to conduct home searches without warrants if they had reason to believe that evidence of a crime would be found. Although the Constitution and statutes prohibited arbitrary arrest and imprisonment, the penal code did permit public prosecutors to detain suspects for up to forty-eight hours without charges. Magistrates could order longer detention of up to four months, provided that monthly reports were filed with the Ministry of Justice justifying continued detention. In the 1980s, periodic but short-lived anticrime campaigns resulted in massive detentions. The Ivoirian government abolished capital punishment for political crimes and had not employed it for criminal offenses since independence.

Prison System

As in most Third World countries, prison conditions in Côte d'Ivoire were harsh. Prisons often were crowded, dietary conditions were poor, and medical and sanitation facilities were minimal. Family members were encouraged to bring food to prisoners to supplement the meager prison diets. Prisons served as punitive and custodial facilities rather than as rehabilitative institutions. Visits by prisoners' attorneys were permitted, but the vast majority of inmates could not afford legal assistance. The few court-appointed lawyers could not effectively represent the large numbers of persons assigned to them. There was virtually no vocational training, and although prisoners routinely performed labor, like cleaning public markets or maintaining roads, they did little or no gainful work. Prison staffs and guard forces were small relative to the inmate population, had minimum education and professional training, and could scarcely maintain control of the inmates and prison facilities. In July 1983, for example, a group of armed Burkinabé made a night raid on the large prison in Bouaké and freed forty-five of their countrymen.

The prison population in 1966 was 3,754 inmates, of whom 2,953 had been sentenced and 801 were accused but not yet convicted or sentenced. By the early 1970s, the prison population had increased sharply to between 5,000 and 7,000 inmates. The two largest prisons, at Yopougon near Abidjan and at Bouaké, accounted for about one-half the total prison population. The former facility had about 1,100 inmates, and the latter had between 1,600 and 2,000. Ten years later, the number of inmates in the Bouaké prison was estimated at 1,400, and by 1985 the total number of convicted prisoners in the country had doubled to some 13,000. A large proportion (perhaps even a substantial majority) of the inmates in Ivoirian penal institutions were expatriate Africans from neighboring countries. If the 1966 prison population figures are representative of a fairly stable ratio of inmates awaiting sentence to those actually serving sentences, then Côte d'Ivoire compared very favorably with the Third World norm in which the majority of prisoners were awaiting trial because of the judicial backlog.

Periodically, Houphouët-Boigny granted wholesale amnesties to prisoners. For example, in October 1975 he pardoned about 5,000 common law prisoners serving prison terms for embezzlement and theft. At the same time, he pardoned many political prisoners, including 145 who had been implicated in the Gagnoa uprising of 1970 and 12 soldiers who had been held since the 1973 coup plot. Ten years later, on December 7, 1985, in commemoration of the twenty-fifth anniversary of Côte d'Ivoire's independence, the president ordered the release of nearly 10,000 of the country's prisoners who were not incarcerated for violent crimes or armed robbery.

Incidence and Trends in Crime

Crime in Côte d'Ivoire has been linked to abrupt socioeconomic and cultural change related to uncontrolled and rapid urbanization, industrialization and associated labor migration, unemployment and underemployment, the proliferation of urban slums, the absence or collapse of urban and human services, and the inability of government authorities to enforce law and order. In the 1980s, serious crime increased markedly, particularly in Abidjan and other urban areas. Like other modernizing countries, Côte d'Ivoire experienced increases in theft, armed robbery, myriad petty crimes, prostitution, and drug and alcohol abuse. The most frequent offenders were young men and juveniles, although women also increasingly resorted to crime.

Police Response to Increased Crime

In July 1987, the minister of internal security estimated that the Ivoirian police required about 800 recruits a year—nearly three times the recruitment level at that time—to cope with increasing crime. In the 1980s, law enforcement officials conducted periodic large-scale crime sweeps and law-enforcement crackdowns to deter and disrupt illegal activities. In July 1983, for instance, police detained more than 3,500 people during a ten-day sweep of Abidjan that involved both directed and random searches of people, vehicles, and homes. Special police units were formed to counter the increasingly sophisticated and brazen tactics used by criminals. In July 1984, the minister of internal security formed a new "antigang brigade" with special training, equipment, and weapons. In early 1987, in response to the proliferation of bank robberies in Abidjan, the ministry established a bank surveillance brigade with fifteen vehicles donated by the Professional Association of Banks.

In the 1980s, the government stepped up drug enforcement efforts to prevent the production, smuggling, sale, and use of illegal drugs, such as marijuana, amphetamines, barbiturates, heroin, and cocaine. In 1986 the police narcotics squad handled 718 drug cases. Nevertheless, the government failed to make a serious dent in an alarming problem that continued to outstrip enforcement resources. In May 1987, Côte d'Ivoire hosted a two-week international symposium on the prevention and treatment of drug abuse and alcoholism. At the insistence of the United States Federal Aeronautics Administration (FAA), the police instituted strict new security measures in October 1987 at the Abidjan-Port Bouët International Airport to meet international standards. The measures included personal searches, metal detectors, baggage x-rays, access cards for airport service personnel, and strict access controls for persons and vehicles seeking to enter the airport.

Public Response: "Psychose Sécuritaire"

Crime and security have become major public concerns in Côte d'Ivoire. The alarming increase in crime rates, particularly in Abidjan, has induced a *psychose sécuritaire* (obsession with security) among Ivoirians. Frequently thefts and armed robberies, often accompanied by violence, have led some neighborhoods and businesses to form defense committees to protect their lives and property. Private security firms also have prospered in the cities, especially in

Abidjan, filling the growing gap between levels of crime and police protection. Various communal and business interest groups have provided equipment and resources to the overtaxed and under-equipped public security forces. The most notable recent example was the Abidjan bankers' contribution of motor vehicles to the new bank surveillance unit. The Union of Burkinabé in Côte d'Ivoire also donated ten vehicles to the police during 1983 and 1984. The Lebanese community, whose estimated 100,000 to 300,000 members control much of the retail trade, contributed twenty vehicles and 200,000 liters of fuel to security forces, and the Italian business community donated fifty-five Fiat vehicles to the police. France also has furnished substantial assistance to the paramilitary forces. After Houphouët-Boigny made an obviously undeliverable promise in November 1983 to rid the country of banditry within five months, the French government promptly donated about 100 Peugeot-504 diesel vehicles to the National Gendarmerie. In 1984 France also dispatched a special police brigade to reinforce Ivoirian counterparts. Despite such self-help and French support, in early 1988 there was no indication that the magnitude of Côte d'Ivoire's crime problem would diminish or that the capacity of the security forces to control it would improve.

* * *

Given the specialized nature of the material and the protectiveness of Ivoirian security services, there is no comprehensive study covering Ivoirian national security. Much of the material in this chapter came from periodicals like *Afrique défense,* its English-language counterpart *Africa Defence, Africa Research Bulletin, Marchés tropicaux et méditerranéens,* and *Frères d'armes.* Other sources were annual publications, such as *The Military Balance* published by the International Institute for Strategic Studies, *World Military Expenditures and Arms Transfers* produced by the United States Arms Control and Disarmament Agency, and *Country Reports on Human Rights Practices* produced by the United States Department of State. Material on the administrative structure of security forces came from *L'Administration ivoirienne,* by Hugues Tay and *Guide des institutions politiques et administratives* by Albert Aggrey. The main sources for information on crime and the criminal justice system included the Ivoirian daily *Fraternité matin* and the Abidjan Institute of Criminology's published conference proceedings titled *First West African Conference in Comparative Criminology.* Also useful was *Crime and Modernization* by Louise Shelley. (For further information and complete citations, see Bibliography.)

Appendix

Table 1. Metric Conversion Coefficients and Factors

When you know	Multiply by	To find
Millimeters	0.04	inches
Centimeters	0.39	inches
Meters	3.3	feet
Kilometers	0.62	miles
Hectares (10,000 m²)	2.47	acres
Square kilometers	0.39	square miles
Cubic meters	35.3	cubic feet
Liters	0.26	gallons
Kilograms	2.2	pounds
Metric tons	0.98	long tons
....	1.1	short tons
....	2,204	pounds
Degrees Celsius	9	degrees Fahrenheit
(Centigrade)	divide by 5 and add 32	

Table 2. Gross Domestic Product by Sector, Selected Years, 1965–84
(in billions of CFA francs at constant prices; base year 1984) *

Sector	1965	1970	1975	1980	1983	1984
Agriculture	485.6	605.0	680.1	856.3	767.1	767.9
Industry	104.8	204.9	287.5	511.5	493.0	374.1
Services	257.3	409.1	844.2	105.0	1,062.1	1,013.9

* For value of the CFA franc—Communauté Financière Africaine franc—see Glossary.

Table 3. Major Economic Aggregates, Selected Years, 1970–87
(in millions of United States dollars)

	1970	1975	1980	1982	1984	1986	1987
Gross national product	1,369	3,580	9,951	7,059	6,092	8,657	9,439
Exports of goods and services ..	566	1,503	3,640	2,844	3,042	3,705	3,624
Imports of goods and services .	584	1,741	4,761	3,498	2,833	3,482	3,881
Current account balance	−38	−379	−1,826	−1,016	−54	−135	−624

Source: Based on information from World Bank, "Country Tables" in *World Debt Tables*, 2, Washington, 1988, 98.

Table 4. Agricultural Production, Selected Years, 1979–87
(in thousands of tons)

Commodity	1979–81 [1]	1985	1986	1987
Cereals	1,090	1,048	1,084	1,000
Rice	438	541	561	595
Maize	352	480	420	415
Roots and tubers	3,429	4,671	4,799	4,704
Cassava	1,067	1,500	1,500	1,500 [2]
Yams	2,079	2,900	3,000	2,900
Coconuts	n.a.	390	400	400
Palm oil	157	160	187	215
Sugar cane	1,373	1,270	1,500	1,750
Bananas	163	163	140 [2]	136 [2]
Coffee	298	277	265	260
Cocoa	427	580	575	570
Cotton (fiber)	54	88	75	91
Cotton-seed	74	117	115	122

n.a.—not available.
[1] Annual average.
[2] Estimate.

Source: Based on information from United Nations, Food and Agriculture Organization, *FAO Production Yearbook, 1987,* Rome, 1988, 113–244.

Table 5. Exports, Imports, and Balance of Trade, Selected Years, 1965–84
(in millions of United States dollars)

	1965	1970	1975	1980	1983	1984
Exports						
Coffee	104.9	186.2	301.6	644.2	410.6	450.2
Cocoa	39.4	89.0	240.6	793.3	427.0	964.0
Other agricultural products	22.7	18.6	70.3	105.0	77.9	127.0
Forestry products	60.7	84.7	162.6	474.3	198.1	217.0
Petroleum products	7.2	5.2	67.9	212.0	239.3	308.0
Food processing	24.2	42.5	218.4	362.1	356.1	296.6
Textiles and shoes	4.7	17.7	59.2	131.0	103.9	136.9
Wood products	21.4	17.7	50.2	98.5	119.0	117.6
Other manufactures	40.8	20.7	113.0	192.2	151.6	169.4
Total exports	326.0	482.3	1,283.8	3,012.6	2,083.5	2,786.7
Imports						
Agricultural products	42.2	41.8	113.7	249.4	251.3	231.4
Petroleum products	13.0	15.3	133.8	557.1	343.3	432.8
Manufactures	204.0	326.3	967.7	1,807.1	911.7	1,115.7
Total imports	259.2	383.4	1,215.2	2,613.6	1,506.3	1,779.9
Balance of trade	66.9	93.0	68.9	399.0	585.2	1,007.6

Table 6. Principal Trading Partners, 1985
(in millions of United States dollars)

Country	Exports	Imports
France	527.7	511.0
United States	507.0	76.7
West Germany	300.7	69.3
Italy	287.5	59.7
Netherlands	192.1	87.3
Britain	135.6	41.5

Source: Based on information from *Africa Research Bulletin* [Exeter, United Kingdom], 24, No. 6, July 31, 1987, 8769.

Table 7. Balance of Payments, Selected Years, 1965–84
(in millions of United States dollars)

	1965	1970	1975	1980	1983	1984
Goods and services balance	61.2	96.5	5.6	−570.3	60.4	755.9
Interest, transfers, and remittances	−52.3	−88.2	−324.1	−1,262.3	−986.7	−891.8
Current account balance *	8.9	8.3	−318.4	−1,832.6	−926.4	−135.9
Capital account balance (private and public)	3.6	29.5	191.6	1,020.9	392.6	269.1
Overall balance *	12.6	37.8	−126.8	−811.7	−533.8	133.2

* Figures may not add to totals because of rounding.

Table 8. Total Debt and Debt Service, Selected Years, 1970–87
(in millions of United States dollars)

	1970	1975	1980	1985	1986	1987
Long-term debt	266	1,008	4,742	8,490	9,733	11,714
Short-term debt	n.a.	n.a.	1,059	725	787	1,265
IMF credit used [1]	0	13	0	622	623	576
Total debt [2]	266	1,021	5,801	9,837	11,142	13,555
Debt service	43	143	943	1,235	1,540	1,477

n.a.—not available.
[1] International Monetary Fund—see Glossary.
[2] Figures may not add to totals because of rounding.

Source: Based on information from World Bank, "Country Tables" in *World Debt Tables*, 2, Washington, 1988, 98–99.

Table 9. Army Equipment Inventory, 1987

Type and Description	Country of Origin	In Inventory
Tanks		
AMX-13 light	France	5
Armored vehicles		
AML-60	-do-	10
AML-90	-do-	6
ERC-90 Panhard reconnaissance	-do-	7
M-4 armored personnel carrier	United States	16
VAB 4 × 4	France	13
Air defense		
20mm M693 towed and self-propelled		
(air defense gun)	France and United States	14
40mm towed antiaircraft gun	France	5
Towed artillery		
M-1950 105mm howitzer	United States	4
Mortars		
120mm AM-50	France	16
Antitank weapons		
89mm STRIM	France	n.a.
Recoilless rifles		
106mm M-40	United States	n.a.

n.a.—not available.

Source: Based on information from *The Military Balance, 1987–1988*, London, 1987, 129;
Barbara Pope, ed., *World Defense Forces*, Santa Barbara, California, 1987, 62; and
Defense and Foreign Affairs Handbook, 1986, Washington, 1986, 379.

Table 10. Naval Equipment Inventory, 1987

Type and Description	Country of Origin	In Inventory
Fast attack craft		
(equipped with missiles)		
PR–48 Patra class	France	2
Patrol craft		
PR–48 Patra class	France and Belgium	2
Karlskrona CG.27	Sweden	3
Amphibious landing ships		
Batral class	France	1
LCVPs		1 *
Fast assault boats		
Rotork-type	Britain	10
Service craft		
Barracuda-class launch	United States	1
Arcor	France	8 *
River patrol craft		
Comoé class	–do–	1
Training vessels		
Shimazu training ship	Japan	1

* Estimate.

Source: Based on information from Jean Labayle Couhat, ed., *Combat Fleets of the World,*
1986–1987, Annapolis, 1986, 282–83; and *Jane's Fighting Ships, 1978–1988,* London,
1987, 300.

Table 11. Air Force Equipment Inventory, 1987

Type and Description	Country of Origin	In Inventory
Ground attack		
Dassault-Breguet light attack/trainer	France	6
Trainer		
Aérospatiale Rallye 160 basic	–do–	1
Aérospatiale Rallye 235 basic	–do–	1
Riems Aviation/Cessna 150H basic	–do–	2
Beech F33C Bonanza basic	United States	6
Transport		
Grumman Gulfstream II and III	–do–	2
Rockwell Aero Commander 500B	–do–	2
Liaison and transport		
F-28 Mk 4000 Fellowship VIP	Netherlands	1
Helicopters and transport		
SA–313B Alouette IIs,		
SA–316B Alouette IIIs,		
SA–365C Dauphin 3s,		
SA–330 Pumas	France	11

Source: Based on information from *The Military Balance, 1987–1988,* London, 1987, 129;
"Republic of the Ivory Coast," *Air Forces of the World, 1986,* Geneva, 1986, 285–86,
and "Ivory Coast," *Flight International,* November 29, 1986, 47.

Bibliography

Chapter 1

Ajayi, J.F. Ade, and Michael Crowder (eds.). *History of West Africa,* 2. New York: Colombia University Press, 1974.

Bakary, Tessilimi. "Elite Transformation and Political Succession." Pages 21–56 in I. William Zartman and Christopher Delgado (eds.), *The Political Economy of Ivory Coast.* New York: Praeger, 1984.

Binger, Capitaine Louis Gustave. *Du Niger au golfe de Guinée par le pays de Kong et le Mossi.* (2 vols.) Paris: Librairie Hachette, 1892.

Campbell, Bonnie. "The Ivory Coast." Pages 66–116 in John Dunn (ed.), *West African States: Failure and Promise.* Cambridge: Cambridge University Press, 1978.

_____. "The State and Capitalist Development in the Ivory Coast." Pages 281–303 in Paul M. Lubeck (ed.), *The African Bourgeoisie: Capitalist Development in Nigeria, Kenya, and the Ivory Coast.* Boulder, Colorado: Lynne Rienner, 1987.

Cohen, Michael A. "The Myth of the Expanding Center—Politics in the Ivory Coast," *Journal of Modern African Studies* [London], 11, No. 2, June 1973, 227–46.

_____. *Urban Policy and Political Conflict in Africa.* Chicago: University of Chicago Press, 1974.

Economist Intelligence Unit. *Quarterly Economic Review of Ivory Coast, Togo, Benin, Niger, Upper Volta: Annual Report.* London: The Economist, 1983.

Gbagbo, Laurent. *Côte d'Ivoire: Economie et société à la veille de l'indépendance (1940–1960).* Paris: L'Harmattan, 1982.

Handloff, Robert Earl. *The Dyula of Gyaman: A Study of Politics and Trade in the Nineteenth Century.* (Ph.D. dissertation.) Evanston, Illinois: Northwestern University, 1982.

Harrison-Church, R.J., Richard Synge, and Edith Hodgkinson. "Côte d'Ivoire." Pages 397–415 in *Africa South of the Sahara.* (17th ed.) London: Europa, 1987.

Hecht, Robert M. "The Ivory Coast Economic 'Miracle': What Benefits for Peasant Farmers?" *Journal of Modern African Studies* [Cambridge], 12, No. 1, March 1983, 25–53.

Jackson, Robert H., and Carl G. Rosberg. *Personal Rule in Black Africa.* Berkeley, California: University of California Press, 1982.

July, Robert W. *A History of the African People.* New York: Scribner's Sons, 1974.

Legum, Colin (ed.). *Africa Contemporary Record: Annual Survey and Documents* (annuals 1980–1981 through 1985–1986). New York: Africana, 1981–1986.

Loucou, Jean-Noël. "Histoire." Page 25 in Pierre Vennetier (ed.), *Atlas de la Côte d'Ivoire*. (2d ed.) Paris: Jeune Afrique, 1983.

Morgenthau, Ruth Schachter. *Political Parties in French-Speaking West Africa*. Oxford: Clarendon Press, 1964.

Mundt, Robert J. *Historical Dictionary of the Ivory Coast*. (African Historical Dictionaries, No. 41.) Metuchen, New Jersey: Scarecrow Press, 1987.

Potholm, Christian P. *Four African Political Systems*. Englewood Cliffs, New Jersey: Prentice-Hall, 1970.

Shaw, Thurstan. "The Prehistory of West Africa." Pages 33–71 in J.F. Ade Ajayi and Michael Crowder (eds.), *History of West Africa*. (2d ed.) London: Longman, 1976.

Staniland, Martin. "Single-Party Regimes and Political Change: The P.D.C.I. and Ivory Coast Politics." Pages 135–75 in Colin Leys (ed.), *Politics and Change in Developing Countries*. London: Cambridge University Press, 1969.

Thompson, Virginia, and Richard Adloff. *French West Africa*. New York: Greenwood Press, 1969.

Toungara, Jeanne Maddox. "Political Reform and Economic Change in Ivory Coast: An Update," *Journal of African Studies* [London], 13, No. 3, Fall 1986, 94–101.

Weiskel, Timothy. "Mission civilisatrice," *The Wilson Quarterly*, 12, No. 4, Autumn 1988, 97–113.

Welch, Claude E., Jr. "Côte d'Ivoire: Personal Rule and Civilian Control." Pages 172–94 in Claude E. Welch, Jr. (ed.), *No Farewell to Arms? Military Disengagement from Politics in Africa and Latin America*. Boulder, Colorado: Westview Press, 1987.

Zolberg, Aristide R. *One-Party Government in the Ivory Coast*. Princeton: Princeton University Press, 1964.

(Various issues of the following periodical were also used in the preparation of this chapter: *Africa Confidential* [London], 1979–84.)

Chapter 2

Adepoju, Aderanti. "Patterns of Migration by Sex." Pages 54–75 in Christine Oppong (ed.), *Female and Male in West Africa*. Boston: Allen and Unwin, 1983.

Alland, Alexander, Jr. *When the Spider Danced*. Garden City, New York: Anchor Press, 1976.

Arnaud, S., and J.-C. Arnaud. "Ethnies." Page 27 in Pierre Vennetier (ed.), *Atlas de la Côte d'Ivoire.* (2d ed.), Paris: Jeune Afrique, 1983.

Asante, Molefi Kete. *The Afrocentric Idea.* Philadelphia: Temple University Press, 1987.

Bakary, Tessilimi. "Elite Transformation and Political Succession." Pages 21–56 in I. William Zartman and Christopher Delgado (eds.), *The Political Economy of Ivory Coast.* New York: Praeger, 1984.

Bakayoko, Adama, and Sylvestre Ehouman. "Ivory Coast." Pages 69–99 in John Dixon (ed.), *Social Welfare in Africa.* (Comparative Social Welfare Series.) London: Croom Helm, 1987.

Bourke, Gerald. "A Tarnished Miracle," *Africa Report,* 32, No. 6, November–December 1987, 62–64.

Bozeman, Adda B. *Conflict in Africa: Concepts and Realities.* Princeton: Princeton University Press, 1976.

Campbell, Bonnie. "The State and Capitalist Development in the Ivory Coast." Pages 281–303 in Paul M. Lubeck (ed.), *The African Bourgeoisie: Capitalist Development in Nigeria, Kenya, and the Ivory Coast.* Boulder, Colorado: Lynne Rienner, 1987.

Charlick, Robert B. "Access to 'Elite' Education in the Ivory Coast: The Importance of Socio-Economic Origins." *Sociology of Education,* 51, July 1978, 187–200.

Cohen, Michael A. "The Myth of the Expanding Center—Politics in the Ivory Coast," *Journal of Modern African Studies* [London], 11, No. 2, June 1973, 227–46.

_____. *Urban Policy and Political Conflict in Africa. A Study of the Ivory Coast.* Chicago: University of Chicago Press, 1974.

Côte d'Ivoire. Embassy in Washington. "Education." (Unpublished document.) Washington: 1987.

"Côte d'Ivoire: Direction of Trade with Major Trading Partners," *Africa Research Bulletin* [Exeter, United Kingdom], 4, No. 6, July 31, 1987, 8769.

Daddieh, Cyril Kofie. "Ivory Coast." Pages 122–44 in Timothy M. Shaw and Olajide Aluko (eds.), *The Political Economy of African Foreign Policy.* New York: St. Martin's Press, 1984.

David, Philippe. *La Côte d'Ivoire.* Paris: Karthala, 1986.

den Tuinder, Bastiaan A. *Ivory Coast: The Challenge of Success.* Baltimore: Johns Hopkins University Press, 1978.

Diallo, Helga. *Le chasseur Lobi: Une étude ethnosociologique.* Vienna: Elisabeth Stiglmayr, 1978.

Dieterlen, Germaine. "The Mandé Creation Myth," Pages 634–53 in Elliott P. Skinner (ed.), *Peoples and Cultures of Africa.* Garden City, New York: Doubleday/Natural History Press, 1973.

Economist Intelligence Unit. *Country Report: Ivory Coast, 1986-1987.* London: The Economist, 1987.

Fieldhouse, D. K. *Black Africa, 1945-1980: Economic Decolonization and Arrested Development.* London: Allen and Unwin, 1986.

Fortes, Meyer. "Kinship and Marriage among the Ashanti." Pages 252-85 in A.R. Radcliffe-Brown and D. Forde, *African Systems of Kinship and Marriage.* London: Oxford University Press, 1950.

_____. "The Structure of Unilineal Descent Groups," *American Anthropologist,* No. 55, 1953, 17-41.

Gbagbo, Laurent. *Côte d'Ivoire: Pour une alternative démocratique.* Paris: L'Harmattan, 1983.

Gozo, K.M. *Crise et pauvreté en Côte d'Ivoire.* Addis Ababa, Ethiopia: Bureau International du Travail, Programme des Emplois et des Compétences Techniques pour l'Afrique, June 1983, 61-65.

Halaoui, Nazam, Kalilou Tera, and Monique Trabi. *Atlas des langues Mandé-sud de Côte d'Ivoire.* Paris: Agence de Coopération Culturelle et Technique, 1983.

Harrison-Church, R.J., Richard Synge, and Edith Hodgkinson. "Côte d'Ivoire." Pages 397-415 in *Africa South of the Sahara.* (17th ed.) London: Europa, 1987.

Hecht, Robert M. "The Ivory Coast Economic 'Miracle': What Benefits for Peasant Farmers?" *Journal of Modern African Studies* [Cambridge], 21, No. 1, 1983, 25-53.

Humana, Charles. *World Human Rights Guide.* New York: Facts on File, 1986.

Jackson, Robert H., and Carl G. Rosberg. *Personal Rule in Black Africa.* Berkeley: University of California Press, 1982.

Kilson, Martin. *Political Change in a West African State.* Cambridge: Harvard University Press, 1966.

Liebenow, J. Gus. *African Politics.* Bloomington: Indiana University Press, 1986.

Little, Kenneth. "Political Functions of the Poro." Pages 257-88 in Colin M. Turnbull (ed.), *Africa and Change.* New York: Alfred A. Knopf, 1973.

Monnier, Yves. "Végétation." Page 17 in Pierre Vennetier (ed.), *Atlas de la Côte d'Ivoire.* Paris: Jeune Afrique, 1983.

Moussa, Alfred Dan. "Quota of Scholarship Grants Restored." *Fraternité Matin* [Abidjan], April 6, 1987, 28.

Mundt, Robert J. *Historical Dictionary of the Ivory Coast.* (African Historical Dictionaries, No. 41.) Metuchen, New Jersey: Scarecrow Press, 1987.

_____. "Internal Criticism of the Ivoirian Political Regime." (Paper presented at African Studies Association Annual Meeting.) Denver, Colorado: November 20, 1987.

Murdock, George Peter. *Africa: Its Peoples and their Culture History.* New York: McGraw-Hill, 1959.

Niamkey, Paul-André. "La grogne des enseignants." *Africa International* [Paris], February 6, 1987, 24–26.

Oppong, Christine (ed.). *Female and Male in West Africa.* Boston: Allen and Unwin, 1983.

Paulme, Denise. "Oral Literature and Social Behavior in Black Africa." Pages 525–42 in Elliott P. Skinner (ed.), *Peoples and Cultures of Africa.* Garden City, New York: Doubleday/Natural History Press, 1973.

Potholm, Christian P. *Four African Political Systems.* Englewood Cliffs, New Jersey: Prentice-Hall, 1970.

Rattray, R.S. *Ashanti.* London: Oxford University Press, 1923.

_____. *Religion and Art in Ashanti.* New York: AMS Press, 1979.

Shaw, Timothy M., and Olajide Aluko (eds.). *The Political Economy of African Foreign Policy.* New York: St. Martin's Press, 1984.

Skinner, Elliott P. "Intergenerational Conflict among the Mossi: Father and Son," *Journal of Conflict Resolution,* 5, No. 1, 1961, 55–60.

Skinner, Elliott P. (ed.). *Peoples and Cultures of Africa.* Garden City, New York: Doubleday/Natural History Press, 1973.

Third World Resources Institute and the International Institute for Environment and Development. *World Resources, 1986.* New York: Basic Books, 1986.

Toungara, Jeanne Maddox. "The Changing Status of Women in Côte d'Ivoire." (Paper presented at African Studies Association Annual Meeting.) Denver, Colorado: November 20, 1987.

_____. "Political Reform and Economic Change in Ivory Coast: An Update," *Journal of African Studies* [London], 13, No. 3, Fall 1986, 94–101.

Turnbull, Colin M. (ed.). *Africa and Change.* New York, Alfred A. Knopf, 1973.

United Nations. Department of International Economic and Social Affairs. Statistical Office. *1986 Demographic Yearbook.* (38th ed.) New York: 1988.

_____. Department of International Economic and Social Affairs. Statistical Office. *Statistical Yearbook, 1983–84.* (34th issue.) New York: 1986.

_____. Educational, Scientific, and Cultural Organization. *International Yearbook of Education,* 32. New York: 1980.

_____. Statistical Office. *Bulletin mensuel de statistique.* 41, No. 8, New York: August 1987.

_____. Statistical Office. "Survey of Economic and Social Conditions in Africa, 1985–1986." (Report presented to the Twenty-second Session of the Economic Commission for Africa.) Addis Ababa, Ethiopia: April 23–27, 1987, 159–74.

United States. Department of Defense. Global Epidemiology Working Group. *Global Disease Surveillance Report.* Frederick, Maryland: January 1988.

Vennetier, Pierre (ed.). *Atlas de la Côte d'Ivoire.* (2d ed.) Paris: Jeune Afrique, 1983.

Weekes, Richard V. (ed.). *Muslim Peoples: A World Ethnographic Survey.* Westport, Connecticut: Greenwood Press, 1978.

Welch, Claude E., Jr. "Côte d'Ivoire: Personal Rule and Civilian Control." Pages 172–94 in Claude E. Welch, Jr. (ed.), *No Farewell to Arms? Military Disengagement from Politics in Africa and Latin America.* Boulder, Colorado: Westview Press, 1987.

Westermann, Diedrich, and Margaret A. Bryan. *The Languages of West Africa.* (Handbook of African Languages, Part 2.) New York: Oxford University Press for the International African Institute, 1952.

_____. *World Development Report, 1986.* Washington: 1986.

World Health Organization. *Progress Report Number 2.* Washington: Special Program on AIDS, November 1987.

_____. "Update: Acquired Immunodeficiency Syndrome." (Global Program on AIDS, unpublished report.) Washington: February 1988.

Young, Crawford. *Ideology and Development in Africa.* New Haven, Connecticut: Yale University Press, 1982.

Zartman, I. William, and Christopher Delgado (eds.). *The Political Economy of Ivory Coast.* New York: Praeger, 1984.

Zolberg, Aristide R. *One-Party Government in the Ivory Coast.* Princeton: Princeton University Press, 1964.

(Various issues of the following periodicals were also used in the preparation of this chapter: *Africa Confidential* [London]; *Africa Economic Digest* [London]; *Africa Report* [London]; *Africa Research Bulletin* [London]; *Afrique-Asie* [Paris]; *Christian Science Monitor;* Foreign Broadcast Information Service, *Daily Report: Subsaharan Africa; Frères d'armes* [Paris]; *Jeune Afrique* [Paris]; *Marchés tropicaux et méditerranéens* [Paris]; West Africa [London].)

Chapter 3

Alschuler, Lawrence R. *Multinationals and Maldevelopment.* New York: St. Martin's Press, 1987.

Amin, Samir. "Capitalism and Development in the Ivory Coast." Pages 277–88 in I.L. Markovitz (ed.), *African Politics and Society.* New York: Free Press, 1970.

————. *Le développement du capitalisme en Côte d'Ivoire.* Paris: Minuit, 1967.

Amnesty International. *Amnesty International Report, 1986.* London: 1986.

Berg, Robert J., and Jennifer Whitaker (eds.). *Strategies for African Development: A Study for the Committee on African Development Strategies.* Berkeley: University of California Press, 1986.

Blackburn, Brigitte. "L'Afrique poignardée par l'occident: Le cas de la Côte d'Ivoire," *Africa International* [Dakar, Senegal], No. 194, April 1987, 13–16.

Bourgoin, Henri, and Philippe Guilbaume. *La Côte d'Ivoire: Economie et Société.* Paris: Stock, 1979.

Brayton, Abbott A. "Stability and Modernization: The Ivory Coast Model," *World Affairs,* 5, No. 141, Winter 1979, 235–49.

Brooke, James. "Abidjan Journal: Black Africa's Oddities, Preserves of White Power," *New York Times,* August 20, 1987, A-3.

Campbell, Bonnie. "The Ivory Coast." Pages 66–116 in John Dunn (ed.), *West African States: Failure and Promise.* Cambridge: Cambridge University Press, 1978.

————. "The State and Capitalist Development in the Ivory Coast." Pages 281–303 in Paul M. Lubeck (ed.), *The African Bourgeoisie: Capitalist Development in Nigeria, Kenya, and the Ivory Coast.* Boulder, Colorado: Lynne Rienner, 1987.

Cohen, Michael A. *Urban Policy and Political Conflict in Africa.* Chicago: University of Chicago Press, 1974.

Côte d'Ivoire." *Budget spécial d'investissement et d'équipement, année 1987,* 2. Abidjan: Imprimerie nationale, 1987.

————. Ministère de l'économie et des finances. *Population de la Côte d'Ivoire.* Abidjan: Imprimerie nationale, 1984.

————. Ministère de l'économie et des finances. *Projet de loi de finances pour la gestion 1986: Rapport économique et financier.* Abidjan: Direction des budgets et comptes, 1986.

————. Ministère du plan et de l'industrie. *Plan quinquennal de développement économique, social et culturel 1981–1985.* (3 vols.) Abidjan: 1983.

"Côte d'Ivoire: Industrial Sector Requires Adjustments," *Courier* [Brussels], No. 105, September–October 1987, "Industrial Opportunities" insert, 1–2.

La Côte d'Ivoire en chiffres. Dakar, Senegal: Société africaine d'édition, 1987.

den Tuinder, Bastiaan A. *Ivory Coast: The Challenge of Success.* Baltimore: Johns Hopkins University Press, 1978.

Dunn, John (ed.). *West African States: Failure and Promise.* Cambridge: Cambridge University Press, 1978.

Economist Intelligence Unit. *Country Report: Ivory Coast, 1986–1987.* London: The Economist, 1987.

"EIB Loan for Modernising and Replacing Textile Mill Installations in Côte d'Ivoire," *Telex Africa* [Brussels], No. 309, September 4, 1987, 8–9.

Eponou, Thomas. "Development Schemes and Their Effect on the Cultural Environment," *Courier* [Brussels], No. 100, November–December 1986, 83–86.

Fauré, Y.-A. "Le complexe politico-économique." Pages 21–60 in Y.-A. Fauré and J.-F. Médard (eds.), *Etat et bourgeoisie en Côte d'Ivoire.* Paris: Karthala, 1982.

Fauré, Y.-A., and J.-F. Médard. "Classe dominante ou classe dirigeante?" Pages 125–48 in Y.-A. Fauré and J.-F. Médard (eds.), *Etat et bourgeoisie en Côte d'Ivoire.* Paris: Karthala, 1982.

_____. *Etat et bourgeoisie en Côte d'Ivoire.* Paris: Karthala, 1982.

Fieldhouse, D.K. *Black Africa, 1945–1980: Economic Decolonization and Arrested Development.* London: Allen and Unwin, 1986.

Gbagbo, Laurent. *Côte d'Ivoire: Pour une alternative démocratique.* Paris: L'Harmattan, 1983.

Glewwe, Paul. *The Distribution of Welfare in Côte d'Ivoire in 1985.* (Living Standards Measurement Study Series, Working Paper No. 29.) Washington: World Bank, 1988.

Hardy, Chandra. "Africa's Debt: Structural Adjustment with Stability." Pages 453–75 in Robert Berg and Jennifer Whitaker (eds.), *Strategies for African Development: A Study for the Committee on African Development Strategies.* Berkeley: University of California Press, 1986.

Harrison-Church, R. J., Richard Synge, and Edith Hodgkinson. "Côte d'Ivoire." Pages 397–415 in *Africa South of the Sahara.* (17th ed.) London: Europa, 1987.

Hecht, Robert M. "The Ivory Coast Economic 'Miracle': What Benefits for Peasant Farmers?" *Journal of Modern African Studies* [Cambridge], No. 21, March 1983, 25–53.

"Interaction News and Events," *Monday Developments,* 6, No. 5, April 4, 1988, 1–9.

"Ivory Coast." Pages B65–B75 in Colin Legum (ed.), *Africa Contemporary Record: Annual Survey and Documents, 1985–1986.* New York: Africana, 1987.

Kurian, George Thomas. "Ivory Coast." Pages 982–99 in George Thomas Kurian (ed.), *Encyclopedia of the Third World,* 2. (3d ed.) New York: Facts on File, 1987.

Lloyd's Ports of the World, 1987. Essex, United Kingdom: Lloyd's of London Press, 1987.

Loucou, J.-N. "Histoire." Pages 39-45 in Pierre Vennetier (ed.), *Atlas de la Côte d'Ivoire.* (2d ed.) Paris: Jeune Afrique, 1983.

Ndulu, Benno J. "Governance and Economic Development." Pages 83-110 in Robert Berg and Jennifer Whitaker (eds.), *Strategies for African Development: A Study for the Committee on African Development Strategies.* Berkeley: University of California, 1986.

Nyong'o, Peter Anyang'. "The Development of Agrarian Capitalist Classes in the Ivory Coast, 1945-1975." Pages 185-245 in Paul Lubeck (ed.), *The African Bourgeoise.* Boulder, Colorado: Lynne Rienner, 1987.

_____. "Liberal Modes of Capitalist Development in Africa: Ivory Coast," *Africa Development* [London], 3, No. 2, April-June 1978, 69-87.

Régie des chemins de fer Abidjan-Niger. *Rapport annuel exercice, 1982-1983.* Abidjan: Imprimerie nationale, 1983.

"République de Côte d'Ivoire," *Europe outremer* [Paris], No. 686-7, March-April 1987, 78-86.

"Thèmes des interventions pour 1988," *Afrique industrie* [Paris], No. 372, July 1, 1987, 41-43.

Toungara, Jeanne Maddox. "Political Reform and Economic Change in Ivory Coast: An Update," *Journal of African Studies* [London], 13, No. 3, Fall 1986, 94-101.

Touré, Abdou. "Paysans et fonctionnaires devant la culture et l'état." Pages 231-51 in Y.-A. Fauré and J.-F. Médard (eds.), *Etat et bourgeoisie en Côte d'Ivoire.* Paris: Karthala, 1982.

Touré, I. "L' U.G.T.C.I. et le 'développement harmonieux'," *Politique africaine* [Paris], No. 24, December 1986, 79-90.

United Nations. Food and Agriculture Organization. Economic and Social Policy Department. *1988 Country Tables.* Rome: 1988.

_____. Food and Agriculture Organization. *FAO Production Yearbook, 1987.* Rome: 1988.

_____. "World Trade by Countries and Regions," *Monthly Bulletin of Statistics,* 41, No. 8, August 1987, 112-13.

United States. Department of Agriculture. *World Indices of Agriculture.* (Statistical Bulletin, No. 744.). Washington: GPO, July 1986.

_____. Department of the Interior. Bureau of Mines. *Mineral Industries of Africa.* Washington: 1984.

Vennetier, Pierre (ed.). *Atlas de la Côte d'Ivoire.* (2d ed.) Paris: Jeune Afrique, 1983.

World Bank. *World Debt Tables.* Washington: 1988.

World Resources Institute for Environment and Development. *World Resources, 1986.* New York: Basic Books, 1986.

Young, Crawford. "Africa's Colonial Legacy." Pages 25–51 in Robert Berg and Jennifer Whitaker (eds.), *Strategies for African Development: A Study for the Committee on African Development Strategies.* Berkeley: University of California Press, 1986.

_____. *Ideology and Development in Africa.* New Haven: Yale University Press, 1982.

Zartman, I. William. *International Relations in the New Africa.* Englewood Cliffs, New Jersey: Prentice-Hall, 1966.

(Various issues of the following periodicals were also used in the preparation of this chapter: *Africa Confidential* [London], 1980–88; *Africa Economic Digest* [London], 1985–88; *Africa Report,* 1980–85; *Africa Research Bulletin* [Exeter, United Kingdom], 1985–88; *Bulletin de l'Afrique noire* [Paris], 1985–88; Foreign Broadcast Information Service, *Daily Report: Subsaharan Africa,* 1985–87; *Jeune Afrique* [Paris], 1983–88; *Jeune Afrique économie* [Paris], 1986–87; Joint Publications Research Service, *Africa/Middle East,* 1985–87; *Le Monde* [Paris], 1985–88; *Marchés tropicaux et méditerranéens,* [Paris], 1980–88; *Telex Africa* [Brussels], 1985–88; and *West Africa* [London], 1985–88.)

Chapter 4

Aggrey, Albert. *Guide des institutions politiques et administratives.* (Guides pratiques du droit ivoirien Series.) Abidjan: Juris-Conseils, 1983.

Alschuler, Lawrence R. *Multinationals and Maldevelopment.* New York: St. Martin's Press, 1987.

Amin, Samir. "Capitalism and Development in the Ivory Coast." Pages 277–88 in I.L. Markovitz (ed.), *African Politics and Society.* New York: Free Press, 1970.

_____. *Le développement du capitalisme en Côte d'Ivoire.* Paris: Minuit, 1967.

_____. *Neo-Colonialism in West Africa.* New York: Monthly Review Press, 1973.

Amondji, Marcel. *Côte d'Ivoire: Le PDCI et la vie politique de 1944 à 1985.* Paris: L'Harmattan, 1986.

_____. *Félix Houphouët et la Côte d'Ivoire.* Paris: Karthala, 1984.

Bach, D. "L'Insertion dans les rapports internationaux." Pages 89–121 in Y.-A. Fauré and J.-F. Médard (eds.), *Etat et bourgeoisie en Côte d'Ivoire.* Paris: Karthala, 1982.

Bakary, Tessilimi. "Elite Transformation and Political Succession." Pages 21–56 in I. William Zartman and Christopher L. Delgado (eds.), *The Political Economy of Ivory Coast*. New York: Praeger, 1984.

Baulin, Jacques. *La politique intérieure d'Houphouët-Boigny*. Paris: Eurafor Press, 1982.

Blackburn, Brigitte. "L'Afrique poignardée par l'occident: Le cas de la Côte d'Ivoire," *Africa International* [Dakar, Senegal], No. 194, April 1987, 13–16.

Bourgoin, Henri, and Philippe Guilbaume. *La Côte d'Ivoire: Economie et société*. Paris: Stock, 1979.

Bourke, Gerald. "A Tarnished Miracle," *Africa Report*, 32, No. 6, November–December 1987, 62–64.

Brayton, Abbott A. "Stability and Modernization: The Ivory Coast Model," *World Affairs*, 5, No. 141, Winter 1979, 235–49.

Brooke, James. "Abidjan Journal: Black Africa's Oddities, Pressures of White Power," *New York Times*, August 20, 1987, A-3.

Campbell, Bonnie. "The Ivory Coast." Pages 66–116 in John Dunn (ed.), *West African States: Failure and Promise*. Cambridge: Cambridge University Press, 1978.

_____. "The State and Capitalist Development in the Ivory Coast." Pages 281–303 in Paul M. Lubeck (ed.), *The African Bourgeoisie*. Boulder, Colorado: Lynne Rienner, 1987.

Chabal, Patrick (ed.). *Political Domination in Africa*. (African Studies Series.) Cambridge: Cambridge University Press, 1986.

Chauveau, J.P., and J. Richard. "Une 'périphérie recentrée' à propos d'un système local d'économie de plantation en Côte d'Ivoire," *Cahiers d'études africaines* [Paris], 17, No. 68, 1977, 485–523.

Chipman, John. *French Military Policy and African Security*. London: International Institute for Strategic Studies, 1975.

Cohen, Michael A. "The Myth of the Expanding Center—Politics in the Ivory Coast," *Journal of Modern African Studies* [London], 11, No. 2, June 1973, 227–46.

_____. *Urban Policy and Political Conflict in Africa*. Chicago: University of Chicago Press, 1974.

_____. "Urban Strategy and Development Strategy." Pages 57–76 in I. William Zartman and Christopher L. Delgado (eds.), *The Political Economy of Ivory Coast*. New York: Praeger, 1984.

Côte d'Ivoire. *Constitution de a République de Côte d'Ivoire*. Abidjan: Imprimerie nationale, 1980.

_____. Ministère de l'économie et des finances. *Projet de loi de finances pour la gestion 1986: Rapport économique et financier*. (Unpublished report.) Abidjan: Direction des budgets et comptes, 1986.

_____. Ministère du plan et de l'industrie. *Plan quinquennal de développement économique, social et culturel, 1981-1985.* (Unpublished document, 3 vols.) Abidjan: 1983.

Delorme, Nicole. "The Foreign Policy of the Ivory Coast." Pages 118-135 in Olajide Aluko (ed.), *The Foreign Policies of African States.* London: Hodder and Stoughton, 1977.

Delury, George E. (ed.). *World Encyclopedia of Political Systems and Parties.* (Facts on File Series, 1.) New York: Facts on File, 1987.

den Tuinder, Bastiaan A. *Ivory Coast: The Challenge of Success.* Baltimore: Johns Hopkins University Press, 1978.

Diallo, Thierno. "Les sociétés et la civilisation des Peul." Pages 227-40 in Mahdi Adams and A.H.M. Kirk-Greene (eds.), *Pastoralists of the West African Savanna.* Manchester: Manchester University Press, 1986.

Dunn, John. *West African States: Failure and Promise.* Cambridge: Cambridge University Press, 1978.

Fauré, Y.-A. "Le complexe politico-économique." Pages 21-60 in Y.-A. Faure and J.-F. Médard (eds.), *Etat et bourgeoisie en Côte d'Ivoire.* Paris: Karthala, 1982.

Fauré, Y.-A., and J.-F. Médard. "Classe dominante ou classe dirigeante?" Pages 125-48 in Y.-A. Fauré and J.-F. Médard (eds.), *Etat et bourgeoisie en Côte d'Ivoire.* Paris: Karthala, 1982.

Fauré, Y.-A. and J.-F. Médard. *Etat et bourgeoisie en Côte d'Ivoire.* Paris: Karthala, 1982.

Fieldhouse, D.K. *Black Africa, 1945-1980. Economic Decolonization and Arrested Development.* London: Allen and Unwin, 1986.

Frelastre, Georges. "Côte d'Ivoire: Nouvelle politique de développement rural sur les rails," *Le mois en Afrique* [Paris], Nos. 249-250, October-November 1986, 97-104.

Gastellu, J.M., and S. Affou Yapi. "Un mythe a décomposé: La 'bourgeoisie de planteurs'." Pages 149-180 in Y.-A. Fauré and J.-F. Médard (eds.), *Etat et bourgeoisie en Côte d'Ivoire.* Paris: Karthala, 1982.

Gbagbo, Laurent. *Côte d'Ivoire: Pour une alternative démocratique.* Paris: L'Harmattan, 1983.

_____. *La Côte d'Ivoire: Economie et société à la veille de l'indépendance (1940-1960).* Paris: L'Harmattan, 1982.

Green, Reginald H. "Reflections on Economic Strategy, Structure, Implementation, and Necessity: Ghana and Ivory Coast, 1957-1967." Pages 231-64 in Philip Foster and Aristide R. Zolberg (eds.), *Ghana and Ivory Coast: Perspectives on Modernization.* Chicago: University of Chicago Press, 1971.

Groff, David. "When the Knees Began Wearing the Hat: Commercial Agriculture and Social Transformation in Assikasso, the

Ivory Coast, 1880–1940." Pages 97–135 in Paul M. Lubeck (ed.), *The African Bourgeoisie.* Boulder, Colorado: Lynne Rienner, 1987.

Harrison-Church, R.J., Richard Synge, and Edith Hodgkinson. "Côte d'Ivoire." Pages 397–415 in *Africa South of the Sahara.* (17th ed.) London: Europa, 1987.

Hecht, Robert M. "The Ivory Coast Economic 'Miracle': What Benefits for Peasant Farmers?" *Journal of Modern African Studies* [Cambridge], 12, No. 1, March 1983, 25–53.

Jackson, Robert H., and Carl G. Rosberg. *Personal Rule in Black Africa: Prince, Autocrat, Prophet, Tyrant.* Berkeley: University of California Press, 1982.

Kurian, George Thomas. "Ivory Coast." Pages 982–99 in George Thomas Kurian (ed.), *Encyclopedia of the Third World,* 2. (3d ed.) New York: Facts on File, 1987.

Lamb, David. "A Different Path," *The Wilson Quarterly,* 12, No. 4, Autumn 1988, 114–131.

"La Liberté de la presse en Côte d'Ivoire," *Peuples noirs—Peuples africains* [Paris], 7, No. 41–2, December 1984, 104–140.

Leys, Colin (ed.). *Politics and Change in Developing Countries.* London: Cambridge University Press, 1969.

Loucou, Jean-Noël. "La deuxième guerre mondiale et ses effets en Côte d'Ivoire," *Annales de l'Université d'Abidjan, série I* [Abidjan], 8, 1980, 183–207.

Médard, J.F. "La régulation socio-politique." Pages 61–88 in Y.-A. Fauré and J.-F. Médard (eds.), *Etat et bourgeoisie en Côte d'Ivoire.* Paris: Karthala, 1982.

de Miras, C. "L'Entrepreneur ivoirien ou une bourgeoisie privée de son état." Pages 181–230 in Y.-A. Fauré and J.-F. Médard (eds.), *Etat et bourgeoisie en Côte d'Ivoire,* Paris: Karthala, 1982.

Morgenthau, Ruth Schachter. *Political Parties in French-Speaking West Africa.* Oxford: Clarendon Press, 1964.

Mundt, Robert J. *Historical Dictionary of the Ivory Coast.* (African Historical Dictionaries, No. 41.) Metuchen, New Jersey: Scarecrow Press, 1987.

_____. "Internal Criticism of the Ivoirian Political Regime." (Paper presented at African Studies Association Annual Meeting.) Denver, Colorado: November 20, 1987.

Naipaul, V.S. *Finding the Center.* New York: Vintage Books, 1984.

Neuberger, Benjamin. *National Self-Determination in Postcolonial Africa.* Boulder, Colorado: Lynne Rienner, 1986.

Nyong'o, Peter Anyang'. "The Development of Agrarian Capitalist Classes in the Ivory Coast, 1945–1975." Pages 185–245 in Paul Lubeck (ed.), *The African Bourgeoisie.* Boulder, Colorado: Lynne Rienner, 1987.

_____. "Liberal Modes of Capitalist Development in Africa: Ivory Coast," *Africa Development* [London], 3, No. 2, April–June 1978, 69–87.

Potholm, Christian P. *Four African Political Systems.* Englewood Cliffs, New Jersey: Prentice-Hall, 1970.

Semi-Bi. Zan. "Genèse de la démocratie à l'ivoirienne," *Le mois en Afrique* [Paris], No. 249–50, October–November 1986, 15–31.

Staniland, Martin. "Single-Party Regimes and Political Change: The P.D.C.I. and Ivory Coast Politics." Pages 135–75 in Colin Leys (ed.), *Politics and Change in Developing Countries.* London: Cambridge University Press, 1969.

Tay, Hugues. *L'Administration ivoirienne.* (Encylopédie Administrative Series.) Paris: Berger-Levrault, 1974.

Tice, Robert D. "Administrative Structure, Ethnicity, and Nation-Building in Ivory Coast," *Journal of Modern African Studies* [London], 12, No. 2, June 1974, 211–29.

Toungara, Jeanne Maddox. "Political Reform and Economic Change in Ivory Coast: An Update," *Journal of African Studies* [London], 13, No. 3, Fall 1986, 94–101.

Touré, Abdou. *La civilisation quotidienne en Côte d'Ivoire.* Paris: Editions Karthala, 1981.

_____. "Paysans et fonctionnaires devant la culture et l'état." Pages 231–51 in Y.-A. Fauré and J.-F. Médard (eds.), *Etat et bourgeoisie en Côte d'Ivoire.* Paris: Karthala, 1982.

Touré, I. "L'U.G.T.C.I. et le 'développement harmonieux'," *Politique africaine* [Paris], No. 24, December 1986, 79–90.

Ungar, Sanford J. *Africa: The People and Politics of an Emerging Continent.* New York: Simon and Schuster, 1986.

United States. Department of State. *Ivory Coast Post Report.* Washington: GPO, December 1985.

Vennetier, Pierre (ed.). *Atlas de la Côte d'Ivoire.* (2d ed.) Paris: Jeune Afrique, 1983.

Weiskel, Timothy. "Independence and the *Longue Durée:* The Ivory Coast 'Miracle' Reconsidered." Pages 347–80 in Prosser Gifford and William Rogers Louis (eds.), *Decolonization and African Independence.* New Haven: Yale University Press, 1988.

_____. "Mission civilisatrice," *The Wilson Quarterly,* 12, No. 4, Autumn 1988, 97–113.

Welch, Claude E., Jr. *No Farewell to Arms? Military Disengagement from Politics in Africa and Latin America.* Boulder, Colorado: Westview Press, 1987.

Young, Crawford. *Ideology and Development in Africa.* New Haven: Yale University Press, 1982.

Zartman, I. William, and Christopher L. Delgado. "Introduction." Pages 1–20 in I. William Zartman and Christopher L. Delgado (eds.), *The Political Economy of Ivory Coast.* New York: Praeger, 1984.

———. *The Political Economy of the Ivory Coast.* New York: Praeger, 1984.

Zolberg, Aristide R. *Creating Political Order.* (Rand McNally Studies in Political Change Series.) Chicago: 1966.

———. *One-Party Government in the Ivory Coast.* (rev. ed.) Princeton: Princeton University Press, 1969.

———. "La Redécouverte de la Côte d'Ivoire," *Politique africaine* [Paris], No. 9, March 1983, 118–131.

(Various issues of the following periodicals were also used in the preparation of this chapter: *Africa Confidential* [London], 1980–88; *Africa Economic Digest* [London], 1985–88; *Africa Report,* 1980–85; *Africa Research Bulletin* [Exeter, United Kingdom], 1985–88; *African Defence* [Paris], 1985–88; *Afrique-Asie* [Paris], 1985–87; *Afrique Défense* [Paris], 1985–88; Foreign Broadcast Information Service, *Daily Report: Subsahara Africa,* 1985–87; *Fraternité matin* [Abidjan], 1985–88; *Guardian* [Manchester], 1986–87; *Jeune Afrique* [Paris], 1983–87; *Jeune Afrique économie* [Paris], 1986–87; Joint Publications Research Service, *Africa/Middle East,* 1985–87; *Le Monde* [Paris], 1985–88; *Marchés tropicaux et méditerranéens* [Paris], 1980–88; and *West Africa* [London], 1985–88.)

Chapter 5

Abidjan Institute of Criminology. *First West African Conference in Comparative Criminology.* Abidjan: June 1972

Aggrey, Albert. *Guides des institutions politiques et administratives.* Abidjan: Juris-Conseils, 1983.

Air Forces of the World, 1986, Geneva: Interavia Data, 1986.

Amnesty International. *Amnesty International Report, 1986.* London: 1986.

Andrade, John M. "Ivory Coast." Page 106 in John M. Andrade (ed.), *World Police and Paramilitary Forces.* New York: Stockton Press, 1985.

Asiwaju, A.I. "Control Through Coercion: A Study of the *Indigénat* Regime in French West African Administration, 1887–1946," *Bulletin de l'institut fondamental de l'Afrique noire* [Dakar, Senegal], 41, No. 1, January 1979, 35–71.

———. "Migrations as Revolt: The Example of the Ivory Coast and the Upper Volta Before 1945," *Journal of African History* [London], 17, No. 4, 1976, 577–94.

Balesi, Charles John. *From Adversaries to Comrades-in-Arms: West Africans and the French Military, 1885-1918.* Waltham, Massachusetts: Crossroads Press, 1979.

Campbell, Bonnie. "The Ivory Coast." Pages 66-116 in John Dunn (ed.), *West African States: Failures and Promise.* Cambridge: Cambridge University Press, 1978.

Clinard, Marshall B., and Daniel J. Abbott. *Crime in Developing Countries: A Comparative Perspective.* New York: John Wiley and Sons, 1973.

Cohen, Michael A. *Urban Policy and Political Conflict in Africa: A Study of the Ivory Coast.* Chicago: University of Chicago Press, 1974.

Couhat, Jean Labayle (ed.). *Combat Fleets of the World, 1986-1987,* Annapolis: Naval Institute Press, 1986.

Côte d'Ivoire. Ministère de la fonction publique. *Recueil de textes et documents.* Abidjan: Imprimerie nationale, 1974.

_____. Ministère de l'information. *Annuaire administratif.* Abidjan: Imprimerie nationale, 1980.

Davis, Shelby Cullom. *Reservoirs of Men: A History of the Black Troops of French West Africa.* 1934. Reprint. Westport, Connecticut: Negro Universities Press, 1970.

Defense and Foreign Affairs Handbook, 1986, Washington: Perth, 1986.

Delorme, Nicole. "The Foreign Policy of the Ivory Coast." Pages 118-35 in Oaljide Aluko (ed.), *The Foreign Policies of African States.* London: Hodder and Stoughton, 1977.

Dennis, Barry M. "Ivory Coast." Separate pamphlet in A.P. Blaustein and G.H. Flanz (eds.), *Constitutions of the Countries of the World.* Dobbs Ferry, New York: Oceana, 1978, with 1980 update.

Fauré, Y.-A., and J.-F. Médard. *Etat et bourgeoisie en Côte d'Ivoire.* Paris: Karthala, 1982.

France. Ministère des affaires étrangères. *Côte d'Ivoire: Mission Hugues Le Roux.* Paris: Imprimerie Jean Cussac, 1918.

Gastil, Raymond D. "Ivory Coast." Page 320 in Raymond D. Gastil (ed.), *Freedom in the World: Political Rights and Civil Liberties, 1985-1986.* Westport, Connecticut: Greenwood Press, 1986.

Gbagbo, Laurent. *Côte d'Ivoire: Pour une alternative démocratique.* Paris: L'Harmattan, 1983.

Goldsworthy, David. "Armies and Politics in Civilian Regimes." Pages 97-18 in Simon Baynham (ed.), *Military Power and Politics in Black Africa.* New York: St. Martin's Press, 1986.

_____. "Civilian Control of the Military in Black Africa," *African Affairs* [London], 80, No. 318, January 1981, 49-74.

Hanning, Hugh. "Ivory Coast." Pages 133-40 in Hugh Hanning (ed.), *Peaceful Uses of Military Forces.* New York: Praeger, 1967.

Harrison-Church, R.J., Richard Synge, and Edith Hodgkinson. "Côte d'Ivoire." Pages 397–415 in *Africa South of the Sahara.* (17th ed.) London: Europa, 1987.

Harshé, Rajen. *Pervasive Entente: France and Ivory Coast in African Affairs.* Atlantic Highlands, New Jersey: Humanities Press, 1984.

Hughes, Arnold, and Roy May. "Armies on Loan: Toward an Explanation of Transnational Military Intervention Among Black African States, 1960–1985." Pages 177–202 in Simon Baynham (ed.), *Military Power and Politics in Black Africa.* New York: St. Martin's Press, 1986.

Humana, Charles, "Ivory Coast." Page 145 in Charles Humana (ed.), *World Human Rights Guide.* New York: Facts on File, 1986.

"The Ivory Coast." Pages 378–84 in Charles S. Rhyne (ed.), *Law and Judicial Systems of Nations.* (3d ed.), Washington: World Peace Through Law Center, 1978.

"Ivory Coast." Pages B65–B75 in Colin Legum (ed.), *Africa Contemporary Record: Annual Survey and Documents, 1985–1986.* New York: Africana, 1987.

"Ivory Coast." Pages 197–209 in Sidney Taylor (ed.), *The New Africans.* New York: G.P. Putnam and Sons, 1967.

Jackson, Robert H., and Carl G. Rosberg. *Personal Rule in Black Africa: Prince, Autocrat, Prophet, Tyrant.* Berkeley: University of California Press, 1982.

Jane's Fighting Ships, 1987–1988. London: Jane's, 1987.

Krivinyi, Nikolaus. "Ivory Coast." Pages 44–45 in Nikolaus Krivinyi (ed.), *World Military Aviation.* (rev. ed.) New York: Arco, 1977.

Kurian, George Thomas. "Ivory Coast." Pages 982–99 in George Thomas Kurian (ed.), *Encyclopedia of the Third World, 2.* (3d ed.) New York: Facts on File, 1987.

Labayle Couhat, Jean. "Ivory Coast." Pages 282–83 in Jean Labayle Couhat (ed.), *Combat Fleets of the World 1986–1987.* (Trans., A.D. Baker, III.) Annapolis, Maryland: Naval Institute Press, 1986.

Lubeck, Paul M. (ed.). *The African Bourgeoisie: Capitalist Development in Nigeria, Kenya, and the Ivory Coast.* Boulder, Colorado: Lynne Rienner, 1987.

Marenin, Otwin. "Policing African States: Toward a Critique," *Comparative Politics,* 14, No. 4, July 1982, 379–96.

Mathews, Lloyd. "Ivory Coast." Pages 320–21 in John Keegan (ed.), *World Armies.* (2d ed.) Detroit: Gale Research, 1983.

The Military Balance, 1986–1987. London: International Institute for Strategic Studies, 1986.

The Military Balance, 1987–1988. London: International Institute for Strategic Studies, 1987.

Moose, George. "French Military Policy in Africa." Pages 59–97 in William J. Foltz and Henry S. Bienen (eds.), *Arms and the African*. New Haven: Yale University Press, 1985.

O'Sullivan, John M. "The Franco-Baoulé War, 1891–1911: The Struggle Against the French Conquest of Central Ivory Coast," *Journal of African Studies*, 5, No. 3, Fall 1978, 329–56.

Pabanel, Jean-Pierre. *Les coups d'état militaires en Afrique noire*. Paris: L'Harmattan, 1984.

Pope, Barbara H. "Ivory Coast." Page 62 in Barbara H. Pope (ed.), *World Defense Forces*. Santa Barbara, California: ABC-CLIO, 1987.

Potholm, Christian P. *Four African Political Systems*. Englewood Cliffs, New Jersey: Prentice-Hall, 1970.

_____. "The Multiple Roles of the Police as Seen in the African Context," *Journal of Developing Areas* [London], 3, No. 2, January 1969, 139–57.

Sellers, Robert C. "Ivory Coast." Pages 113–14 in Robert C. Sellers (ed.), *Armed Forces of the World: A Reference Handbook*. (4th ed.) New York: Praeger, 1977.

Shelley, Louise I. *Crime and Modernization: The Impact of Industrialization and Urbanization on Crime*. Carbondale, Illinois: Southern Illinois University Press, 1981.

Tay, Hugues. *L'Administration ivoirienne*. Paris: Berger-Levrault, 1974.

Taylor, Charles Lewis, and David A. Jodice. *World Handbook of Political and Social Indicators*. (2 vols.) (3d ed.) New Haven: Yale University Press, 1983.

Teya, Pascal Koffi. *Côte d'Ivoire: Le roi est nu*. Paris: L'Harmattan, 1985.

Thompson, Virginia M. *West Africa's Council of the Entente*. Ithaca: Cornell University Press, 1972.

United States. Arms Control and Disarmament Agency. *Arms Control and Disarmament Agreements: Texts and Histories of Negotiations*. Washington: GPO, 1982.

_____. Arms Control and Disarmament Agency. *World Military Expenditures and Arms Transfers, 1986*. (Annual Series, No. 127.) Washington: GPO, April 1987.

_____. Central Intelligence Agency. *The World Factbook, 1987*, Washington: GPO, 1987.

_____. Department of State. *Country Reports on Human Rights Practice for 1986: Report submitted to the Committee on Foreign Relations,*

U.S. Senate, and Committee on Foreign Affairs, U.S. House of Representatives. Washington: GPO, February 1987.
_____. Department of State. Office of the Legal Adviser. Treaty Affairs Staff. *Treaties in Force, 1987.* Washington: GPO, 1987.
_____. Department of State. *Report to Congress on Voting Practices in the United Nations.* Washington: GPO, April 23, 1987.
Welch, Claude E., Jr. "Côte d'Ivoire: Personal Rule and Civilian Control." Pages 172–94 in Claude E. Welch, Jr. (ed.), *No Farewell to Arms?* Boulder, Colorado: Westview Press, 1987.
World Armaments and Disarmament: Stockholm International Peace Research Institute Yearbook, 1986. Oxford: Oxford University Press, 1986.
Woronoff, Jon. *West African Wager: Houphouët Versus Nkrumah.* Metuchen, New Jersey: Scarecrow Press, 1972.
Zartman, I. William. *International Relations in the New Africa.* Englewood Cliffs, New Jersey: Prentice-Hall, 1966.
Zartman, I. William, and Christopher Delgado (eds.). *The Political Economy of Ivory Coast.* New York: Praeger, 1984.

(Various issues of the following periodicals were also used in the preparation of this chapter: *Afrique Défense* [Paris], 1985–87; *Défense Africaine* [Paris], 1985–87; and *Fraternité matin* [Abidjan], 1985–88.)

Glossary

barrels per day (bpd)—Production of crude oil and petroleum products is frequently measured in barrels per day, often abbreviated "bpd" or "bd." A barrel is a volume measure of forty-two United States gallons. Conversion of barrels to tons depends on the density of the specific product. About 7.3 barrels of average crude oil weigh one ton; gasoline and kerosene average closer to 8 barrels per ton.

canton—During the colonial era, referred to a group of neighboring villages linked either by ethnicity or by direct family ties.

CFA franc—The African Financial Community (Communauté Financière Africaine—CFA) franc, the currency of Côte d'Ivoire. In 1988 CFA F315 equaled US$1. The CFA, an organization that includes France and most former French colonies in Africa, administers currency policy in the franc zone. As of 1988, the CFA maintained a currency parity between French francs (FF) and the CFA francs of West Africa at the rate of FF1 = CFA F50. Issuing the CFA francs is the Central Bank of West African States (Banque Centrale des Etats de l'Afrique de l'Ouest—BCEAO), which is based in Paris.

coopérants—French technical assistants and teachers under contract to the Ivoirian government for a fixed period. *Coopérants* generally received higher salaries than local counterparts and were exempted from many customs regulations. Until 1986 the Ivoirian government assumed responsibility for paying *coopérants;* after 1986 their salaries were included in the foreign aid provided by France.

coutumes—Literally, "customs, mores, or practices." Fixed, annual fees paid by colonial authorities to local rulers to secure trading rights or permission to establish permanent settlements. Payment of *coutumes* constituted a de facto recognition of lower status and ceased when the colonial administration felt it could impose its will on local chiefs.

fiscal year (FY)—the calendar year.

French West Africa (Afrique Occidentale Française—AOF)—The collection of territories under French colonial rule until 1960. French West Africa comprised what in 1988 was Mauritania, Mali, Burkina Faso, Guinea, Côte d'Ivoire, Niger, Togo, and Benin.

gross domestic product (GDP)—A measure of the value of domestic goods and services produced by an economy over a period of time, such as a year. Only output values of goods for final consumption and investment are included because the values of primary and intermediate production are assumed to be included in final prices. GDP is sometimes aggregated and shown at market prices, meaning that indirect taxes and subsidies are included; when these have been eliminated, the result is GDP at factor cost. The word *gross* indicates that deductions for depreciation of physical assets have not been made.

gross national product (GNP)—The gross domestic product (*q.v.*) plus net income or loss stemming from transactions with foreign countries. GNP is the broadest measure of the output of goods and services by an economy.

indigénat—Refers to denizenship and rights of natives. In colonial French West Africa (*q.v.*), the colonial system of discipline characterized by arbitrary and summary judgments accorded Africans living in rural areas. The *indigénat* was abolished in 1946.

International Monetary Fund (IMF)—Established along with the World Bank (*q.v.*) in 1945, the IMF is a specialized agency affiliated with the United Nations and is responsible for stabilizing international exchange rates and payments. The main business of the IMF is the provision of loans to its members (including industrialized and developing countries) when they experience balance of payments difficulties. These loans frequently carry conditions that require substantial internal economic adjustments by the recipients, most of which are developing countries.

London Club—A noninstitutional framework within which bank advisory committees conduct negotiations between debtor countries and the private banks holding the loans. The advisory committees form in response to requests for debt restructuring and consist of individuals representing major loan holders in the key creditor countries. The London Club typically reschedules principal falling due and principal in arrears; interest is not covered by any agreement and must be paid along with any outstanding arrearages before any agreement can take effect.

Paris Club—A noninstitutional framework whereby developed nations that have made loans or guaranteed official or private export credits to developing nations meet to discuss borrowers' ability to repay debts. The organization, which met for the first time in 1956, has no formal or institutional existence and no fixed membership. Its secretariat is run by the French treasury, and it has a close relationship with the World Bank (*q.v.*), the International Monetary Fund (*q.v.*), and the United Nations Conference on Trade and Development (UNCTAD).

Western Sudan—That part of French West Africa (*q.v.*) comprising in 1988 the state of Mali.

World Bank—Informal name used to designate a group of three affiliated international institutions: the International Bank for Reconstruction and Development (IBRD), the International Development Association (IDA), and the International Finance Corporation (IFC). The IBRD, established in 1945, has the primary purpose of providing loans to developing countries for productive projects. The IDA, a legally separate loan fund but administered by the staff of the IBRD, was set up in 1960 to furnish credits to the poorest developing countries on much easier terms than those of conventional IBRD loans. The IFC, founded in 1956, supplements the activities of the IBRD through loans and assistance designed specifically to encourage the growth of productive private enterprises in the less-developed countries. The president and certain senior officers of the IBRD hold the same positions in the IFC. The three institutions are owned by the governments of the countries that subscribe their capital. To participate in the World Bank group, member states must first belong to the International Monetary Fund (IMF—*q.v.*).

Index

Abbé people, 56

Abidjan: concentration of population in, 26; courts in, 151–2; crime in, 211; Ebrié population in, 56; land concessions in, 77; life expectancy in, 86; as military region, 189– 90, 192; petroleum fields near, 125; as port, 131; as principal city, 16; as railroad terminal, 129; roads in, 130; social unrest in, xxx; telecommunications in, 133; university in, 81, 84

Abidjan-Niger Railroad (Régie du Chemin de Fer Abidjan-Niger: RAN), 129–30

Abidjan-Port Bouët International Airport, 132–33

Abidjan Stock Exchange (Bourse de Valeurs d'Abidjan), 104

Abidjan University (see also National University of Côte d'Ivoire), 27

Abidji people, 56

Abolition of Slavery, Supplementary Convention (1956), 206

Abouré people, 56

Abron (Brong) people, xxiv, xxvi, 7, 56

Academy of Oceanographic Sciences and Technology, 197

accords, military (1961), 197–98

Adioukrou people, 56

administration, government (see also military organization; specific ministries), 24, 146, 207; autonomous communities as, 155–56; cercles (French colonial), 13–14; divisions of, 25–26, 207; prefectural administration of, 24–25, 153–54, 189, 207; Subprefectural Council of, 155; subprefectures (sous-préfetures) of, 24–25, 154–55, 207

Administrative Section (Supreme Court), 152

Advisory Labor Committee, 108

African Agricultural Union (Syndicat Agricole Africain: SAA), 4, 17; opposition of, 73–74; pressure for colonial reform of, xxv, 20

African Civic Action Program, 200

African Democratic Rally (Rassemblement Démocratique Africain: RDA), 19, 20

African Development Bank, 138

African Financial Community (Communauté Financière Africaine), 102

Agip, 126

Agni (Anyi) people, xxiv, xxvi, 7, 28, 49; Christianity among, 72, 73; culture of, 54–56; rebellion of, 7, 28, 55

agricultural sector (see also cocoa industry; coffee industry; exports; food processing industry; planter class): expansion of, 93; exports of, xxvii, 4, 26, 30, 94–95, 109–10, 112–17, 121–22, 134; food crops of, 117–20; foreign workers in, xxvi, 106–7, 205; forest and savanna regions of, 110–11; labor force employment in, 105; livestock and poultry in, 120; performance of, 109–10; plantation elite in, 19, 73; under Vichy government, 16

Ahmadiya brotherhood, 70

Aid and Cooperation Fund (Fond d'Aide et de Coopération: FAC), 138

AIDS, 87–88

Air Afrique, 133

air bases, 191–92

air fields, 129, 133, 192

air force (see also Ivoirian Air Force), 183

Air France, 133

Air Ivoire, 133, 191

airports, 129, 132–33

Air Transport Union (Union des Transports Aériens: UTA), 133

Akan people (see also Agni (Anyi)), xxvi, 7, 47, 48; influence of, 61; religions of, 66, 68; society of, 53–56

Albania, 173

Alépé, 45

Algeria, 177, 185

Alladian people, 56

Alliali, Camille, 158

Angoulvant, Gabriel, xxiv, 11

AOF. See French West Africa (Afrique Occidentale Française: AOF)

armed forces (see also Armed Forces of Côte d'Ivoire; conscription; military training; veterans), 169–70; chain of command in, 187; expansion of, 186; of French in Côte d'Ivoire, 170, 198–99;

259

Published Country Studies

(Area Handbook Series)

550-65	Afghanistan	550-87	Greece
550-98	Albania	550-78	Guatemala
550-44	Algeria	550-174	Guinea
550-59	Angola	550-82	Guyana and Belize
550-73	Argentina	550-151	Honduras
550-169	Australia	550-165	Hungary
550-176	Austria	550-21	India
550-175	Bangladesh	550-154	Indian Ocean
550-170	Belgium	550-39	Indonesia
550-66	Bolivia	550-68	Iran
550-20	Brazil	550-31	Iraq
550-168	Bulgaria	550-25	Israel
550-61	Burma	550-182	Italy
550-50	Cambodia	550-30	Japan
550-166	Cameroon	550-34	Jordan
550-159	Chad	550-56	Kenya
550-77	Chile	550-81	Korea, North
550-60	China	550-41	Korea, South
550-26	Colombia	550-58	Laos
550-33	Commonwealth Caribbean, Islands of the	550-24	Lebanon
550-91	Congo	550-38	Liberia
550-90	Costa Rica	550-85	Libya
550-69	Côte d'Ivoire (Ivory Coast)	550-172	Malawi
550-152	Cuba	550-45	Malaysia
550-22	Cyprus	550-161	Mauritania
550-158	Czechoslovakia	550-79	Mexico
550-36	Dominican Republic and Haiti	550-76	Mongolia
550-52	Ecuador	550-49	Morocco
550-43	Egypt	550-64	Mozambique
550-150	El Salvador	550-35	Nepal and Bhutan
550-28	Ethiopia	550-88	Nicaragua
550-167	Finland	550-157	Nigeria
550-155	Germany, East	550-94	Oceania
550-173	Germany, Fed. Rep. of	550-48	Pakistan
550-153	Ghana	550-46	Panama

550-156	Paraguay	550-53	Thailand
550-185	Persian Gulf States	550-89	Tunisia
550-42	Peru	550-80	Turkey
550-72	Philippines	550-74	Uganda
550-162	Poland	550-97	Uruguay
550-181	Portugal	550-71	Venezuela
550-160	Romania	550-32	Vietnam
550-37	Rwanda and Burundi	550-183	Yemens, The
550-51	Saudi Arabia	550-99	Yugoslavia
550-70	Senegal	550-67	Zaire
550-180	Sierra Leone	550-75	Zambia
550-184	Singapore	550-171	Zimbabwe
550-86	Somalia		
550-93	South Africa		
550-95	Soviet Union		
550-179	Spain		
550-96	Sri Lanka		
550-27	Sudan		
550-47	Syria		
550-62	Tanzania		

DATE DUE

DATE DUE